DECODING THE SHAMAN WITHIN

A METAPHYSICAL JOURNEY

O.M. KELLY

COPYRIGHT

Copyright © 2023 Margaret Ann Kelly (Omni)
All rights reserved. This book may not be reproduced, wholly or in part, or transmitted in any form whatsoever without written permission from the author, O.M. Kelly, www.elanea.com.

The author of this book does not dispense medical advice or prescribe the use of any technique as a form of treatment for physical, emotional, or medical problems without the advice of a physician, either directly or indirectly. The intent of the author is only to offer information of a general nature to help you in your quest for emotional and spiritual well-being. In the event you use any of the information in this book for yourself, which is your constitutional right, the author assumes no responsibility for your actions.

AUTHOR

Author O. M. Kelly, known as Omni to her clients and students is an accomplished author and lecturer, on Metaphysics, Philosophy and understanding the Collective Consciousness. Omni consults for Member States of the European Commission as a Conciliation Advisor and Rhetoric Counsellor for other International Companies throughout Europe. Omni now resides on Australia's beautiful Gold Coast, writing books, and works as a Life Mentor and Business Coach.

Omni's cumulative years of personal research and dedication to her journey, has lead to discoveries and initiations into the mathematical language of the unconscious mind (higher mind), all compiled into a nine volume masterpiece, *Decoding the Mind of God*. Omni discovered that the Biblical Agenda, Greek Myths, Egyptology and the Asian Principles all explained the same story throughout the ages in hidden language. Omni revealed the secrets of the Collective Consciousness, showing how we can realize the potential of the human mind through belief in ourselves. The Laws of the Universe are identical to the Collective Consciousness, they reveal an answer to every question we are capable of asking.

CULTURAL SENSITIVITY WARNING

Australian Aboriginal readers are warned that there are words and descriptions that may be culturally sensitive and which might not normally be used in certain public or community contexts.

CONTENTS

Introduction and Acknowledgements		1
Chapter 1	My Maternal Grandmother was an Alchemist	5
Chapter 2.	Discovering the Way	18
Chapter 3.	Introduction to the Ancient Wisdom	22
Chapter 4.	Initiation Into The Ancient Wisdoms	26
Chapter 5.	Initiation Into The Tribal Law	29
Chapter 6.	Receiving My Shamanic Tools	33
Chapter 7.	Inner And Outer Worlds Of Whorls	40
Chapter 8.	Expanded Consciousness	43
Chapter 9.	Secrets To Live My Own Universal Law	50
Chapter 10.	Death of Loved Ones	61
Chapter 11.	The Masters Of Time	71
Chapter 12.	Opening The Heart And Decoding Ancient Egyptian Metaphysical Codes	82
Chapter 13.	Expanded Consciousness	91
Chapter 14.	Visitors From The Next Dimension Of Time	97
Chapter 15.	Extreme Spiritual Messages	101
Chapter 16.	The Mathematics At The Time Of Your Birth Created A Cosmic Program	116
Chapter 17.	We Are The Ones, We Have Been Waiting For	124
Chapter 18.	The Language Of The Shamanic Principles	130
Chapter 19.	Vision World of Extra Terrestrial Energy	140
Chapter 20	Vision World For Healing	148
Chapter 21.	Discovering The 'Dark Night Of The Soul'	152
Chapter 22.	Quest For Life	163
Chapter 23.	The Rainmaker	168
Chapter 24.	The Three Phases Of Surrender	172
Chapter 25	Changing The Alchemy Of Our Body	181
Chapter 26	Dolphin—Free Will And The Earnings Of Freedom	186
Chapter 27.	The Shaman Within	189

Chapter 28.	Secrets Of The Medicine Wheel	198
Chapter 29.	The Sacred Alphabet	201
Chapter 30.	Numerology	210
Chapter 31.	Totem Energy	218
Chapter 32.	Last Chapter	227

A Shaman is trained to accept and become the measurement of the emotional harmonics of all the species that have evolved on this planet.
Omni

Introduction and Acknowledgements

The shaman is a person, male or female, who has an overwhelming psychological experience that turns him totally inward. The whole unconscious opens up, and the shaman falls into it.
Joseph Campbell

Through the 'Totem' energy of all, the ancient species that have evolved before us, represent an emotional inheritance that we can rely on to sustain our moment. They will become the beneficial advisers to help us with our own intelligence when our mind is in the fields of doubt. As we release the Shamanic Principles from within, Metaphysics describes how every myth was an inner kingdom that each human could find within themselves. Through the Collective Consciousness, we connect unconsciously with every story that has ever been written, spoken, and collected.

A Shaman is trained to accept and become the measurement of the emotional harmonics of all the species that have evolved on this planet. During the inheritance of our Totem, our energy fields are multifaceted; that energy then collects and builds up into a force field, which is of exactly the same mathematics as the electromagnetic fields of the planet. Every Shaman must learn to realize the frequencies that each animal, plant, or mineral commits to the Collective for them to have also inherited their Earth.

We gain the ability to have that energy at our beck and call. I can work with different species for the different energies that I need, and then send them to other areas where I am asked to work through on behalf of the Collective Consciousness. I connect with those vibrations through my telepathic communication. I have the ability to vibrate them throughout different states of consciousness that are freely available and presented to me from the Collective Mind.

This book is my Shamanic Metaphysical journey. It would be termed a contemporary Shamanic journey; a powerful one in reference to the codes of evolution and the Quest of Life. Throughout my training to receive the breath of Shamanism, many Elders from other cultures came to Australia and initiated me into their own tribal laws. Most of these Elders were men who arrived on my doorstep uninvited; I received only four women. Those magnificent people who had also earned their Shamanic experiences, only stayed long enough to give me their gift of consciousness and to initiate me into my new name, which their tribe had bestowed on me, and then they disappeared out of my life as quickly as they had come into it. They came to Australia representing the cultures that had evolved before mine.

The Shamanic path is the oldest pathway of the tribal law through the evolution of humanity. The Shaman is trained in the ancient language (metaphysically) that is instilled in every genetic code that humanity carries in their DNA, you either have the opportunity to open it up and use it, or you just don't bother and choose to ignore it! It is as simple as that!

When one begins to write their story, they open themselves up to the subject at hand. The more they relax into explaining what they would like to write, their inner storehouse of information opens up to explain their own biblical agenda, which is the blueprint of their own DNA. Recorded in this blueprint is every experience that their previous generations and they, have lived. This information is freely available to be used in concordance with the subject at hand. The unconscious mind clicks in to the subject as it has every recorded moment of the author's existence and the reader also realizes that this story is also for them as well, as their own unconscious mind (higher mind) is alerting them to the fact! There has to be an ongoing conversation between the author and the reader for the story to be heard!

Hopefully by now you have read my books *Decoding the Mind of God* as to how we learn to understand the hidden language that was exponential as it spread its way forward through each generation into our DNA. Please also read my previous book *Decoding the Revelation of Saint John the Divine: Understand the role you inherit*. The Shaman has to become St John the Divine and earn each page to become the Book of Revelations. This wonderful last book of the Bible is written in the Divine Intelligence, and it is the third and final initiation of humanity's earnings—and this is where we reach the land of philosophy and discover the embedded codes in the seven sacred seals within us. More importantly discover the principles that lay behind Egyptology, the Biblical Agenda and also our Medical Sciences; that are explaining the same identical story! These natural laws remain hidden from us until we realize the importance of learning more about our self. It is during this journey, that we begin to realize that this language is something that we mathematically earn, and allows us to unravel our genetic inheritance. There is nothing magical about it; this language is explaining the next evolutionary step of human intelligence.

My heart rests now, through the teachings of those who taught me how to succumb to this information, with my thanks and adoration to my team who worked tirelessly assisting me to bring the story together. Special thanks to Maree Hubbard (dedication to the dictation), Sharhraiah Wright (social media consultant), and many others for the comfort and support given when needed. Enjoy the read!

See everything around you—
all of it is waiting for you.
Omni

It is the relationship of self that connects us to the energy of our total evolution.
Omni

Imagine someone, who is courageous enough to withdraw all his illusions and the projections thereof. That creates an individual who is fully aware of a considerable shadow.

Such a human knows that, whatever is wrong in the world, it is within himself, too, and, if only he could learn to cope with his own shadow.
Carl G. Jung

Chapter 1
My Maternal Grandmother Was An Alchemist

My maternal grandmother was an Alchemist, she was a very powerful and charismatic woman. When she spoke, she held peoples respect and they stopped their inner mind chatter and listened to her. She was a marvelous story teller; her listeners were enthralled with her speech. Her herbal and spiritual knowledge was a part of my daily life. When anyone walked into her house, the overcoats of their persona, (those feelings of fear they had wrapped around themselves) fell off at the front door immediately, all of their layers disintegrated and they were left standing naked in their spiritual garment; which when decoded through the sacred language their inner language, is explaining to them that they are baring their truth, as they know it to be, to others in that moment. In other words, they are not hiding behind their excuses that they use, to support them as they walk forward into their future.

We lived a long way out of the small town that had a mercantile store that supplied us with petrol and farming needs. We killed our own meat and grew our own vegetables and fruit, we preserved and bottled and pickled and salted and made brawn, we relished and made chutney, and created the finest jams and marmalades. You could smell the aroma of our fresh baked cakes and pies for miles. Our puddings were as light as a feather and as sweet as a kiss. We made our own candles and soap to wash ourselves therefore we became quiet self sufficient.

We had our own church service in our large sitting room every Sunday. People travelled for hours to attend our services and when you walked in the sitting room, you could smell the lavender, peppermint, rosemary and rose essences. A roast lamb was slowly cooking in the large combustion oven to be enjoyed as a meal once the service was over.

On a very hot day when you walked into each room, you could smell oranges, lemons, grapefruit; the essences from the odors of the fruit cooled our body down. The oranges were studded with whole cloves, there was something about the two odors blending and harmonizing with one another. The lemons were studded with the bark from the cinnamon tree that one of the elders had brought the seeds back from his journey overseas and the mandarins were studded with a crushed nutmeg.

My mother was not interested in my grandmother's ways. My mother was the needle worker and embroiderer. She made blankets for the beds, the rugs for the floors, and was a marvelous cook. We had the finest tablecloths, always white and starched, with crisp white damask napkins, placed in bright silver rings.

My father was interested in my grandmother's ways. When time permitted he sat for hours and listened, as my grandmother explained her ways to him. As a child, I would walk past the sitting room which seemed dark to keep the heat out and watch their animation. They seemed to be in their own world, where they could only see and hear one another. They spoke softly to one another; they never raised their voices. No one would dare to disturb them. It is a beautiful memory. As I grew up, she turned to me and initiated me into many of her ways. I am so sorry now, that I only half listened some of the time. I listened to her words, but I never heard the words register in my inner alphabet (the words we would use, when we are busily thinking our thoughts). Therefore, the memories were scant, they come back to haunt me now that I have opened up more of my DNA in small glimpses and her words continue down to me from that moment. What I thought I had forgotten was still there embedded in me, just waiting for the opportunity to serve me, when it was needed.

My father was an Elder of our church and also a healer. My uncles were also Elders of the church. Since his Passover, my father has still been a wonderful guide to show me my way; especially in explaining the biblical agenda. He provides insights for me to change my mind to see metaphysical interpretation in other easy. It is just a word here or there, enough to encourage me to create and expand my thinking.

Our Christianity was in every moment of our lives. I heard the Biblical stories explained lovingly through my family, which we all still remember to this day. I left home when I was seventeen; I went out into the world and fell in love and finally married and my life continued.

I remember that my grandmother had over one acre of garden

around her house and as a child, I would walk with her as she gathered her flowers and herbs to decorate the table and her cooking was always exquisite to the pallet. For the setting on the breakfast table we would have a vase of freshly cut herbs, which would release their essence to strengthen our thoughts for the day. These herbs were used in the forthcoming meals. Flowers were placed on the table in the evening and a mixture of herbs brushed into the floor and also on the carpet square with a damp straw broom which would crush the essence of the herbs to relax the mind after a busy day. These herbs were not allowed to be crushed until just after four o'clock in the afternoon, after the pressure lamps had been pricked and primed ready to serve us with light for the evening meal. Their essence could release and remove the odor of kerosene without overpowering the men when they took off their boots and hats and had scrubbed up in preparation for the evening meal after the end of a long day in the paddocks.

The garden was all coordinated and grandmother planted the colors according to the colors of the rainbow. Herbs were sprinkled throughout as a companion to the flowers. You were introduced into the white flowers when you walked outside the door, its color cleared the cluttered mind and as you stepped forward you walked into the soft pinks; continuing down through the lilacs, into the blues of the cornflowers, then the greens which were the soft green of the Canterbury bells and onto the richer colors of lemons, oranges, reds and browns and as a child, it was like walking through a rainbow. My grandmother said that the colors were compatible with our inner alphabet as they urged us forward; our inner alphabet related to the words we would use, when we were busily thinking our thoughts. It was like an inner cleansing and healing of the chakras, as it is known today, back in my time it was known as Joseph's coat of many colors or the inner rainbow healing our self.

I knew how important each flower was by the color they emitted from the plant. You could read the value of the flower and what it had to offer you by the strength of its color. Even down to which part of the body it would be called to heal. The deeper the color, the more it connected to the problem in the lower section of the body. The lighter the color, the higher vibration was created. This is exactly the same as the colors we automatically release from our mind as we think each thought! We all have this inner rainbow that mathematically collects and arks its way up through our spinal column, when we think positive thoughts. These colors permeate their way throughout our aura, where they are reflected out to others. Now you can understand the Biblical story of Joseph (remember, as mentioned in my other works that Joseph is decoded as 'Youseph'. The word Youseph interprets as 'yourself'—through the codes of the unconscious mind—higher mind and his coat of many colors!).

And in the center of grandmother's land was the rose garden. There was a large rectangle green lawn, bordered with around a hundred rose bushes, all coordinated of course. We would pose for photos in the rose gallery, whether it was an engagement, Christmas gathering, wedding, anniversary or someone's birthday party. It did not matter if the weather was hot or cold, there was always a section of the garden that we could stand in front of and pose! That is the nice thing about my country, there is always a flower in bloom all year long. We saved the washing up water after the dishes were done, the bath water after we had finished our scrub up, the washing water when the clothes had been hung up to dry— all collected and bucketed out on to the garden. The men in the family did all of the preparation work to the soil and when the earth was ready, it was up to the women to put in the cuttings and strew the seeds.

My grandmother cooked her scrumptious meals, full of fresh vegetables and herbs, which were always ground in the mortar and pestle that she had brought back from China in the beginning of the 1900's, where she had studied Chinese herbal medicine, and the art of painting on ceramics, plus food preparation for three years; her order of the day was little and often, feeds the man; as this is the Asian way, in which she was taught. This stimulates the alchemy of their brain where they are always walking ahead of themselves and not lagging behind.

She was always explaining herbs and spices that she learned about in China during the preparation of each meal. "Be careful of curry, don't rob the meal of its own flavor, it is there to enhance the meal and the spices are to retrain the lining of the stomach as well as feed the endocrine system, and then work its way through to the immune system", she would say. "Be very careful of chili, it is only to be used once a month, if then. Why do I tell you this? We speak the English language; you don't need to inflame or stimulate your ego into distancing itself from taking a step forward. It needs to keep within its own boundaries to allow your emotions and feelings to also take their place within your vocabulary. Chili disturbs the language we speak, where we have a tendency to become more abrupt and callous with our choice of words".

Through research, and the lessons learned from customers who came into our restaurant and wanted more chili in their meals,

I quickly read their body language and realized that they were trapped in their thinking and were desperate to try and perpetuate their mind. Chili gave them that instant rush of cortisol which tied them over, (cortisol, the primary stress hormone, increases sugars— glucose, in the bloodstream, enhances the brain's use of glucose and increases the availability of substances that repair tissues). I discovered that the chemical elements in chili force the body to go beyond its normal comprehension, where it becomes addictive to the consumer through the ego's demands. Their tired and stressed voice is usually the first things we begin to notice, then to their own detriment, they become aggressive and quick to show their anger, as their overstressed ego tries to regain control over their thoughts in all situations and conversations. Due to the body's over production of cortisol, over time, people become lethargic and develop a weakened immune system. They will crave for more chili, as the mind of their ego becomes inflamed and reaches for a perpetual escape as their original thinking has been annulled, through the ego's vilification.

Chili is a plant of medication, to be used sparingly in healing. It lifts the layers of the stomach lining and distributes the toxins that are caught up in that area; all created through your repetitious thinking of an old thought or idea that has still not been digested correctly; those old thoughts have already served their purpose to you. Therefore, by you overdosing on chili there is no need to purge or permanently cleanse yourself of everything you have placed in your mouth. I noticed in hot countries if used sparingly, it is a healer to cool the body down when one becomes overheated and overloaded, where too many thoughts are running rampant with nowhere to reside as they have not let go of their past thinking. Now do you understand the haunting of old thoughts forced upon us by our own ego, as to how we create the diseases that occur in later life?

Please take a look at the countries that use chili in their hot and spicy meals; they are still at loggerheads with one another, as well as their neighbor next door. Why? They repress themselves when they cannot find contentment to their own inner sanctum. Their mind is measuring with other like mindedness, as they become deterred with their own thinking. This is the stage where they search for compatibility of thought, as they cannot find satisfaction within themselves; they feel that there is a part of themselves that are missing and on an unconscious level they connect to one another and automatically group together.

The latest information released, is the new research being conducted in relationship to chili and the connection to dementia, which is now affecting young people in their early twenties as their mind tries desperately to reshape itself. Fifty years ago, when I was taking an interest in the healing modalities, dementia began to awaken itself in the human chain as we moved into our late sixties, early seventies. How come we have brought the statistics down to the person who is only twenty years old? Another theory is the testing on chili and the new cancer strains that are mutating so quickly. What has drastically happened to our immune system, over such a short period of time, to disturb our thinking to such an extent?

Oh! The memories flood into my mind when I allow my memory bank to release its information. I have spoken of my grandmother's words in many seminars around the globe; of course, the chili addicts scoffed at my explanations. The parents and other siblings all agreed with me and were grateful for the information.

So, my grandmother was right; her Chinese education taught her to use chili sparingly and less often, to allow the stomach to clean itself naturally. Watch what you eat. Again, I ask you to relook at the countries that use this product for their own excuses, every day in the meal intake. And to end this section of my grandmother, before leaving China to migrate to Australia, she also studied Confucianism for a number of years, which continued right throughout her life. This information was passed down to the family as we grew into adult hood.

On a present note, one in ten babies born in my land, have allergies to food. We are number one in the world for allergies, and yet we have the healthiest fruit and vegetables that I have seen, as I travelled around the world. And yet so many have become allergic to this miracle. Why? Millions of dollars are spent in research to find an answer to this difficult situation.

An allergy is an immune system response or an over-reaction to the food you eat; or the animal you connect too. The same goes for the mold on the walls, dust mites, medication, insect bites and stings, to name a few. Now for the big one, an allergy is opened up on an inner level to react negatively through your thinking becoming blocked; all through you not expressing your desire to equate to the thought of your moment. You are busy designing, expressing an idea and not thinking it through to its completeness. This intolerance can be overcome much quicker through you finishing the ideas that are bouncing forward to be acknowledged, when you are in too much of a hurry to create a balance to your thinking.

Ninety percent of all illness created in the human body, is created through how you organize your thinking and bring each equation, which is a collection of thoughts on one subject, to a completion, not how you bring each idea together! There is only seven to ten percent created through hereditary conditioning.

Throughout the threading of our DNA the majority of us are implanted with every disease known to man. This threading becomes cross wired, when our inner energy cannot follow its own pathway. Each thought that has not earned its own satisfaction is constantly repeated over and over again, where it chokes up the neural highways to create a constant traffic jam.

What fascinated me more, was for me to understand as the years of study went by, that our food habits changed, as our intellect advanced to unfold itself. How did this occur? Our body communicates to itself every second of our existence, having the most amazing conversations with one another, if our mind is not chattering away through old thoughts constantly repeating themselves, we are able to hone in on the inner conversations, just as our thoughts combine with one another to form our sentences. As we stepped forward intellectually, our ego was quick to deny our new found grace; therefore we would again crave our old food habits, which automatically slowed us down.

Our old thinking patterns would come back to haunt us! We seemed to be living the same experiences over and over again, as our body could not make headway to comprehend these current new ideas. There was no harmonizing and balancing of our mind. This held our thinking at bay and made our new education harder for us to accept. The Guardian in charge of these thoughts is in the hands of the Pituitary Gland, as it assesses the value of each thought, through them continuing their communal growth. Hopefully this explains to you how our diseases have free reign over all thoughts, if we are constantly walking backwards on our self. Thank you for reading these paragraphs.

We had our own meat from the chickens, turkeys, ducks, and geese; then there were the sheep, pigs, wild goats and cattle. We could supply our own terrines, brawns, casseroles, pickled and smoked meats, roasts, milk, cream, butter and cheese. We had our own hives, which supplied our honey and assisted us in making our own candles with ground up lavender heads to rest our mind throughout the night. We had soap that could be used throughout the day, and a different blend for the night wash.

We planted our own orchards for fruit, jams and preserves,

vegetables to share with our meals and chutneys and relishes. We baked our own bread, cakes and biscuits from the harvest of the wheat, oats, rice, millet, maize, and barley that we harvested each year.

We made our soap mixed with oats and lavender and calendula for the women to replace the moisture in our skin. Grandmother's knowledge of Aromatherapy was amazing as she explained the use of flowers owing to her training in China. There was ground up barley and softly sieved sand for the men to lift the grease off their hands as they washed them. These gifts from the eternal kingdom served us in many different ways. There were six meals per day, three large and three smaller ones. No one became ill, as our mind had been forewarned with our herbal concoctions.

Grandmother was also known as the local healer of the area. Her alchemy through the knowledge of herbs and spices were brilliant. There was no doctor in nearly a hundred and fifty kilometers and when someone in the area was sick, she would either receive a phone call or someone would come by the property and out she would go talking to her plants and gathering her herbs and her special big black cast iron pot would go on the old wood stove and the herbs were rendered down into a concoction of "one tablespoon a day please for seven days and then have three days off, to allow the body to catch up with the herbs and work on your illness." As a young child, my position in the house was to bless the bottles once they had come out of the sterilizer and sit alongside of her when she had poured the mixture in and make sure the cork was ready to place into the bottle. Of course, the people were healed in their given moment as they had turned their worries over to my grandmother. She always knew how strong their illness was and when to tell them to make an appointment in the nearest town to see the local doctor. And, sure enough they would go to town and have their operation, then come back to her for a checkup. I now know where I have inherited this information from. We don't follow in our parent's footsteps; we follow in the pathways our grandparents carved out for us to walk forward to inherit. As explained in my previous works, the ego tries to control the parent, and yet reveres the previous generation, which is released through a religious veneration that is generated through our mind and body balancing as a complete unit.

As the grapes that grew over the arbor at the rear of the house started to produce their new seasons growth, this helped keep the rooms cooler. Every child had to eat ten green grapes before they were ripe. This was to purify our blood and cleanse it after the short winter where we were rugged up all day. It worked! We were more than prepared for the long hot summer months ahead.

Grandmother never said "No! Don't touch." When I asked to rub a leaf together to emit the essence she would say, "yes, snip the fresh leaves cleanly from the top with your fingers, they are the freshest part of the plant and sniff the essence deep down into your lungs and anything nasty in the way of viruses, or pending diseases that is hanging around you looking for a place to reside and create itself, will soon leave home. Remember, we are all taught that God's gift to us is his garden." She also taught me how to plant my seeds with companion herbs. I learned the difference between herbs and weeds. A herb would benefit and a weed would hinder my flowers and vegetables. I learned to watch what weeds found their way forward into evolving their next evolutionary step, as they sprung up around my new seedlings, to see if they were a robber that would interfere with the energy of the new plant or if they were a friend which would form a relationship to strengthen the plant. The robber would feed itself on the innocence of the new growth; it was like a parasite and had to be removed.

Grandmother explained that the garden had much to teach us, as our body also worked on the same parallel as the garden. If we had thoughts that could not find their own strength, then there was a parasite that would create a nest for it to strengthen itself and a disease became immanent. My crops of vegetables were always successful. I learned to understand how the plant kingdom is identical to the human kingdom.

And we all know by now, that every species that has evolved on this planet, is indelibly imprinted and is mathematically registered within the genes of every human.

I now feel honored to finally understanding the magnificence to the language of the mathematical universal laws that every human must abide by. They are explaining how our genes communicate with one another to harmonize and balance our body; which prepares the mind for the words that autonomously release for us to speak. Who do I thank? I would like to thank God (when decoded it is explaining to us the **G**reatest **O**racle of the **D**ivine) which all belongs to our inner language, the one that keeps us on the straight and narrow, for anointing us with this genetic engineering which has become my most precious gift.

To return back to the story, my grandmother taught me back in the late-forties through to the mid-fifties, where and how to attract energy through planting the dried cow horns which were filled with their own waste products and buried, then months later were taken out of the ground and buried in the new garden bed. She also liked some of the cow horns to be filled with fresh sea sand once a year. When we had killed the beast, the horns were severed and placed on top of the ant nests; which were built up into mounds behind the toilet and this was half way down the paddock and a good three-minute walk away. I often wondered why the meat ants had collected to build their nests behind there. Anyway, the ants would clean the fibrous tissue out of the horns. We also used the cow horns as beakers to drink out of; flower vases on the table or cupboard, and they were lovingly polished with bee's wax where they glowed through the lamp light on the table. It wasn't until the generators came out that we could enjoy the power of electricity with our 25-watt globes, which was only allowed for two hours of a night.

When members of the family would go for holidays to the ocean once a year after the wheat harvest, they had to bring back a fresh bucket of sand from the beach for grandmother. The silica and salt of the sand once buried inside the horns would change the molecular structure of the soil and no matter how tired or parched it felt, it would purify the soil and spring into life once again.

Grandmother having spent those three years in China in 1903-6, was taught how to hum to her vegetables and she would walk through her garden humming to her plants, which I now understand was creating a vibration firstly for the plants, as well as assisting her to reach her own resonance to promote her own sound. I can still recall how some of them seemed to bow to her as she walked down her rows. This fascinated me as there wasn't any wind to move them; they knew her sound and were honoring her.

We now understand that the symbol OM or AUM when chanted creates its own frequency, where we lift the eternal layers of consciousness to create a field of levitation which can occur, and my grandmother lived it around 140 years ago.

I can still recall the smell of the ocean when I put my head over the bucket as a child. It stayed fresh and never went sour and the smell was there all year long. There were millions of tiny little shells in the sand and these were ground up in the mortar and the pestle and grandmother would create them into a paste and this was scattered around certain plants who were not feeling too well. She explained to me that the shapes of these tiny shells were in perfect unison to God's original plan and that they would help to heal whatever they came into contact with. These old wives tales are still used as a reflection of today's intuitiveness, as they were all chemically free and correct at that time of our evolution. Today we have continued on with their story and advanced upon the knowledge of the past. Their mathematical shape would release the correct prescription to the plant. Today we are more aware of the spiral the golden mean creates as reflected in a sea shell.

Once again it was the men's job to collect the sand, as they had to make sure that it was not spilt on the way home, which was just on nine hundred kilometers away, over rough dirt roads. One memory that still abounds in my mind is that I can recall the thrill of driving on a bitumen road. The car seemed to glide over the road and I often stuck my head out of the car window to see if the tires were really on the road. I felt like we were flying as I could not feel the bumps of the corrugated dirt roads!

As my childhood expanded, I became fascinated with how things worked. I loved being outdoors; it was much safer than the kitchen. I had my own motorbike by the time I was nine. I learned to drive a semi-trailer from one gate to the next, when I celebrated my tenth birthday, I also received my first watch as I was now in double figures, therefore I had more responsibility to live up to and was to become more aware of time. I was propped up with wheat bags so that I could reach the brakes and accelerator with my father as the passenger guiding me through the gears. Another surprise was for my eleventh birthday when I received a 22 rifle with a box of shells that had to last me twelve months so there was not too much sky larking around. I could pull down a rabbit or two for the oven, but, if I took its life, I had to tell it a story of how it would benefit the family and thank it for its service to us.

I then had to skin and clean it myself and then I could take it into the kitchen, where it had to be soaked in coarse salt and water to clear the carcass of any toxins. I then had to place the pelt inside out on the u-shaped wire to dry and say thank you for the gift it had given me. As the pelts added up, they were sent to Sydney where they were tanned and made into the softest blankets one could imagine, we also made floor rugs and slippers, a small hat to keep our ears from chilblains and mittens to keep the hands and feet warm on cold and frosty mornings.

I could stop a goanna in his tracks as he was about to devour the eggs in the hen house or a snake who was about to devour the hens! The carcasses were dragged behind the toilet and placed on the ant's nest where in time we could view the skeletal structures bone by bone. My younger brother would compare them to the ancient prehistoric animals. No one bothered to stay in the toilet too long to read the scraps of paper, as the stench from the rotting carcass could be unbearable for a few days.

Another teaching of grandmother's was how to coil a piece of copper pipe and plant it into the ground; the end of the pipe had to be planted six inches into the ground to transfer the energy around the vegetable beds. She placed three copper coils around the rows in a triangle shape. It could not be four; that didn't work as four would divert the energy and could cancel itself out. Needless to say, we were again reminded that God's gift to us was in his garden.

I loved the stories she told, when she taught me all about the plant kingdom. That everything that God had designed had to earn its place on this planet. (Learning comes from explanations that we receive from someone else; earnings are released to us from your inner self). Every plant, every tree, all needed their own temperament to encourage them to grow, to advance themselves. They needed the minerals from under the earth and the elements in the earth to sustain them. Their territory became their boundary, they never ventured outside of their own perimeter, until the species of the planet assisted. Just as our own body needs the elements of the earth and minerals to keep us alive. Their seed could be carried along with the birds, the wind, the fire or the water, which propagated further down the track where they found a new home in soil of same mind. And that goes for every species on the planet as well; they have all had to earn their place to exist on the earth.

I can still recall some of her sayings when we were down in the mouth, "now remember, every cloud has a silver lining" or maybe it was "this too will pass" to assist us with what we were going through in the moment. If the same thought was still there the next morning, then we had held onto it for too long to support us, therefore we were hindering our own growth. As I write these words to you now, there are so many stories waiting to be shared with you. One that has stood by me all of my life was 'Aim for the highest; there is room at the top.' And as always after our church service had finished on Sundays, she would remind us children that at the end of our day there had to be something that we had learned to carry us forward into tomorrow and if we felt we had earned something, it would support us for the rest of our life! Do not allow your mind to keep on repeating its thoughts. If we had learned nothing, then we had totally wasted our day!! We all remember that message to this day.

This was my life as a child. And of course, I carried these teachings into my life as a married woman and passed them onto my children. Now it's the grandchildren's time and the great grandchildren's turn. If I was shaped like a phone or an iPad and had a keypad, maybe I would be heard more clearly!

Please have a long glass of water after reading this chapter, you have earned the cleanse. Thank you for listening to my story.

*There is a fundamental order underlying all things,
there is a grand design...*
Albert Einstein

Chapter 2
Discovering The Way

On the 11th November, 1977 I received my introduction into a higher level of the next intellectual language, where it began in earnest. My late husband and I owned a property in Central Queensland, in Australia. It is one of the hottest and most humid parts of Australia and when the monsoons known as the wet season, introduced themselves to us over the peak of the summer months, we were deluged with rain. It had a strength that we as a family had to keep up with and grow into and more importantly, accept and respect. These four months of the year really tested one's senses. We had a large creek that ran through the property, which worried me slightly when I began to sense the heaviness of the rain that seemed to bucket down from the sky; everything flooded so quickly. There was many a night when I would try to go to sleep with my leg dangling on the floor outside the bed, so that the floodwaters would wake me when they entered the house. At that particular time, I had cancer of the cervix and was receiving chemotherapy. I was at my wits end as to how I could overcome this disease. It was not the verdict I wanted to accept! I had five young children to rare and explain to them how they could reach adulthood. I did not think that I could step down onto the last rung of my own ladder, as there were no more, for me to step back onto. My emotional mind had been pushed under the carpet so to speak and I was walking all over myself and trampling myself into the ground.

It was also during this time that the family had come to stay so that we could spend Christmas together; we had nineteen family guests staying with us, as well as the seven of my own, so there were twenty six people to feed and take care of and my relaxation time came when I was down in the dairy with my cows. I loved their smell, their homeliness and their contentment. They seemed to fix any immediate problem that was busily manifesting around me. I walked away with my buckets full of rich sustenance for the family to grow and thrive on through the butter and cheese that I made, the cream and all of those cakes and baked puddings and this left me feeling satisfied that there was always plenty of food on the table.

One evening as I was milking the last cow, I was depleted emotionally and feeling sorry for myself. 'Give me the strength to do what I had to do' was my plea to the heavens. There is not enough time to enjoy the fun. The trouble was, I had always been such a perfectionist with knowing that everyone must be happy and contented; I seemed to forget myself, which is a typical mothering attitude. The second dose of chemotherapy was making me want to be sick all of the time and I just had to find the strength to go on. As I waited for my last cow to drop her milk down, I felt a vibration run up my back, and this vibration felt different to anything I had ever experienced before. I could feel a drumming in my head, and I could also feel different energies pulsating through different sections of my body.

We had a carpet snake that lived in the dairy, and we called him Jack. He was ten feet or 3.3 meters long and ate the rats in the grain shed, so he became a friend in need. When Jack wanted milk, he would slide along the top rafters and hang down close to the back of the cow and we would tilt the teat of the cow up, and squirt the milk into his mouth. I thought that this was the vibration I had been sensing and I looked up but he was not there.

As this vibration coursed up and down through my vertebrae, I felt very calm and peaceful, so I buried my head into the flank of the cow and milked her until the bucket was full. As I did this, I could feel my strength returning, my emotions settled and my mind became silent and still. Half an hour seemed to go by in just one minute.

When the bucket was finally full, I stood up to let the cows out, and as I opened the gate, I felt that vibration travel up my spine again. I looked across the creek to the paddock on the other side and saw three lights bobbing along the ground. I thought it might have been my sons over there, with the pressure lamps, so I coo-eed out over the paddock to what I thought were the boys. This attracted my husband who was working on a tractor in the machinery shed and he came over to see what I was doing. I asked him why the boys were out in the paddock and I showed him the lights and said I was worried because the grass was still tinder dry in parts and the smallest spark could have started a fire. My husband carried the milk to the house and told me that they were all inside the house, but he would go and see who it was anyway, just in case it was someone who was about to maverick one of the cattle to assist them with their Christmas and who had no right being there.

There were nine men in my house, so loaded with guns and riding motorbikes, tractors, cars and trucks, they headed off to investigate the lights. A short while later the men started forming a tighter circle with the vehicles, I saw from the cattle yards the three lights lift up off the ground and hover above the trees. The men stopped dead in their tracks to view the phenomenon. The lights started dancing around in the sky, but, as the men walked towards them, the lights flew off over the hill. The men returned to the house and the kettle went on for a big pot of tea. It was the quietest evening we had spent together in a long time. We could not explain the phenomena. The conversations began many times, and yet there was a difficulty to finish them. We were all quite stunned.

Within two days of that experience, I knew that my cancer had gone. Knew what? I just knew that my death sentence had been lifted. Little did I know that this was my introduction into the sacred laws of Shamanism, which I now realize is a giant step into the collective Laws of the Universe.

My life began to change rapidly after this event; Christmas came and went in a happy and fulfilling way. Laughter reigned supreme! Gifts were exchanged. We roasted the pig and the lamb on the spit as well as the young steer and there was enough food prepared to symbolically feed the five thousand who seemed to arrive at the door, with a ham, cake, pie, casserole or beer in their hands. Our yearly celebration exceeded our expectations. We thought that this maybe the last time we would spend together as I had been given the death sentence. I settled their minds as we all said our good-byes to one another, emotions were rife and my final words to them was that I would like to have them again next year for Christmas.

As I settled back into the chores with a quieter house, I began to test myself each day to see how far my strength was returning. One of my tests came when I could pick up my two twenty gallon buckets, that I carried full of water down the paddock to water my mango trees. During my treatment my strength had depleted and I became weaker, I only had the energy to half or quarter fill the buckets and my body screamed for attention when I had finished; so, into the bedroom I would go for half an hour to recuperate. As time went on, with a focused mind I began to put a little more in the buckets each time I watered. When I could fill those two twenty gallon containers to near the top I would place my yolk around my neck, hook up the buckets and shuffle off down the paddock, I knew I was well on the way to recovery.

I had forgotten my next appointment for chemotherapy and only became aware when my doctor came out to our property to find out why I had not come to him. I told him that all was well, I was in remission; I had no need to come again. He wanted to know why and started to call me a foolish woman as I explained the only way I knew how, which was through my innocence; that my cancer had been taken from me. I explained about the lights and of course he was flabbergasted to think that I believed in such a thing. Give me time to get the children back to school and I will come in for tests, was my reply. Three months after the event I went back into town for my check-up. My hair had started to grow back again and I felt female and human once again. I was screened and tests were done over and over again and all to no avail; the cancer was in remission and had all but nearly disappeared.

When I despair, I remember
That all throughout the pages of history,
The way of Truth and Love has always won.
Mahatma Gandhi

Chapter 3
Introduction To The Ancient Wisdoms

It was through the changes I had made to my old belief system, that those lights came into my life once again. I had completed the next stage of my life's program to my satisfaction. My only fear was the immensity of the knowledge I found myself stepping into; could I remember it all; could I explain it correctly; would I forget the important parts!

My introduction into the educational training of the Ancient Wisdoms began once again. The lights made contact again two years later (in 1979) at my daughter's engagement party. The time was 11:11 pm.

As the guests danced into the night, those three bright lights appeared, dancing in the sky to the beat of our music. We had invited 120 people that evening, and this phenomenon stunned them all. They laughed and cheered at the movement of those lightships swaying in the night sky. My late husband and a friend went over in the direction of the lights and Whoosh! The lights disappeared very quickly over the next hill and out of sight. As you can imagine, it took us all quite a while to get back to dancing! These lights that appeared in the sky never fazed the locals as they had grown up with them most of their lives and they never made any problems. Often the locals would ring the local Airport, which was thirty kilometers away to enquire, but they could not offer them an explanation, as there were no planes in the area. We were off the beaten track. I found out many years later when it came time to sell our property that we were on an energy grid. After we had moved away from the area a power station was built on these grids.

Why had I been introduced to this intelligence of knowledge known as Extra Terrestrial; what were they to do with my life? The lessons I began to learn throughout the following ten years were difficult ones emotionally, as I had to begin to disconnect from my daughter, as she had now grown up and had chosen to join another member of one of the twelve Tribes.

Remember as previously explained in my other works, there are only twelve of us walking the planet; every human belongs to one of the twelve tribes of Israel as explained through the codes written in the Old Testament. These twelve tribes are each echoing a strand of our DNA. This relates to each pregnancy being delivered unto (from above) the mother, through the relationship of her mind! If she is still creating excuses for her own thinking, then the pregnancy will occur, where the child will come forth to remind her of the courage she will strive to earn, to rare the child. As we already know, each child has its own set of values.

My daughter was breaking away from her childhood home and had chosen her new partner. My mother had taught her the arts of knitting, crocheting, embroidering, darning and replacing zips and her specialty, which was cooking. She was quick to learn as she did not argue with my mother. They laughed a lot. I taught her the art of arranging the home, cooking, herbal knowledge, preserving, etiquette, and the secrets attached to old wives tales that I had learned from my grandmother. My daughter was becoming my emotional age. Her thoughts were focusing on her new life, her future. I still had the rest of the family to be responsible for, until their turn came. Are you noticing the way I am speaking to you? My daughter was becoming my emotional age? She was now a woman and experiencing her own freedom and was in training through the responsibility of her unconscious mind (higher mind) as to how she had to react through her next phase of intellect. She had to handle these new emotions correctly for her to attain her own satisfaction.

You are now being introduced to the metaphorical or metaphysical language also known to us as the language announcing the 'matter of physics' which is explaining itself to you through your inner wisdom. This metaphorical language is permanently reacting to the worlds of your inner thoughts. Not necessarily, how you speak to others. It is making you aware of accepting the language of your DNA, as to how your alphabet (the words we would use, when we are busily thinking our thoughts) has been collected over the millennium. My daughter was born with my mathematics and her father's; therefore, she had to understand and grow through her emotional dilemmas first to understand herself, before she could acknowledge her own inner strength. Just as we all must do.

That second contact took away my fear of extra-terrestrial intelligence. We had been visited twice and no harm was done. I went on to rear my children to adulthood and was then emotionally driven to begin to fulfill my own dreams. I wanted time for pottery; expand my cake decorating and the correct procedure involved with flower arranging. I had a fascination for Ikebana, and played with it for many years, until I could do a course and learn correctly, also to polish up my painting skills. I was already a good cook and great gardener and could make beautiful soap and candles, which I have to thank my mother and grandmother, as they had both excelled in these fine arts and they had shared their knowledge and taught me both of these gifts at an early age. I now had to learn to re-awaken the daughter in me, once mine had grown and equalized my emotional age; this prepared me to accept the responsibilities of stepping forward into my next world of educating myself into the next lessons of my intellectual light.

As I moved into these new experiences I realized that everything we learn to do, must equate with the world of our inner mathematics. These mathematical seeds had been endowed to us before we were born, through the intellect of our past generations. They were the creation of our DNA. These seeds propagated themselves as we released our next positive thought! Therefore, we were living the same thought forms as our grandparents had acquired in their lifetime. The difference was that we could advance ourselves on from them to add to the congruence we had inherited.

Teachers came to the outback and took over the local halls for the day where we could all attend to experience something new. They taught me all of those gifts of adding to my fields of pottery, floristry etc; that I wanted to understand; as I learned and earned my next step. I entered my chutneys and pickles and flower arranging into shows and collected my certificates. Little did I realize that these teachers had always been there to offer their gifts to others. It was just that I had not been ready at that time to accept their knowledge. I soon realized that it was me who had to grow up!

Just a quick explanation about our brain/mind. Our brain has two hemispheres—two parts. The left brain is our logic (conscious mind). The left brain is our masculine side; our ego, our primal fear, and as stated our logic. It represents how we are representing ourselves to others through releasing from within. The right brain is our emotions (subconscious mind). The right brain is our feminine side, our inner creativity. We give out to others with the right side, and our energy in motion—or emotion—creates itself from how we are giving and receiving to and from the self. The right brain represents what we are doing to ourselves within, and what we are capable of receiving through ourselves—through our being aware of that giving.

The people who live in their logical ego sense are perfect, and so, too, are the people who live in their creative emotional sense. In understanding the logical sense, we understand through our primal inheritance, where it begins to fit with common sense. The mind of logic is the echo from whatever is created, and it is also, what we attract in our outer worlds; the emotional mind sits within and takes care of our sense of responsibility.

We cannot survive on this planet without both ego and emotions. Our journey is to learn how to balance both brains so that we may become more aware of the supportiveness of our unconscious mind, (called by many names such as the higher mind, supra-consciousness etc.). The unconscious mind is the freedom with which we can tune into ourselves, but only when the other two parts of our brain have balanced through our attitude to our self. We touch and connect to our unconscious mind, as the other two brains encompass the Soul through looking into one another.

If we like to take this further. Our left brain, our conscious self, is responsible for the first and second-dimensional mind. Our right brain, our subconscious self; is responsible for the third dimension and the relationship to the introduction of the fourth dimension. The balance of both brains is the doorway up into our unconscious mind, which allows it to be responsible for the temple of self to live up to its expectations. Temple of self means we are training our self, moment by moment, to have control over our thinking. Our unconscious mind is the make-up of our Divine Inheritance—or the language of our Soul—it is our life force. The unconscious mind is the world of telepathic communication.

They can because they think they can.
Virgil

Chapter 4
Initiation Into The Ancient Wisdoms

Over the following years I learned as much as I could and knew that I was ready for the next educated step of my life to continue. We sold the farm and my late husband and I went into another venture and purchased a construction company where we were given a contract for eighteen months rebuilding the roads in the centre of Australia. He received a contract with a larger construction company to build up the road from Adelaide up through the centre of the outback to Alice Springs. We were to make the highway an all-weather road, which was suitable for both the wet season and the dry weather conditions as the traffic was becoming heavier due to the introduction of the four-wheel drive. Everyone wanted to tour the 'Outback' at that time, as it was very fashionable. During those years, there was my husband, the last two children and myself living in the town of Coober Pedy, which was approximately a five-hour drive south of Uluru, known previously as Ayres Rock, and approximately eight hours south of Alice Springs. When I had finally arrived into this area after a three-day drive, I felt that I had entered the twilight zone; the land seemed to be caught between other worlds where somehow, I had to be able to see both sides of the same coin. It seemed so unnatural with its eerie landscape. I felt like my mind had shrunk to the size of a pea through its pure vastness; I also felt that I was becoming an animated object. I could taste the metallic energy in my teeth.

I had a quick look at my two beautiful young boys who had the 'look of expectation' in their eyes that said "Welcome to your new home for the next twelve—eighteen months!" Their first reply was "But mum there's no trees, there's no grass, it's not normal, there's nothing as far as the eye can see, just a few tin sheds here and there!"

My home was a cave in the side of the hill, which is known as a 'dugout,' which was approximately 24 metres below the surface of the ground. My younger brother had just passed over at the age of thirty eight years of age and when we lose a member of our family, it seems to make us more aware of our own short comings and the experiences we need to finish in our own life, so it was a great move for us to go into this area and take up another challenge in our lives. The name Coober Pedy was named by the indigenous Australians perplexed by the early settlers' preference for subterranean living.

This name means 'white man who stands up in a burrow' and the town is renowned for the opals, which have made their home in this area of the planet. The Mad Max movies and also the movie 'Priscilla Queen of the Desert' and many others were all made in this magnificent outback area. So, if you have seen these movies, you may have seen the familiarities of the land I am continuing to speak about.

The land was sparse and trees were stunted and few and far between. I was to meet my father's side of my family for the first time. They had lived in the area for over forty years digging the opals out of the ground. The family had magnificent dugouts that were so modern and cool in the summer, and cozy and warm in the winter, where the inside temperature regulated around 21 degrees Celsius all year round. You could build each room as large as your imagination, the larger the room, the cooler it was during the heat. The air ducts were the width of a 44 gallon drum all the way from the ceiling, up to the top of the hill. Sometimes 30 metres high, so the natural current of air was always available, making the inside of the house breathe. My new cousin's wives were teachers in the local school and nursing sisters in the hospital and introduced me to the people and into the area.

We rented a beautiful roomy dugout which was spray painted white and stayed in this area for just on eighteen months until the job had finished. While we lived there, I took on a voluntary position working with the South Australian Education Department, working with children who had difficulties with understanding and accepting their own levels of education. I also had the opportunity to attend courses which were provided by the Government and available to the outback women. I learned how to sew and make my garments with stretch sewing classes. I made my boys their warm track suits for the snappy and cold winter, which we were not prepared for.

The desert has its own climate and knows the ways of reproducing itself when there is no rain. The plants need that snap of ice for the previous generations to bare their seeds on the desert floor to continue the species and allow the next season to retrain them back into what they already have accomplished. The same goes for us humans. We need a cold snap in the weather to retrain our thoughts from becoming too lethargic. When those wild flowers birth out of the ground after this snappy winter, they are a joy to behold. Millions of them seem to grow and flower in less than three weeks. Their season is so quick to bloom. They were a sight for my eyes, which never seemed to want to leave those thousands of hectares that were colored by the rainbow spread right on top of the ground. When the flowers are full, the colors mutate with the landscape which becomes a painter's paradise as far as the eyes can see. My favorite flower is known as Sturt's Desert Pea. It grows in the waterless red desert and spreads itself out softly over the sand, sometimes in a circular fashion which is up to 2-3 metres in circumference and when its flowers come out of the centre of the bush they are a feast for the mind. From their gestation, it takes the flowers around four months to reach their fulfillment. They become a pure deep rich red in color with a piercing black centre. They are spread over the sand for around five to six months of the year.

Over time I began to work more with the Aboriginal children, where I quickly realized that I had to change my way of thinking in order for me to understand their way of evaluating a difficult situation, as it was so different to mine. They seemed to be speaking not only a different language but they viewed and accepted their communication of what they were saying, through different eyes. They viewed their truth being returned back to them through their softly spoken words. It took me many months to adjust to their way of thinking. This was the beginning of my initiation into the world of the Ancient Wisdoms. I am so pleased that I began with the children as I was being initiated correctly. This precious elder race of humanity from my land have lived in their unconscious mind (higher mind) for millennia; it is where they have the gift of being able to see through what they are explaining to others. Something we are now eager to return too; to look back into. My respect grew for them over the coming months as I learned to shape shift my mind into their worlds of thought. I knew for me to succeed with the children, I had to think and become an Aborigine.

*My totem was beginning to evolve as
my intelligence took its new shape.*
Omni

Chapter 5
Initiation Into The Tribal Law

While living in Coober Pedy, I spent those glorious months working mostly with one of three tribes who lived in the area and the tribe that stepped forward for me to learn from was the Pitjanjatjarra tribe, which through their pronunciation, it was spoken to me as 'Pit-yan-yat-yarra.'

Allow me to show you how to take this word back into what we understand as the principles of the early Egyptian codes and how it was originally pronounced, and we say the word 'Pit-An-Hat-Ha-Rha.' If we take notice of the last two syllables we find the word 'Ha-Rha' is the word for Soul in the ancient Vedantic language or to be more precise through the sacred alphabet this word means 'HA—in the name of the—RAH—the one who reigns.' Through my previous works, you will understand how this word is created through the power of our speech, as it stems up from our thyroid gland and moves into the energy of the Pituitary gland. Do you recall in my book, 'Decoding the Mind of God', how we learned to understand the energy of our glandular system is stimulated up through our inner alphabet to help us produce the words we speak?

Are you beginning to see the Universal Language of Babylon? This same language is also in the tribal knowledge of Papua New Guinea where we speak to them in the Pityan or Pitjan Language. Most people refer to this as 'Pigeon English' (Pidgin) so you can see how the mind understood this word. The pigeon, through the Shamanistic language, is the message or the inner messenger. The messenger is the connection to our sonic sound i.e., as to how we subconsciously receive a message delivered to us from our unconscious mind (higher mind). When we think a thought, it is registered in the Collective Consciousness which is known to us through the language of Shamanism, as the Soul mind. The pigeon relies totally on its sonic sound for it to survive. It is never lost! It has the same hearing as every other bird; they register and hear our thoughts before we have finished our sentences. This wonderful species of the divine plan, known as the Collective Consciousness, is representing our guardian angel; it just appears before us to assist us in the heaviness that we have created in our mind, all through us not digesting our thoughts correctly. So, this tribe was known and referred to by other tribes as—the messengers, the ones who are able to hear the right message, in the name of the one who reigns. In other words, the ones who are in charge of themselves.

I could quote hundreds of stories from people who came to ask for assistance, as to how the pigeon appeared at their window, strutted up and down the window ledge and emptied itself out, and then took off! What is the message it is delivering? Let's read it metaphysically! Pigeon is asking us to open the window of our mind and to balance our thinking by strutting backwards and forwards, bring both hemispheres of our brain together, and to let go of the past! How many of you realize that these natural laws create the language of Metaphysics (or the matter of physics); all of which is now referred to as the mathematical laws that every living species on the planet receives and obeys. These laws have been here for us to tune into, ever since the world began! It is an introduction into the telepathic enhancement which becomes our inheritance; that keeps this planet in its own continuous orbit and is available to all of you. It is the next educated step of humanities earnings! Until you have earned the right to step into this next realm of intelligence you will stay innocently unaware of this global responsibility, that each species endures all of their lives. Please remember everything out there, reflects an instantaneous message to what your thoughts are creating inside your mind at this moment in time.

I gradually came into contact with the parents of the children of the Pitjanjatjarra tribe and then earned my way up to be able to communicate with the Elders. They spoke with a depth of pride regarding their little ones and with such emotional understanding for what was expected of their children, through our teachings. They knew of the difficulties that their children had to try and understand the new world of thought, we were introducing to them. More importantly, they had to try to accept our ways, which were just plain common sense to our intelligence and formed a different sense of responsibility to theirs. Their priorities were connected more to the teachings of the family and were much higher than ours; they were more on an inner spiritual level. Only when I had allowed myself to sacrifice to them, i.e., when I had the opportunity to release my ego, where I could begin to think in an emotional context, did they begin to show me their ways. The Elders were always asking me to go steady, and not to push their future generations or their family too fast and high. "This is all new to them, teach them slowly Kelly Missus and they will learn to get it right" was the Elders call to me.

One of the younger Elders who was in training to become a Kadaitcha Medicine Man of the tribe, had received the Christian name of Peter, from the missions, became my good friend. He was reared in the

Ernabella Mission area, a few hundred kilometers away. Peter wanted to be treated as white and wanted me to relate to him through his Christian name. "You look at me Missus, the same way I look at you and we will learn from one another and then we can walk and talk with the sticks." he used to say to me.

There are hundreds of stories that spring into my mind as I write this story from my memory banks. I was always in an exalted state of mind as I listened to Peter training me into his ways. I was excited to be introduced into my inner language, as I was being re-educated into accepting a different explanation to my way of life. There was and still is, not allowed any sympathy with his explanation to this ancient knowledge.

As my initiation grew, Peter started to collect and gather my tools that he thought I needed to assist me as I earned them throughout my education. The first gift came after three months and it was the Winnow dish that had been carved out of a tree and allowed to drop when it had collected its own sap. They referred to it as the u-an-na dish. It was worn down over the years and the inside of the bowl was as smooth as silk. It takes time for these items to be prepared. As they found the tree which was applicable to the item they wanted to form, they would chip the shape of the dish they wanted to create from around the trunk of the tree and would return when the sap had gradually released and had dried and the tree had healed its first wound, then they would go back again and chip a bit deeper into the trunk. This process would go on over time until the dish would lift itself away from the trunk of the tree naturally and when it had dropped off the tree onto the ground it would be ready to rub down and used. This is exactly the same way they created the form of the boomerang, also their canoe. It took time for the branch or trunk of the tree to release what they were creating. There was a respect and a knowing for nature that was different to ours; we chop down the tree and see what we can construct out of the whole thing! Many of those trees are still alive and growing to this day. Time always seemed to be on their side.

All through their time of procuring the tools they needed, there was no destruction to the tree as it healed itself during the whole process. The newly created dish would not warp as it had not died of destruction; it had learned to procure a percentage of its own sap as it grew apart from the tree and had taken on its own life force. Similar to what we now refer to as cloning, don't you think? It was hollowed out with round flat stones into a smooth shape as the seeds they used were of a finite variety owing to the lack of rain in the area. This gift was for me to prepare my seeds of thought into a form of fine creamy flour, which would be easy to digest to nourish and feed myself.

At the end of the next three months, I received my rod-shaped digging tool, with a sharp hook at the end that I could place around the roots to reinforce my strength to bring them to the surface. This was for me to dig out my roots, which would heal me and keep me in contact with the elements of the earth. These elements that I could take from the plants would sustain me no matter what I had to confront, in my future. Remember what grows under the ground is the sustenance we need for the gravity fields of the mind and body, to keep honing in on one another. This creates the knowledge as to how we can understand our inner strength, which gives us the sustenance, to create our own opportunity to outgrow our previous thoughts.

My totem was beginning to evolve as my intelligence took its new shape. I was sampling new food and to remind you of my grandmother's words that this is where we must teach our children to eat all of their vegetables; as the essence of each species of food is registered in our brain, which strengthens and creates a chemical reaction that is autonomously produced inside the light membranes of the brain. The easiest way to do this is to mash and mix each vegetable or puree the components together. Our brain needs the species of these mathematical laws to help prepare itself. It is not the taste of each vegetable; it is the element of that species that is needed to strengthen and refurbish our body. Again, we are earning our inner Totem Power.

Once we have eaten a species of vegetable, the mathematical intensity of it stays with us for the rest of our life. Take a moment to reflect back into your own lives to remember what vegetables you rejected as a child? What did you miss out on? It's never too late; eat or juice them now to stimulate your senses into creating new ideas, also to be of service to you in your future.

The universe we live in, is an enormous quantum computer, where we find everything is beginning to become an earning, not just a learning!
Omni

Chapter 6
Receiving My Shamanic Tools

Around nine months into my teachings with Peter, he presented me with my clapping sticks; I learned to hear the sound of the wind. Both sticks were engraved with the symbols of the air. He explained that I could always call on the wind; so that I could always hear my own thoughts come home to me and know that I would never be lost. I had to be able to hear the echo that they created when I began to call on the spirit of the Rainbow Serpent to realize what I was capable of attracting and available to me, owing to the direction I was standing in, whether it is North, South, East or West. Each direction supplies its own energetic force field.

This took time for me to realize that it was the way I brought my sticks together, it was not the hit that brought the energy together, it had to create the sound of a clap and this movement created the echo. Similar to the Asiatic substance that creates their Fung Shwa (Feng Shui). If I was facing in the direction of the east, the sound was different to me facing west, the north or the south. I found that the sound was deepened when I was facing the south, and flatter if I was facing the west. It rebounded if I was facing the east and became lighter if I was facing the north. There were many hours of practice to earn this field of education. Thank goodness for my training in music as to how I learned the sound of sharps and flats when incorporated into the musical score.

There were five distinct decibels all completing a full octave, the center which had a neutral sound, just like a hum as it was close to my body, plus the four directions, again the medicine wheel at work. I always knew the direction of North as I wore a little compass around my neck for many years. I found that I was learning to see the shape of the divine sound in geometrical symbols, which creates itself according to the scales of A-E-I-O-U or through the way we pronounce our learned language. This symbolic structure collected itself mathematically according to the direction I was standing in. If I was standing, facing in a Northerly direction it seemed to be coming in through the top of my head. Easterly I could feel it through my heart, where it seemed to swirl throughout my body. Southerly it seemed to enter through the top of my legs and the vibrations continued up to my navel. If I was standing in a Westerly direction, my arms were extended, this allowed my peripheral vision to broaden for me to see more, therefore I could take my time to work out what was important for me to support my intentional thought. I then learned to hear the sound of these symbols through the combination of the air waves and my directional sonar, which was a combination of my consciousness, automatically connecting to the consciousness of the Laws of the Universe.

It reminded me of my musical training through my theory work and also the black line at the bottom of the swimming pool. As I struck the sticks, it seemed like every second note rang its truth. Fung Shwa (note the difference in spelling from the Chinese 'Feng Shui') is a transference of our own energy, which automatically becomes harmonically balanced when it is measured against itself, is also calculated the same way, always energy attracts attention. If I could attract and see the movement or shape of the Rainbow Serpent come into my vision worlds or the 'Whorls' (Spirals) as Peter spoke the word, through my sticks vibrating, then I knew that my message had gone out to where I was being heard right across the land. I began to realize that again I was viewing the mathematics of the consciousness at work! I could change the direction of the way the wind was blowing, through changing my direction and calling the elements to shift the consciousness that surrounded me.

Allow me to explain to you again, that this is explaining why we do not follow in our parent's footsteps, even if we have the same genetic inheritance; we align our mind through the thoughts of our grandparents, who are the second generation. Why? Our ego cannot feed itself through the sound repeating itself, it must alter its role; therefore the emotional structure of our thought reverberates through the vibrational energy produced through our heart, which automatically rebalances our thinking!

The trees could hear my thoughts, as strong and stubby as they were, they quivered gently to alert me, that they were supporting my thoughts. There was many a stunted tree that I practiced on. The rocks could collect and grow into their strength and work with me, and the grass could become stronger and taller and nourish me. Even the desert sands moved in unison to my thinking. I felt safe and protected. When I was talking to the Librarians of Timbuktu in Mali, the oldest library on the planet, also the Berber Tribes in Morocco many years later, they explained to me exactly this same story, as to how they were also trained to work with the vibrations that were created through the elements of silver. My vision world began to form and take shape inside my mind. Everything in the Aboriginal world of expression was asked for; it was never taken for granted. I quickly learned this important lesson, as it was to sustain me throughout the next thirty odd years and even to this day.

Following on was the gift of the 'Nulla-Nulla' which was to crack the seeds of the nuts which fell from the trees and were gathered from the hardy bushes. The women looked for the seeds that were left over from the last seasons growth, as they were of a greater value to the new seasons growth. They had to be dried out to make the flour. I had to place them on a flat slightly curved stone which fitted around the Nulla-Nulla and I could smash the nuts; in this way, I did not lose the nut. These nuts were to give me the strength I needed for my regeneration and for me to allow the new ways that would come to me from the spirit of the bush. As you are aware, I was receiving the complete essence of the whole plant, as it propagated itself. Once they were released from their confinement, I could ground them up in my winnow dish. I also had designs of mountains carved into the base of my Nulla-Nulla. Symbolically this was to give me the strength to climb over any difficulty that stood in my way.

And then came along the gift that I had the privilege to use was Peter's 'Bull Roarer'. This instrument was usually given to a man, Peter had informed me. He allowed me to use this instrument, as I had made my claim with the Khadiacha through his approval of what I had earned. The Khadiacha was the highest venerated position in the tribe and therefore neither male nor female, as through their journey of working with the Universal Laws, they had earned a balanced mind of both male and female. Peter told to me to repeat the sound in my mind and to send it out across country, if ever I needed help, as it would call the Elders who had walked before, to work with me. Again, with patience I learned to twirl the rope of hair around my body and up and over my head and hear the roar of spirit ready to answer my thoughts. In the beginning, I noticed that my energy seemed to be planting itself in the ground around me as though it pulled my aura up and strengthened my thoughts where they could travel further out into the consciousness. In other words, I was not holding on to them to support my fear of the unknown.

To my amazement I began to realize, that there was never a mistake that was given or presented to us throughout the consciousness, everything that was mathematically created for us to earn, was always for the right reason.

Again, I was creating my whorls of sound, pulse and tone to work on my behalf! This energetic sound is carried through the outback for many miles, just the same as a drum sends its sound through the bush in Africa, or the call from one elephant to its nearest, as well as its most furthered neighbor. I also noticed in my vision world, that the same sound connected to the ley lines of the earth. This was also heard through the energy of the ocean which was autonomically magnified through the water, which the whales used for communication to one another. And don't forget this same experience is waiting for you, when you have learned to be in control of your thinking, where the eternal mathematics opens up your consciousness to place the disciplined teacher before you! Remember, when the student is ready, the teacher appears.

One of the first things I began to notice was how I connected to other kingdoms, which each had their own laws to obey. The birds ceased their sounds as a form of respect to those around them, as I sent out mine, through their respect, everything became still and silent. We, the birds, the insects, the trees, the desert sands, the wind and I were all waiting for the answers. Even the flies ceased their appraisal of me while I was working and left me alone. I was finding my energy changing through the thoughts that had been confined for so long. I became lighter and as my mind evolved into these other levels of self conduct; I noticed I was entering deeper into the silence of the consciousness; it was in abeyance waiting for my next move and once my mind had measured with the eternal mathematics of the consciousness, I could begin to collect the answer.

Could stilling one's mind create this exalted heavenly feeling? Was my brain re-wiring my DNA? I knew that I was working solely with the Laws of the Universe! I marveled that they were there at the tips of my fingers, to supply me with their wisdom, as well as working for everyone else on the earth at the same time! Therefore, if these Laws of the Universe could accomplish such feats, then so could we, if we bothered to put our mind to it! Who were we as a species, that we have been embedded with this supreme electrical circuit, which allowed each one of us to conduit so much attention from the collective, all at the same time? Wow, we live in an exalted place we call home!

Peter then presented me with my last gift, just before my time was up which was the 'Didgeridoo' which was preciously found in a stubby tree at the bottom of a dry creek bed in the desert. It had a twist in the shape of a spiral and it took Peter and two of his women friends, many months to burn out the center of the narrow log with a hot coal being dropped down again and again. He said that I needed both women's energy to keep my emotions from straggling away from the family. It has a wonderful deep tone. My grandmother's words returned to me that day from years before when she said to me, "There is music to be found in every form of nature, if only you could learn to still your mind long enough to hear it."

The didgeridoo carving began at the base with an introduction of the eternal energy entering into our body upon gestation, (inside the consciousness) were twenty-one (21) spirals, which relates to 3 cycles of 7. Metaphysically there are three worlds (three-dimensional mind) that we live in, and, as we leave one world we are brought up into the next one. This is represented by the names of the three Gods: 'EL', 'AN', 'EA'. Interpreted through the matter of physics—or the Metaphysical language—these three names are here to remind us that we can attain Everlasting Life, Ascending and Nourishing, with an Energetic Attitude. All this is similar to how we introduced our self into our spoken word, which was released to us through our DNA. To accomplish this, our intellect must bring the three Gods together to become one God (one higher mind). We continue on the journey through the Egyptian Philosophies, which explains this area as the seven bands of peace, also known as representing the 'seven churches which are in Asia', which are sealed. They are also known colloquially as the seven seals, as written in The Revelation of St John the Divine (Book of Revelations), the last amazing book of knowledge in the Bible that we must open, which are the seven vertebrae in the neck. Remember as previously explained, our body, also known as the earth, finishes at our neck. The journey into total enlightenment is to open the seals of these seven churches or books to allow us to enter up into the neural pathways of our brain, also known as the heavenly kingdoms or afterlife.

The story continues—around the top of the stem of the didgeridoo, was carved seven fish. It is explained through their story telling, as representing the journey of the seven seals in the last book of the Bible, or the seven chakras all in alignment. When decoded through the codes of Shamanism, fish represent our next thought; the totem energy is announcing to us that we are entering into the doorway of the unconscious mind. Therefore, the didgeridoo is representing our totem pole—and the sound we emit through the pole is coming from the collection of our inner alphabet; now take this information back 40,000 years ago, to see how we are still explaining the same story. There is nothing new on this planet, that same story will keep on repeating itself to us, until we get it right!!

Peter had taken the time to burn and carve all the symbolic pictures, which he had covered completely around the didgeridoo. These represented the stories of the four shields (symbolizing the Medicine Wheel of directions. The meanings of the different directions are: North: Message from above. East: Message from within. South: Message from the past. West: Dichotomy; where we bring the energy of both brains into harmonizing with one another) then the ocean symbol and above the ocean are carved four extra-terrestrials, which awakens within us all as our intelligence evolves. In other words, I was receiving the totem of the complete evolution of the human being, which is implanted in our DNA, to sustain me throughout my life. Each symbol and animal represented an emotion that I needed to sustain me. "Every picture tells a story Missus and the more Aboriginal and like me you become, the more you are able to read and become one with the country." Peter said. Peter informed me that as I had earned the five sacred tools, that this was to be his final gift to me. I was to pass the didgeridoo on to my son whom he knew and respected, and only present it to him when I had found out that it was time for me to move to a new camp. I loved the way he spoke to me. In other words, when I had finished with this world of earning, I could freely move up into my next world and leave the past behind me. I had earned the respect of moving up towards the intelligence that was waiting to guide me into my final initiation of earning my souls right of becoming free to co-join with the unconscious mind (higher mind).

Our tone or the sonar of our sound (sonic sound), is free to collect the energy from our seven seals or chakras as we call them today and keep them all opened for the body to produce our permanence with spirit. Explained more prolifically in my e-book 'Decoding the Revelation of St John the Divine'. In this way we could learn to produce our own bodily tone through understanding who we are and how we were delivered from the mathematics of the sacred laws, to belong to our own tribal law. This litigation is still ongoing to the way the Chinese taught my grandmother, regarding their totem energy at the turn of the last century.

The Aborigines speak of this inner sound as their song lines. This inner sound/or song lines are threaded throughout the universe and are in abeyance to us, until we have found our inner freedom to connect with them. This super organism, which has created itself over the millennium through earning its own truth, is known to many of us, as the global DNA (Collective Consciousness). When the aboriginal people are trekking in the outback, they listen to the pitch of their inner sound to know if they are on the right track. It is a powerful education regarding telepathic communication, where by quietening your mind chatter, the more you are able to tune autonomically into your original sound.

Remember our genes mutate at a faster rate, through us using the same alphabet (the words we would use, when we are busily thinking our thoughts) that our previous generations used. It is already instilled in us, through the embedment of our birthright. We were being primed to listen to the conversation being spoken, during those ninety days of pre-gestation. In other words, the global DNA has been available for us to balance our inner alphabet with less congestion, and at an easier pace. Again, the codes remind us that we can only follow on from the last three generations and then the genes begin to dissipate, as we step out from the past through learning to trust and believe in self. All of which allows our alphabet to be restructured, into realizing our own future, through our genetic adaptations stimulating our DNA; where these old patterns have been given the opportunity to reinvest in themselves, which allows a positive change.

Through this change, we are being reminded of the reason we are here, where we learn to depend on ourselves, not rely on the previous memories of the ones who have walked before us! This is why we have a tendency to follow on from our grandparents, as the ego begins to transform itself through the power and strength that we can emit through respect and love of self. The universe we live in, is an enormous quantum computer, where we find everything is beginning to become an earning, not just a learning! It is embedded with information that corrects and adjusts our thinking, moment by moment.

I have the impression that I received my gifts around every ninety days, which we now understand is the code of recognition through the Collective Consciousness, as it changes the molecular structure of the DNA of every living cell that is living on the planet. Again, we are watching the mathematical laws at work. As explained in my previous works, every cell in the human body regurgitates itself every ninety days. This is an autonomic reaction of cellular recognition to remind the cell of its permanence; its purity; its sanctification, all of which ark together to keep us secure on the planet.

Please remember, an automatic response creates itself through the mathematics aligning from the previous thought which is without feelings; to take this explanation further, an autonomic response is created through our feelings being stimulated through our heart and brought together through our sonic sound, which begins in the porous bone matter behind and just above our ears. An interesting chapter, don't you agree? So, take your time and practice these rituals in your own space and amaze yourself with the outcome. Thank you for reading this chapter.

*It is the relationship of self that connects
us to the energy of our total evolution.*
Omni

Chapter 7
Inner And Outer Worlds Of Whorls

There were times during my teachings when I had to confront the Elders and give them a report as to how the children were coping with their education, I learned to sit outside of the circle as I was a woman and so was considered to take my place through their tribal ways. I didn't want to push my way into their worlds and this I did not mind at all. I knew they were not being offensive to me; it was just their way. I wanted to reinforce their respect in me through their ancient ways of the tribe; therefore, I listened intently as to how they repeated their myth and logic, explaining their inner and outer worlds or whorls. Times have changed over the last twenty years and now the communication is conducted around a table, where chairs are provided under the shade of the sparse trees or in the council house.

During those months, I learned many of their Tribal Laws, which was their religion through their way of life. This was their heritage. I had to learn to trust in the land and the stars, as they are explaining what we understand as Mother/Father God. I had to learn to become the land, the trees, the rocks, the stars and the sky. Forget the water, as there had been no rain and the creeks had been dry, for years. It was in the dry creek beds that they sought the trees to create their boomerangs. The root system of the trees could search for the underground water, which kept their DNA up into their ultimate antennas (highest state of existence) and in tip top condition.

The Aboriginal stories are the same as most of the other earth nations; just the names have been changed through the colloquialism of their own personal language, to suit their story of the moment. Since this time, I have heard the same stories in every land that I have walked the talk. Each land whether it was in Europe, Northern Africa, Central America or in the highlands of the Asiatic nations, all explain their stories through their emotional inheritance, through the language that they communicate to one another.

I have always thoroughly enjoyed listening to my many interpreters relay my message through their interpretation into their own language. They pronounce their vowels differently according to the ancientness of their tribe's first thought.

One story I wish to repeat and write about was when I asked Peter how far it was to travel to a certain hill where I could dig out the soft colored striped rock we referred to as the zebra stone, as it is the birthing of the earliest forms of Jasper, which is the companion rock to the Opal. It is referred to as a mother lode as it creates itself near the surface of the earth. Interesting isn't it, that the mother is always on top of everything. I had heard about 'One Hill' that was a couple of hundred kilometers away to the east towards the next township with the name of Oodnadatta. There were not too many hills to choose from and I thought he may have known an easier way for me to get there. I asked Peter, which was the easiest way for me to drive there and which road should I take. "How long will it take me Peter, to get there" I asked him. "For you Missus, it will take long time, long time, long time," he said. "Three long times for me Peter, how about you, how long will you take?" "Me! I just take one long time," was his reply. "Why can't I take one long time Peter, and get there quicker" was my retort. "Well, you will have to learn what long time is, Missus" he said to me. "OK, please teach me long time." I replied. And so, my lessons began. Over the next few weeks, we met each other often near the brick wall beside the bank in town, where we had a good view over the sparse arid land, where I could see the mirages out in the distance resting on the horizon. There wasn't much to see, just a few sand dunes and three small trees in the distance. "What's out there behind them trees Missus?" he said. "Goodness Peter, I can't see that far away" was my instant reply. He would let out a deep sigh and say "That's why it will take you long time, long time, long time, you still can't find your inner eyes (sight) or your sound" was his instant reply. I did not understand him at that time regarding my sight and sound and I asked him to tell me a story on how I could find it.

"Long time ago, when we walked along the track to move on to the next camp, some people started to lag behind. The tribe could not stop as there was water to find for all the people. "Leave them", said the Elder "they will catch up, they can read our tracks. Walk heavier to leave your mark on the ground; the wind will leave some of the marks (imprint) for them to see". So, they walked on to the next water hole.

Allow me to describe this in the third person from here. As they settled around the water hole, they drank their fill and kept on looking back into the distance for the movement of the others coming forward. The day was finally settling itself into the arms of the night and they still had not arrived, so bone weary from the walk and the heat, the rest of the tribe retired for the night. The elder did not leave the camp site or rest as he had to keep searching for his people, he trekked the others with his mind, he started to chant softly which soothed the weary travelers into a restful sleep.

His sound went lower until he knew that it was just above the ground. It traveled further this way. He flattened his voice out to see it traveling wider over the ground into the four directions of North, South, East and West where two spirals formed and through the Elders resonance of lowering his chant, they began to become attracted to each other, the momentum pulled these whorls or spirals into one another... Peter explained it to me as placing your hand out in front of you and you being able to feel the pressure of the chant create its own sound waves... as you become aware of your fingers starting to lift back from the pressure that is collecting itself, you realized the energy was becoming stronger.

This action created a larger spiral, which picked up the momentum of his sound, where he then realized that his sound would become constant to be carried across the desert floor and also be in touch with him, at the same time. It also became lighter as the gravity fields were less influenced, until it reached the others, and then he knew that he was in constant contact with the rest of the stragglers, so he could rest. (Similar to my grandmother when she hummed to the plants in her garden) The Elder sat up and concentrated on the silence until he could hear other thoughts besides his own, entering into his mind. Slowly these thoughts began to gather until they surrounded him. He knew that the spiral or in their language the whorl, had created his sound and his life force had called and collected the minds of the others, where they knew exactly how far they still had to travel to catch up with the rest of the tribe. He waited for them to enter into the camp light created from the fires.

*We create a wonderful multifaceted hologram of self,
and that hologram is the result of our thinking.*
Omni

Chapter 8
Expanded Consciousness

After hearing this story, I began in earnest to tune into Peter's explanation of his language, so that he could teach me how to view and read the land. I knew from then on, that my sound would come naturally as I learned to earn my own resonance, which would assist me into understanding how I could broaden my pathway to connect me deeper into the consciousness. I found that the more fear we have trapped within our self, the higher our octave becomes; the less fear, the deeper our voice resonates, which allows for our sound to tune into and travel further throughout the width and breadth of the land.

I learned how to always look into the moment at what was in front of my face; and to push that view out from me into the distance, to allow it to follow itself out, to connect with the collective consciousness and then to draw it back to me. Peter explained to me, that the earth would show me what was behind those trees and for me not to force myself. The earth was surrounded by a living body of information that never argued with itself, this momentous electrical circuitry system that guides every facet of energy on this planet, just kept its silence and moved with the energetic flow, whether it be drought, floods, tornado's or fire, I was to ask the land to reveal itself to me. The mathematics must expel its self, for time to recollect and gather itself, for us to move forward.

Recently I began to notice that I seemed to be growing taller, or maybe the land was receding in its stature, as I released my own fear of the unknown and it appeared to be shrinking smaller. I could sit outside with others at night and enjoy the cool breeze as it moved across the desert floor and not spend my time swatting mosquitoes as they no longer bother to bite me. My father taught me this as a child. "Keep the mind free of thought, all of which deters the insect to search for those who are inhibited by their own fear." The energy of my intellectual light was beginning to lift itself above their sonar. Slowly I was learning that these species were here to support me, not the other way around!

My consciousness was concentrating on the job at hand and was being magnified back to me. (I teach this experience now in Business Seminars as to how you can attract further possibilities of rearranging and expanding your financial gains.) As the land slowly revealed itself to me, I knew it was me becoming taller; I was being called up towards the doorways of my unconscious mind (higher mind). I was learning how to view the land through the eyes of the space in what we refer to in the Bible, as beyond the first time; the Aborigines had always lived and many are still living in these worlds or whorls of being able to alter the momentary value of their thinking. I was beginning to understand the importance of my inner sound the more I associated with it, as I was learning to fly in the mind. My intellectual light was creating its own awareness through me releasing the freedom of self discovery.

I found that I was creating my own hologram in my mind (we are indelibly imprinting our own hologram, which begins when the third eye has opened. Our consciousness is comprised within a personal light body hologram which consists of electromagnetic waves. The higher and more powerful your vibrations become through accepting your intelligence and wisdom, the more your waves will have the strength to regenerate the self. String theories are at work here), where through the focused mind I could bring information from 'out there to in here', where it was registered in both hemispheres of the brain at the same time! I could look through the trees into the distance over the other side of the horizon and just ask what was on the other side. There it was hidden in plain sight all of the time. I just had to focus both left and right hemispheres of the brain into becoming one; this allowed the third eye to create the vision that could not be seen in the third dimensional world; through bringing the focus back into two dimensions, one of the moment and one futuristically, everything could follow on from this moment! All combined, this allowed the truth to reveal itself to become the supreme moment.

It could not be distorted. Why? As it registered with the supreme collective consciousness, it could only release the mathematics of the moment! Is this where matter and antimatter are combining to become as one?

Had my energy bounced out to the G-Force (fields of gravity) of the planet to open up the whole picture of what was beyond those trees, which I now know, holds the recorded blue print of this wonderful planet? I could see the whole perspective in the third dimensional reality. The surprising thing to me was that I could walk around each item and view it from all sides. It was as if I had been taken to this site and there I was, right in the middle of the picture I was viewing. I could see how the sand dunes stretched out in front of me for miles and in the distance; I noticed that one old gnarled gum tree had the left side of its branches missing. It seemed to have been snapped off and had rotted into the ground. I brought my attention back to me and I looked at Peter and told him what I had seen and his face broadened into a wonderful smile. I also noticed that throughout my education I was able to connect through the layers of space and not get lost, as there was always a continuation to the next volume of matter.

As each new field began to come to the end of its experience, there was a pause, not an ending; through this pause I had the opportunity to collect what I had focused on. This measurement registered in my brain where it could continue into the next sequence, in this way the same story could advance itself and continue. This is exactly how every human's brain works mathematically through it rewiring itself to connect, to the collective. Our blue print is identical to the blue print of the planet and the universe, as to how we have existed since time began! As we have an experience, autonomically our brain is lying in waiting to give us the continuation of our previous thinking. These lapses are arbitrary, which allows us to create time for us to digest what we are receiving. If we are thinking positive then we are given the green light, which ignites through the connection of the pituitary gland, working in cohesion with the middle ear. If it is a negative reaction, we must live the same experience again, until we change our status quo!

Nothing ever stops! As everything that has previously occurred, is registered throughout the mathematics of the natural laws, it is autonomically re-embedded back into the original blue print. It has its own laws, which is a millennium of layers beyond our thinking. As we create each moment in our life, these laws are permanently adjusting to compensate the excuses and mistakes we each make. Just like our brain, the natural laws live by the same identical law! This is created through multiplying the consequences where they tip the scales to broaden the karmic overload. Now maybe you can understand how our intelligence has multiplied so quickly over the last one hundred years, as we have watched how technology has brought our future closer for us to inherit.

Once this energy has reached its antenna of the current thought form; more and more people become caught up in its reply. We then become aware of another entry into the mathematical law, through the worlds of division. As we give out to others, so shall we receive! If we are not realizing our own truth, we begin to create separate units of the same experiences, which must be brought back into the fold of the cosmic law, before they create catastrophic circumstances. The Collective Consciousness never makes mistakes when it is in its own continuum. The Collective Consciousness is continually searching for a complete equation, where the results are returned to sender for them to justify why they consented to their underhanded behavior. This can also occur through members of our own family in this generation, where the results are then seeded to the forthcoming generation for them to inherit! It never goes away; it is watching and breathing every move we make! This cosmic payment is also returned to us through one of the four elements, water, earth, wind or fire.

I felt confident with my understanding of Peter's story and prepared myself for the trip to the hill where I could dig for the zebra stone. I went and spoke to my uncle who had lived in the area for many years, mining opals. I received quite a lecture about the dangers of the bush and how I had to stock my car with food, plenty of water and petrol. As a Queenslander I always had my trouble box in the back of my car with tinned food, flour, tea, a camp oven, a billy to boil the water, a can opener, a tourniquet in case of bites and a sharp knife. This kept us alive when the creeks were swollen during the heavy rains in the monsoon weather. Sometimes we would have to sit there for two to three days until the water receded enough for us to be able to cross the creek.

I had to buy a silver tarp and have marking pens or a tin of flat black or red paint to write S.O.S on it and place it on the roof of my car in case I broke down. He could not see rhyme or reason, as to why I wanted to do this trip alone. "Wait until the weekend and I will take you out there," he said to me. I convinced him that I needed to do this trip alone and that I would be safe and told him that I would not be more than eight to ten hours in total. I had to draw a mud map as to where I was going and he told me that he knew of this track and hill and so after my promise to him that I would not stray off the track, we made a time for me to report back to him. I rechecked my trouble box, updated my kit and knew I was prepared for the trip ahead. Even provided new batteries to my torch in case I was out there in the dark! The old girl guides motto of "Be prepared" and my grandmother's saying "Better to be safe than sorry" flashed before my eyes.

My day finally arrived and just as I was ready to leave, I mentally saw myself arriving at the hill, filling my car with rock and then saw myself arriving back at the dugout all safe and sound! Therefore, nothing could interfere with my preparation. I left home just as dawn was appearing over the horizon and with the boys waving me off at the front door. I drove in the direction of those three trees in the distance.

In the beginning the hours went by with me staring at a repetitious land mass all around me of nothing but a few kangaroos who seemed to disappear quickly into the predawn. I watched in awe as the sky created soft muted colors to announce the new day. As the sun rose over the horizon the view turned into soft undulating hills, where the colors merged into one another to become tinged with gold around the edges. I could see the birthing of the mirages in the distance as they became brighter and stronger as the sun rose in the sky; the only thing that seemed to move was the shimmer of light and the movement of the odd crow or eagle spiraling upwards in the sky. Remember, crow is the keeper of the sacred laws, and eagle asks me to keep the mind steady and spiral up above the thermals, therefore I knew that I was in safe hands.

The sun became stronger and hotter as the day and time moved on. I had just passed the three trees that I had seen in the distance with Peter that day when we were beside the bank wall and I knew that I was to go straight ahead until I came to a fork in the road and then I had to follow the right one as the other one would finally take me to the settlement of Simpson's Ridge. As I traveled along the right-hand track, I could see in the distance one tree which looked like it was standing in the middle of the road. I traveled towards the tree and as I became closer I noticed that the old gnarled gum tree had the left side of its branches missing I became excited as this was the picture that I had viewed in my mind previously with Peter and the viewing had been correct. When I reached the old gum tree, I jumped out of my car and walked over and picked up a small piece of broken tree branch and tucked it away in a plastic bag and placed it in the glove box of my vehicle.

After traveling another hour, I finally came to the hill that I had viewed in my mind and for the next hour I walked around the rubble and filled up my vehicle with suitable pieces of jasper. I began to visualize the picture that presented itself to me to carve, and I marveled at the colors that nature had provided for me to work with. They were the softest colors of blue and mauve; over in another section I could see the browns and softest beiges. And then there were the stripes of black and white. The stronger the color the more significant the stripes were pronounced. As the colors became muted, they spread out softly through the stone. I could visualize oceans and sand pictures. In another piece of rock, I could see how the clouds were forming; others represented the mountain ranges and trees. The landscape changed through the color formation.

I drove off for home in the heat of the day and never realized how much weight I had put in the vehicle as I thumped and bumped my way back to town, stopping every now and then to release the pressure out of the tires (tyres) as my car limped back to my dugout. I rang my uncle who came around and inspected my treasures. There was so much respect in his eyes for the efforts undertaken on my own. Peter just smiled at me at our next meeting near the bank and I presented him with the piece of wood that I had picked up from my old wounded tree. He asked me questions about how I had spent my birthdays. He once had a birthday party when he was living at the mission as a child and he knew it was a sort of celebration for being good. Their birthdays were held on the day the children were admitted to the mission. Peter thought that this was a good time for me to have one now as he felt I had also been a good girl as well.

It was only when my studies had finished, was I allowed to walk proudly as an Aboriginal. While I was being trained into their way of life, I could be an Aboriginal on the inside and yet I was not allowed to show my teachings to the others of the same Tribe. I first had to become a sister, which meant I had to become a family member of the tribe, and my first name that I was given was Rainbow Wadjinda, which means 'Illumination of the Ocean'. It was easy to see how I earned this name, as I had my eye on a beautiful petrified snail shell which had turned into opal over the millennium of time and I loved the miraculous colors it produced when it was turned through my fingers in the sunlight. We spoke of this fossil often when we came back into town from working out in the bush and I would drop Peter off near the Opal Shop. "One day I am going to be able to afford to buy that sea snail." I would often say to him. I don't need it now, I have become it.

If we look at the word 'Wadjinda' through the Sacred Alphabet, 'Wadj' means 'wisdom ascending through the Divine Justice'. 'Inda' interprets as 'intelligence nourishing through Divine Ascension'—or, simply, 'to search'. When decoded through the Egyptian language, 'Wadj' means 'serpent'. Do you see now how the Aborigines first understood the codes and came to the fruition of the Rainbow Serpent?

I was beginning to notice how my world had changed with this ancient knowledge being instilled amongst my own dictionary of words. Respect in self had blossomed, there was so much learning being offered to me, that I found I could not let myself down. The first thing I noticed was that old friends had stopped ringing me for idle conversation. It was as though I had been delegated into a higher realm of knowledge, which gave the opportunity for new friends to enter. My conversations had changed; my words were pronounced with respect to all concerned. Even my clothing was rearranged in my mind, it didn't take too long before my wardrobe had been altered. I felt clean and tidy; it was good to be alive and a pleasure to start my day. My new world was on the horizon with a light so bright, I could see its aura.

Throughout all of the ancient languages, our DNA is known to us as our Bibliography or our inner binary code. It holds every universal code that equates to the Library of the Universal Mind.
Omni

Chapter 9
Secrets To Live My Own Universal Law

It was coming up to Christmas and the temperature was building up into the mid 40 degrees Celsius and we wanted to get away from the heat. My family and I were going down to Adelaide to spend four lovely weeks by the ocean and cool off. I wished Peter a 'Merry Christmas' and agreed to meet him at the end of January. I kissed him on the cheek as I said "Thank you for your teachings and for having patience with me until I understood your sacred ways." He found the courage to kiss me on the cheek as I was the first white woman to touch him and he told me that he would always be with me forever, as he vigorously shook my hand. He was going on walkabout down south with a group of his friends. Christmas did not register with his way of thinking, but the respite from the heat certainly did.

So down we went to the ocean and had three pleasant weeks walking near the water. My boys found it a bit too cold to swim, as the waters in the Tropics were much softer and warmer. These southern waters were strong and as sharp as needles when we walked along the foreshore as the spray hit the senses of our skin. We had fun and laughed as the salt spray washed over us. I just loved the smell of the ocean. That salty air was so strong and invigorating, it certainly does something to one's body; it seemed to reverberate through every cell of the mind. I made sure that I was showered with the spray every time I walked along the shore. I felt my strength gather and cleanse itself as I prepared to go back to the heat in the outback. I was beginning to realize that this was the baptism that I was receiving from the sacred laws, for all of those previous months of study. We watched as a couple of late whales boomed their way moving down around the South Coast of Australia coming from the East where they had just finished their migration up North near our home town in Queensland to give birth in the warm waters to their next generation. They were on their way to the Antarctic to rear their young.

We returned back into the desert one week earlier than expected. While watching two whales breech themselves in the water when the phone rang; my husband had received word that he was required to travel back to camp as he was needed. We arrived home just after midnight with temperatures boiling up into 45 degrees Celsius plus. It was like a large hot blanket had wrapped itself around my body and I felt that those three weeks by the Ocean, had all been a dream. Early the following morning I made my way down to the supermarket early to purchase fresh milk, butter and fresh meat as it was so much sweeter and tender, than what you could buy in the city. I had brought back heaps of vegetables and packets and canned food back in my four-wheel drive.

As I walked into the supermarket I noticed a group of Aborigine women standing outside the shop. I nodded to them and continued on inside and started to place my order to my friend Maria who owned the supermarket. All of a sudden, I heard this keening (death wail) sound coming from the entrance of the supermarket. I stopped talking about the good times we had and we walked together outside to see what was happening. There were five Aboriginal ladies with staffs in their right hands and they were stamping it into the earth. Their bare feet began to move in unison with their staffs. I felt the goose bumps rise on my skin as I had never seen this action before, especially not from the women. I was used to watching the Aboriginal men when they had a decision impending. They would call on the Spirits in similar ways. The women's voices rose as they chanted louder and louder. One of the women, whose name was Esther kept turning her head and looking down the main street to the right. I turned and followed her eyes and in the distance at the bottom of the main street was the flashings of head lights as far as the eyes could see. Their keening became louder and their bare feet pounded into the ground and their staffs snapped in unison with their feet and more importantly their backs stood tall and straight, as the lights slowly came towards us. "What is this Maria", I stammered to her. "Oh! I forgot to mention it to you, I was so pleased to see you were back, you have only just returned, your friend Peter is getting buried today," she said.

I went into a void of nothing! I found this information hard to digest as we were to start with my studies at the end of the following week. I went over to stand near the women as I so desperately wanted to stamp my feet and to chant with them. I kept my silence as Peter had asked me to do; my tears flowed down my cheeks. Those women knew he was my friend and Teacher, they took no notice of me and they did not stop until the last of the cars went past us. My time with Peter was up. "God Bless you Peter and thank you for allowing our souls to meld as one through your teachings and for having the confidence and patience to explain the wisdom of your knowledge to me," I whispered to him as he went passed me.

Little did I realize at that time that I had been given one of the greatest gifts that we can receive. I had received the spirit of his soul. Do you see why I had to return back to the area before our holiday was finished? Peter had died exactly twenty-one days (three cycles of seven) after we said our good-byes. God works in mysterious ways, so the story goes. The codes of consciousness cannot be interfered with. Why? We as a combined state of consciousness are only a fractional response of the original blueprint! We always receive our dues at exactly the right time. Do you think the Company we worked for, knew that Peter was to return home? What did it have to do with them? They contacted us the day before he died. Why did those two whales breech themselves just as the phone started ringing? These are the important messages from our Divine Inheritance. This is the Law of the Universe answering to my own Universal Law. This is the Collective Consciousness at work, creating the codes that serve the whole of humanities worth. Every single one of us, are treated exactly the same way, as we give, so we shall receive!

Those eighteen months working with the Elders were very important for me to see how through time we have evolved and have released the potentialities of our DNA, connecting to one another throughout the telepathic communication that has and is continually connected through our unconscious language to every human brain. These wonderful people speak 144 dialects of their language throughout my land and each one of those tribes represents different aspects that are in all of us; they are still here representing the personalities that we have already evolved through, with time.

I was viewing my life differently at this stage of my teachings, I could see how our threads were beginning to connect to each other as we became—at one—with one another, to become one Collective Mind.

These are the stories of the 'Twelve Tribes of Israel' written in the Old Testament in the Bible. The 12 x 12 = 144,000, is explaining to us how in the beginning of humanities earnings, the twelve strands of our DNA unfurl their threads to release their intellect, which lifts us up to where we are earning our freedom. They are the first step as to how we release the mathematical codes of our central nervous system. These stories explain how humanity began to collect and connect to the Universal Laws. Each story in the Old Testament is explaining the journey as to how these strands have earned their knowledge; when brought together through us understanding who we are, they then become the foundation of our inner knowledge.

As Peter or P'tah as it is referred to through the codes of Egyptology said, "Upon this rock I will build my church". (Every myth and every story of the Bible is explaining a hidden language through the Metaphysical resonance. It has taken more than 1,500 years to try to understand the stories explained to us in the Bible. The Bible, along with the hieroglyphs on the walls of the temples in Egypt, reveals the hidden codes. It is all the same story, and that story can only be revealed through us entering up into the next phase of the hidden intelligence).The New Testament is explaining the next advanced step of our inner journey; the stories describe to us our own personal laws, which are the pathways to discovering the importance of self. These are how we learn to understand the stories of Jesus and the twelve Apostles as our next inheritance; as to how we earn our next evolutionary step.

We learn to open up our intellect where our emotions are free to walk before our ego, as to how we wise up to this inner knowledge and bring forth our wisdom. Once our knowledge and our wisdom are released, we are free to walk with a balanced mind, known as the path of perpetuity in congruence with everything around us.

From this level of equation through understanding the codes in The Revelation of St John the Divine (Book of Revelations); which is the final exalted step of intellect we unravel, we know now that all of this information is explaining the recorded library of our own personal DNA, which is explaining the exalted teachings of—The Revelation of St. John the Divine—also referred to as the inner light; how we move up higher into the Territories of Christianity, where each word we phrase or speak to others becomes our living testament.

For you to understand how this inner language can release us from our past, we learn to concentrate on each moment, we learn how to balance our thinking where our thoughts are free to come through our heart; firstly, for the betterment of our self, which then automatically flows out to others. This is the road map that the wonderful stories of Egyptology have forwarded on for us to unravel. You will find all of the relevant information in my book 'The Revelation of St John the Divine'. Just as over the years, I have opened up my tree of knowledge, so too; the Lord Buddha sat under the Bodhi tree for his enlightenment, also Muhammad sat on top of his mountain to release and speak the Koran (the Core or Kur 'healing through the heart') we receive through understanding our education system through the second God AN).

And to my surprise the Aborigines also have their tree of knowledge, which is called the Bibolicea tree. This same name is also used in Ethiopia throughout many tribes. Amazing isn't it, to think that thousands of years ago, that these ancient tribes also have their own words for what we refer to today as the Bible. This ancient word is still carried forward into today's language and relates to the same mind. So how old is this word that we refer to as Christianity, also known as the Christ or light of your intelligence within your unity or your united verse (universe).

Throughout all of the ancient languages, our DNA is known to us as our Bibliography or our inner binary code. It holds every universal code that equates to the Library of the Universal Mind; which was created many thousands of years before Christianity was refreshed again in our mind and is the intellectual intelligence, we have called the library of the mind. I refer in other writings of the 144,000 personalities (aspects of self) that each human has the opportunity to use, as they are representing the genes that we have inherited. Remember these numbers were also carved in the skulls of Tutankhamen (decoded as Tut-Ankh-Amen) through the Egyptian Philosophies and also Lord Pacal (decoded as Pa-Ark-Kha-El) of the Mayan Principles. Again, long before Christianity was brought to our attention.

Also this explains the 'Lighthouse of Alexandria'. Alexandria ('EL-Ex-AN-Dri-EA') is known throughout the metaphysical codes as the 'city or home of the three Gods', and is situated high up in the delta of Egypt. It also symbolically represents the crown of the head. It first became famous for its large lighthouse; the story is told that its light could be, and still can be seen, right around the planet. We can add to that previous sentence, much more eloquently, by saying that the lighthouse is also how our thinking releases from the brain back down into our body, which mirrors its reflection out into the aura of self—and, from there, into the Collective Consciousness, where we become a light that is seen by others.

More recently, Alexandria is known to us for its famous library, which supposedly held thousands of books regarding the evolution of humanity. Did it ever occur in reality; or, have the myths designed it for us; is it where our thoughts have released out to create what we think is the truth of reality? Do you see how the myths are created? Or, is it just a vision that has been handed down from father to son, mother to daughter? We have to keep going back into understanding our beginnings, so that we can accept our past—and, thereby, be able to release it in order to create our future. (This answers the myth where we become the lighthouse from Alexandria that is seen from the four corners of the earth, becoming humanity's ultimate aim, where we can live in the library of our mind).

Remember in the book of The Revelation of St John the Divine (Book of Revelations), St. John introduces us to the seven sealed books which are clasped on the back of the book. He refers to them in Chapter 1: verse 4, as the 'seven churches which are in Asia'. These seven churches are representing the seven vertebrae of the cervical spine. The full context of this story is written in my book 'Decoding the Revelation of Saint John the Divine: Understand the role you inherit'.

It is each person's responsibility to open these seals as they journey up into the unconscious mind (higher mind). I also refer to the brain as an advancement to our oracle (our thinking), as it can reimburse us with all of our answers, if we can still our mind long enough to hear the answers. Now you can understand how the thousands of mythical stories written by the learned scholars of the past are explaining these codes of our DNA; whether they are Asian, Arabic, Mayan, Greek, Egyptian and Aboriginal, as to how they have foretold their findings as they unraveled their ancient sacred laws. The secrets of the world were revealed to me by dedicated research to explain this hidden language, and I hope that I have done service and justice to those who walked before me. Every human that has birthed onto this planet is aware of these codes implanted within; it is finding the courage to live, understand, accept and act them that create the furor we must all endure.

If we take a look at the evolution of the Aramaic language they explained the vibration of freedom through to the number seven. And then the sanctification begins with the Prophets earning the number eight. Time has moved on, also with our Aborigines; as through the carvings of the seven kangaroos on my didgeridoo as we make progress we are continually adding and creating another form of consciousness to our DNA. Therefore, the responsibility is ours to live our truth; most importantly to remember it is available for the next generation to accept and inherit.

The Australian Aboriginals have earned their freedom through the codes of Sacred Numerology. They can take us far back into our own evolution. How long have they been here living on and with the earth? Does it really matter? I thank God that the Aborigines are still here to hold the threads of their intellect to induce us back into the ancient ways through us honoring them.

We are always being constantly reminded that we all have the opportunity to remember who we once were. We still have these ancient personalities or genes threaded throughout our consciousness to this day! That is why these stories will remain with us, as they can never become—old fashioned—for the future to appear before us, we must rectify and understand our past!

That introduction into my teachings was very precious to me, as it taught me that it is okay, to change my old ways of thinking and to have the inner strength to extol my mind, and not get stuck in the moment. I realized how much we as humans have progressed, and how expansive the Collective Consciousness has evolved into what it is and has now become. I had been connected back to the earth from whence I had first begun. Maybe it had always been this way for us to learn to understand and to know ourselves. I just had to grow up to notice the wisdom that had and has always been here; it is still available to all of us, since time began. Again, I reiterate, that the more we move forward to harmonize our future, the more we are brought back to rebalance and clear our past!

We also had an Aboriginal family working for us on our sheep station in the Binya Hills, which is an outback area in New South Wales. And as a child, I always referred to them as Mr. and Mrs. McGrath. They had their own quarters away from the house and to us children; it was forbidden territory to play there. Mrs. McGrath was a wonder in the home; she was a good cook and could turn the roast on Sundays while we attended our church services into a melting dream. The smell would waft into the sitting room where we were all gathered, which would stimulate our senses and I can still recall the grumbling of many tummies as we sniffed the essence of the roast lamb deep inside. She worked beside my mother in the house and she would softly sing as she scrubbed and cleaned the house; we only used one cleaner for everything and that was a tin of Ajax powder and this was mixed with kerosene into a paste. Our house sparkled with sunshine as I recall my childhood memories, but the smell of the kerosene always seemed to linger on the tip of my nose. So, to fix the problem, herbs were rubbed into the furniture which made it glisten as the sun filtered into the room; and was also stomped into the carpet square to assist in purifying the odor in each room.

Mrs. McGrath's gentleness was everything to my younger brothers and sister, when they were looking for attention or cried. The McGraths' didn't have any family of their own and so they devoted their lives to us. They understood and knew the grasses and the bark of the trees to gather when we were ill; off Mrs. McGrath would go and collect what was needed to make us feel good. The nearest doctor was hundreds of miles away. My grandmother also lived a long way away. My mother never interfered with Mrs. McGrath. She knew things my mother didn't and it was so. Both women treated each other royally and the respect grew between both of them.

Mr. and Mrs. McGrath were a very softly spoken couple and they were gentle in their speaking in regards to us children. They stayed with us for the rest of their lives, and when it came time for them to reside in God's arms, they wanted their final resting place to be near the family and they were buried in the family plot.

I loved this land, it was good sheep and wheat country and after the winter, the wattle trees came into bloom. We had thousands of them scattered over the hills on our land and they transformed the country with their radiant golden color. I would pick bunches of the blooms and bring them back to the house. My mother had an irritation to their essence and would sneeze all day long. I was soon kicked out of the house with my tins of golden flowers. It was shearing time when they bloomed, so I would take the flowers down to the Shearer's quarters and place the tins outside their door and fill the shearing shed up as well. I thought they looked nice and the smell of them transformed the odor of the sheep. They were a great bunch of men who removed the tins outside and laughed at my folly.

There are not too many old Australian Aboriginal tribes left, as we are coming towards the end of the Lemurian age or the 'Land of Mu' as it is called today. They, like all of us have brought themselves forward, as many have, to extend the rest of the world. It is called progress! The next generation will have to hold the gravity fields, once their Elders have gone. These wonderful people, who have walked before us, are our anchors. Remember that the more we move forward; the more we are pulled back to sustain the previous generations. I remember a saying that I learned from my grandmother as a child, "A ship always finds safety in the harbor, but that is not what ships are built for. It has to move forward to receive its own reward." Release your courage, it is embedded within you for you to achieve in your own right. This is the way the consciousness expands the divine soul for all to inherit! What I have noticed in regards to the young mind is, as the consciousness expands itself, I realize that the younger generation, understand what we have done; where it becomes easier for them to know and accept.

That ancient energy has been carried down through the generations of our own DNA and embedded through each one of us who are left to carry on with the responsibilities of continually re-birthing the intellect of this wonderful planet.

The Indigenous Nations are our original Shamanic Teachers; they still hold the threads of the ancient ways, which are the gravity fields that keep us all stabilized here on the planet. The Indigenous Consciousness is an Ancient Lemurian energy, or as it is sometimes referred to as the original Arian energy. It goes back to the early evolution of the human brain, so they are one of the main root stocks or the preciousness that align us to the beginning of humanity. We began in the Unconscious Mind (higher mind) and up until now we are still coming into our own reasoning and learning to cope with the opportunities that are available to us throughout the wonder of these Universal Laws. This creates our evolution and we find that this energy is not only in Australia, although the Australian Aborigines are one of the oldest races; it is also found throughout the whole Continent of Africa, South America, Arabia, China, Upper Mongolia, and Siberia and it is still alive deep in the Alps of Europe. I know, I now live in all of these places and call them my home.

And now let us return back to the story of my wonderful Aboriginal Teacher, who's Christian name was Peter and had just passed over and returned home. Within two weeks from this time I received the message from my mother that my younger sister Barbara had died in her sleep, she was also thirty eight years of age, the same age as my younger brother. What was this story of life explaining to me as to how we are all woven through the threads of our past generations, to live this life I have right now! I needed answers to my questions! I wanted to go back to the East Coast; I needed family and I knew that for now I had finished with accepting my journey to understand the ancient ways of my land called the 'Outback.' My Shamanic education, experiences and my initiations were now well on the way.

To finish with my journey of learning in the outback, I would like to explain how the energy differs from above the ground, as to how it reconnects under the ground. The temperature in the desert hovers around fifty-four degrees Celsius, during the summer months which can last up to nine months of the year and dive down to minus 10 degrees Celsius in the few short winter months. Most of the people in this area live underground where the inside temperature fluctuates around 20 degrees Celsius in the winter to 25 degrees Celsius in the hot summer months all year round; it is more tolerable and cooler living in the bowels of the earth.

One of the first things I noticed while living in the 'dugout' was that my vegetables did not require refrigeration. They stayed fresher for longer, and as they aged they grew these finite fibrous roots around their skin which looked like a fine spider's web as its essence busily protected its life force. I realized that they were busily preparing themselves to get ready to create their seed. The longer I had them, the stronger their essence became, which added to the flavor of the casseroles and roasts.

My fruit ripened very quickly and had to be used immediately or be refrigerated. Fruit did not hold the same strength in its memory as the vegetable, owing to the amount of sugar it needed to sustain its character. It had difficulties keeping up its own sustenance. Fruit is for the moment to please an excuse we are so often dependant on; it sweetens our moment, until we are ready to digest that thought! The meat had a longer life force when kept in the refrigerator and yet it seemed to tenderize itself over time. What was this? How did living underground create this much difference to live food? What was so different to the eternal memory of evolution regarding living underground, as to living above the ground?

Why? The reason we needed to eat in the first time was to help us support our fear. The elements that came from the earth were more protected by the Universal Law of all that is. I noticed this same thinking when I lived in Europe years later and saw how the women kept their preserves and reserve fruit deep down under the ground in their cellars throughout the winter. If their excess fruit or vegetables were placed in grass or stubble, it had a shorter life span than if it was placed in boxes and covered with sand. The temperature does not fluctuate as much as above the ground and is kept around the same cooling temperature; we see a permanent state of animation which supports the fruit into holding on to its own permanence, especially apples. It became an instant cold storage agreement. These apples would shrink and dehydrate and their flavor would become concentrated where they could still be used twelve months after picking. You could always slice them up to make a delicious apple pie.

This story explains how the consciousness continually expands itself through the threads we weave in our mind. Our thoughts prosper when they are positive and degenerate when they are not!

Another change that happened quickly was the family squabbles ceased to eventuate. We found an inner peace living with one another in this home in the ground. Our energy became suppliant with one another. Our mind seemed to bend and was not obtrusive towards one another. The arguments grew few and far between. We became mellow in our communication with one another and enjoyed being a family. We respected each other's privacy much more eloquently; we also respected each other's solace when we needed to enjoy our own moments. I noticed that our aura became more condensed which seemed to support each thought, where we could digest each word more easily. There were many changes to our lives for the better when we returned back to the East.

*To know how to wait,
Is the great secret of success.*
Joseph De Maistre

Chapter 10
Death of Loved Ones

On this journey, you have the opportunity to learn as much of the Laws of the Universe as you allow yourself to, and, when you understand that law, the Universe opens up its next level, and you walk towards it. It is a never-ending experience that enables you to rearrange your life program.

The Laws of the Universe were being introduced to me, at the time of my younger brothers passing. It was at this time that my first Shamanic teacher, who was an Australian Aboriginal Elder with the Christian name of Peter, entered into my life (as per the previous chapter). My mathematics had collected to allow me to step forward to receive this next education. Through Peter's teachings I was trained in the ancient laws, which was the Pitjantjatjara tribe. He passed over to his next education at the end of my training, while we were down south by the ocean having a well-earned holiday. Exactly eighteen months after my brother's passing, and two weeks after Peter's, my younger sister, who was also age thirty-eight, passed over for my journey.

Let me return to my brother's passing. My brother had been working with his horses and was busy breaking one in. My brother was thrown from his horse; there seemed to be a balancing of egos working itself out between the two of them and the horse had won in the moment. My brother landed heavily on his right shoulder resulting in his right shoulder/arm completely dislocated out of its socket. His horses were stabled at my parent's property and my father and my youngest son were watching him at the time and witnessed the accident. My father took control of the situation and cooeed out to me to come and give a hand. We lived next door at that time, and of course I had just walked out into the yard three seconds before, and heard my father and son yell for me. I ran across the yard and I saw my youngest son running towards me with a terrified look on his face yelling "Quick Mum, uncle has been bucked off his horse and grandfather needs you." I arrived in time to see my father trying to pull the leather belt out of my brother's jeans. "Put this leather between your teeth son and bite hard and I will pop your shoulder back into its socket," were the first words I heard when I arrived. My brother was grey and was very quickly going all shades of black around the face. He was swaying on his feet, so I came up behind him and tried to support him and hold him upright. My brother's breathing was becoming very rapid and his eyes filled with pain, "Oh God, I have never known such pain," he stammered. At my father's suggestion, we supported him over to the house where my father placed the belt between his teeth and made him chomp down hard, my mother who had also heard the call came to the rescue to make sure his tongue was free and then I heard my father say "Okay, my son, with the grace of God, here we go." My father took a firm grip of my brother's arm and pushed with all his might and we heard this squelch and a slight pop, and it was all over, my brother by this time was just on the passing out stage.

Something inside me started to vibrate and I felt a surge travel up my spine as my brother said over and over again "Oh the pain, the pain is tremendous" I pulled my brother back towards me and I balanced him on my breast and I raised my hands and placed them both onto his right shoulder "Here give me your pain?" My voice thundered from deep within me and I felt a burning sensation in my hands and a horrific pain shot up both my arms to my shoulders. My mind snapped and I did not know what to do, this burning continued to get stronger and stronger. I could feel it all around my heart area. "Dad, Dad, I have his pain, it is all in my hands and arms, what can I do?" I said to my father. He looked at me with such a loving expression on his face and with tears in his eyes said to me "Give it back to God girl, and try to wipe that shocked look off your face while you're at it."

Twenty-one days later my brother passed away and I was emotionally devastated along with the rest of the family. He had a huge gathering of friends of over 1,300 people who came respectfully to give their thanks and farewells to a great friend. He had a guard of honor of over 300; there were Stockmen and Rodeo participants who raised their whips and the rest were members of the ski club who raised their skis to the skies. We all walked through this guard of honor tunnel of men whose tears freely flowed all the way to the grave site. My mother and father raised their heads high as they walked behind my sister-in-law and her four small children. The day was very hot and it was as though God had placed a huge umbrella of shade for us to walk under. The service was beautifully spoken and memories were brought to our attention through his friends and our Minister. And the next new phase of life presented itself. My husband, children and I moved to the Outback where I was introduced to the 'Ancient Ways' of the Australian Aboriginal Law.

With the passing of my beautiful sister, I was again shocked to my core. My sister's death had devastated me, we were so very close to one another and the threads of love between us were strong. I remember the last conversation we had with one another the day before she died. It was my wedding anniversary and as always, we made telephone contact with one another on those special days. I was telling her about the loss of Peter and how distraught I felt at his passing. I felt at a loss in my mind and was explaining to her how he had shown me his ways through his teachings. She listened to me and told me she was envious as to how I could take my life in my own hands and without any qualms, just get on with it.

My sister and her husband had returned from three weeks holiday where they had traveled down south to meet up with their friends, and she explained the loving time she had. We offered our love to one another and happily ended our telephone call. I went to bed that night to be woken in the morning by my mother ringing to say my sister had passed away during the night.

Apparently during the last week of my sister's holidays, one of her special close friends had died and she stayed for the funeral and then my sister and her husband travelled the three-day, trip back home. They arrived home just after lunch and unpacked and my sister went about with the washing and ironing. At the same time, she rearranged her husband's wardrobe and re-labeled each draw with the items of clothing that were inside of them. She cooked a roast chicken dinner and baked vegetables with her husband's favorite dessert of rice pudding and stewed fruit. My sister had then rung me and with her husband had settled down to watch a movie on TV. At around 10:30 p.m., my sister said goodnight and went to bed as she was too tired to sit through to the end of the movie. Her husband went to bed twenty minutes later to see her curled up sound asleep. He awoke at 4:30 a.m., when the alarm clock rang, and went into the kitchen to make coffee, surprised that his wife did not follow him into the kitchen as usual. My sister's husband took in a coffee for her to find that she had passed away in her sleep. My sister had a magnificent funeral service of over 1,100 people in attendance. Both of my siblings were loved so much for their service to their friends and the community as a whole. Within the allotted time of ninety days, her best friend Polly also passed over and the mathematical codes of the Laws of the Universe were completed.

Upon returning to the east, the next stage of my life began again. My Healing Centre had been closed while I was in Coober Pedy. I did learn a little of the Aboriginal Herbal modalities, but I knew I was not there for my healing experiences. That came back later into my life. My parents were devastated with the passing over of their two children and I felt a sense of responsibility to help ease their pain in any way I could. I shared my experiences that I had been taught with Peter and my parents and I became closer with one another.

I was very much aware when I returned to my home state, that things were different. My mind had grown beyond my old reasoning and I had difficulties settling back into my old ways. My wisdom had altered into an importance of self. I found difficulties trying to fit back into old friendships. I was beginning to notice that it was my life that had changed, not necessarily theirs. Returning back to repeat the same old conversations became boring and I wondered why I was feeling so uncomfortable and out of union with my friends. Nobody was interested in what I had been learning and their attention spans were limited to my explanations. I felt so utterly alone. I could no longer pick up the phone and dial my brother and sister and receive comfort and could no longer burden my mother and father as theirs was the same as mine; I had to learn to stand on my own two feet!

I called out to the wind and I hugged the trees as I asked for solace for my endless inner chattering. "Help me rearrange my thinking" was my cry to the Universe. I wanted answers. I knew I had to move on. My next son left home to go out into the world to start his own path and that left me with the last child to rare into adulthood. The marriage was becoming temperamental and both of us knew that we had just about used every excuse in the book! We had to invent something new for us to continue on.

At my husband's suggestion, we sold our construction company and purchased a restaurant thinking we would be spending more time with one another. My God! Out of the frying pan and into the fire went our lives. We worked twenty hours per day, seven days per week, over the next four years and yet, I never seemed to be able to release any satisfaction within myself. We never had time to spend with one another and when we did, the first thing we said to one another was "Sorry to disturb you right now, but..." Why the dickens did I always have to start a conversation with an apology? I had this itch that collected all over my body. Off to the doctors I went, trying this and that cream; swallowing groups of tablets and when I had realized nothing was working; I would be placed on to another one. The medications seemed to be taking its toll and yet, I was still scratching this blasted itch. (Later I learned that an itch is an irritation reflecting out through the senses to connect with its outer boundary, which is the surface of the skin. It is given back to us from the thoughts we are busily creating and thinking about and through me not finalising those thoughts, there was nowhere for them to go and of course they were jammed up inside and had to erupt out through the surface of the skin.)

It was at this stage of my life when suicide entered my psyche. I could not find another excuse to bide my time. Inside me was the cry to go back to Coober Pedy and find my Kadaitcha man (Australian Aboriginal medicine man). Only he wasn't around anymore. I tried to relive the stories that Peter had explained to me. My mother and father had our religion, my brother and sister had gone home to rest and I felt pretty darn worthless with myself. Losing a loved one can shatter one's belief in self. We are the ones who are left behind, and now we have to change our old reliance and face the fact that our world that we shared with one another has finished.

Back I went into focusing my mind and recalling all of my past. My God, I have been given so much from others and had not done anything about it. I began to think to myself, now go back and call the wind and use the tools that I had been given. Where the hell were they? I know, I wrapped them up in an old blanket, somewhere deep in the cupboards. I searched and pulled them out and allowed the tears to flow. Why was life such a bitch? I became angry at myself—searched for the value of my real self. Where was my stamina that had sufficed me all of those years? There was a moment of personal insight and the recognition of a connection to an existing higher order, but it was up to me to connect with it. My thoughts rambled on as I lovingly polished each tool that had been given to me and I became determined that I would not make another excuse for my way of living. These sacred codes of the Laws of the Universe, had initiated me into the next paragraph of my hidden library, and my next venture was to regain emotional strength and move on. Love never dies; it continues to live on throughout our lifetime, and it is always regenerated into a new life form of compatible energy.

My next venture began when I deliberately took time off from our business and started to clean out all of the cupboards in our home. Thoughts of suicide stepped in front of me again. A belated declutter of the house which was long overdue, took hold of me. I backed the trailer up to the door and loaded it up and off to the refuse tip or the nearest charity shop I went. I took great delight in emptying out the past. I remembered a saying my grandmother had learned in China "If that cupboard has not been completely used in the last twelve months, then there are unnecessary items that need to be finding another home. If we keep changing our habits, our life changes as well; and it is in this space where we find that we can breathe more freely." But I had been hanging on to everything and so afraid to release it, just in case I might need it some time. I felt my grandmother dance with me around the house as every item that I had not looked at in the last few years, could find another home. I noticed during this time that the rift between my husband and I was stepping forward again and talking it over between each other did absolutely nothing to change the situation! We were beginning to reinvent the same excuses and they seemed to repeat themselves. I thought to myself that my husband would not have to clean the house when I was gone. What was that old saying that was mentioned many times during my childhood? 'A tidy house is a tidy mind.' Three days ticked away and the house had been cleaned from top to bottom and I returned back to the restaurant satisfied that I had done the right thing.

And then the day came when I was going to walk into the water and just keep walking and everything would be okay. My Australian Aboriginal training and my own inner-educated intelligence (my own Universal Law), had been pushed further into the background, where they had just about disappeared from my mind. A customer came in just as I was about to close the doors of the restaurant and asked for change for the pay phone which was outside the building and a small can of coke. The woman was beautiful and dressed in a golden top with royal blue slacks and I thought how regal she looked and without a care in the world.

When she walked out the door, I noticed that we needed more large drinks in the fridge and I proceeded to fill it up and then thought to myself, "Right, now close the door and off you go" I said aloud to myself. Again, as I went to shut the doors, the same woman came back in, this time for more change and a packet of cigarettes; I complied with her wishes and went to close the door when the phone rang. I answered the phone and took a booking for the evening's meal and placed the order in the book and again went to shut the door when the same woman walked back into the restaurant for the third time. She was looking for an address in the local area; so out came the local town map and we searched for the address she wanted. We talked for about ten minutes discussing the quickest route and then she decided to change more money for the public phone.

Well over half an hour had passed and as I was about to close the door again another customer walked in and said they were going to have an early dinner and could they place an order. Time had slipped away and another customer entered the restaurant. The staff arrived early in preparation for the dinner that night and the restaurant became very busy and I was unable to have any thoughts of my own. That evening when I finally closed the doors to the restaurant and walked out the back of the restaurant to my car, I noticed a car parked in front of mine with the motor running. I thought the driver must be waiting for someone, so I reversed out and went home to bed.

My husband returned to the restaurant at 5:30 a.m., to prepare the days ingredients for lunch. He rang and asked me to come to the restaurant as the police were in attendance at the restaurant and wanted to ask questions in reference to a nearby incident. The police questioned me if I had come in contact with a woman that was dressed in a golden top with royal blue trousers, the evening before amongst the customers. I confirmed that I had given change for the pay phone and that she had purchased a soft drink and asked for directions to an address in town. The police informed me that this precious woman had taken her life at the end of that fateful day with a hosepipe connected from the muffler to inside her car, which turned out to be the car that was parked in front of mine in the car park at the back of the restaurant. How fortuitous was this event! She had completed her suicide on my behalf. Over the next few days, I went into limbo. I found this news so devastating and hard to digest.

Gradually we pieced her story together. The address she was looking for was a friend of her daughters. This beautiful woman had been trying to contact her daughter, but her daughter's mobile phone did not answer, so she had decided to go around and talk with her daughter only to find that they had gone to a concert. The beautiful woman returned to the back of the restaurant and took her own life. What was this all about? Why did she choose my place? Did we connect in some ethereal level through our same thoughts and why did she take her life for me? Did she feel a safety harness protecting her because of my thoughts? Had she been attracted to me because of my thinking? Or more importantly had I been attracted to her through my thinking?

The questions ran hot and fast in my mind. Old thoughts came back to haunt me; what had this to do with God or was it just coincidence? I sent out a silent plea. "Let me learn more. Teach me to understand all!" was my cry to the Laws of the Universe.

My restaurant customers came into my life and of course the news of the suicide had circulated around town. The customer conversations were consistently focused on the suicide. I found that the thoughts I was thinking about what had occurred were answered systematically by the conversations in our business. How did these wonders know what I was thinking? I had not mentioned anything at that point in time to anyone. My goodness, this was all becoming too much for me and greater than I ever thought possible. I discovered that each time your eyes look at another human; you look at a reflection of yourself. Others become a mirror of the thoughts that you have in your mind in that moment, and they relay back to you an answer to the questions of that moment. It is this way for each of us, in order for us to begin to understand our hidden intelligence.

The thought of suicide never entered my psyche again. I erased the word from my own personal dictionary.

We placed our business on the market and sold it instantly and purchased a restaurant near the Ocean. It was in a quieter area than the previous one and we thought we would cruise along in a much easier stride. We made a huge success of our BBQ roasts of all gender, gourmet pies and fish that melted in your mouth and again the hours picked up. We thought it would be quieter through the week and that we would have a busy two days over the weekend. Wrong! We worked again for twenty hours per day and the commitment to the public grew and grew. The staff collected and we had nine people running all day with "excuse me please" as we squashed our way past one another. Then there came a time when it was all too much and I collapsed on the floor. I had suffered a diabetic coma and was admitted to hospital.

For fifteen days I was in a coma and on a drip, but I vividly remember my thinking as I came out of it to face the world again. I remembered having been in the land of China, where I had learned so many different stories, and where I had met wonderful High Priests clothed in the most magnificent robes. They were from the Divine equation of the Collective. I felt someone gently slapping my face as I came out of the coma, and I opened my eyes to see a beautiful Chinese woman standing over me and calling my name.

My first words to her were, "Thank you for being here and for the gifts that you have bestowed upon me." She was shocked at first, but then, once I answered the preliminary questions satisfactorily— that is, knowing my name, where I was, my date of birth, and where I lived—Dr Wong (she had filled in for my doctor who was away on leave) asked me to tell her what I could remember about where I had just been. For the next couple of hours, I spoke of my experiences, explaining my story to her. She wrote it all down, asking if she could use the information in her current education—of course I said yes!

She wrote and wrote my words down. I can remember being in another world; it was a world that was in the mountains of China. I was a student being taught the mythical explanations and stories of the world. Wonderful teachers spoke to me and were dressed in the most exquisitely colored garments draped down to the floor. They showed me methods of moving the hands through my body and I watched as that section of the body moved to coincide with their hands. I noticed how the colors changed as their energy rearranged my old thinking. I watched as flowers moved through my body and their perfume changed my cellular structure. I never asked a question; I only had to collect my thinking and the answers were shown to me. I gave the doctor names that I had never heard of. When these wonderful entities wished me to open my own psyche, I was given a circle that looked like a very ornate silver plate and then they asked me questions and I had to give them my answer in measurements.

I remember laughing at these lessons as they reminded me of cutting up the family pie. My husband always received the largest slice with my sons receiving a slightly smaller slice depending on their ages. My daughter and I received what was left on the plate. My daughter, asked for a small portion as she was on a permanent diet. Due to necessity, there were only the crumbs around the edge of the plate that were left for me.

My God! What an exalted way of explaining things to me? This world did not seem to be real. I could recall a few of the stories that my grandmother talked about when I was a child. Her conversations were brief and it was a though I was given half of her story. This was also the world that my father explained to me when he healed his friends! I then remembered how I had healed my brother! Was this the world of fantasy? Somewhere deep inside me I seemed satisfied with what was going on. I felt loved and I knew that I could also send this feeling out to others.

Was this the next step? Was this the world that my Australian Aboriginal brother Peter was talking about when he showed me how to view the horizon? So many thoughts were releasing themselves from my mind? Dr. Wong explained that these visions I was repeating to her were the scenes that were in the Temples of China. The names that I mentioned were Chinese Gods that Dr Wong had been brought up with. I had never heard of them before. The result was many pages to my story and we both laughed about it all at the end of our conversation. I often wondered if there was a connection between my grandmother's training in China from 1903-1907, and the inheritance of my DNA at birth had anything to do with it. Was my grandmother communicating with me while I was in my coma?

I went back to the restaurant and my earthly teachers entered my realms. They came from all over the world and just appeared at my doorstep.

*
Dare to be a Daniel,
Dare to stand alone,
Dare to have a purpose true, and
Dare to make it known.

Those words, my brother's favourite saying, do not mean that you have to live alone; they mean that, in your mind's eye, you can hold your own focus—your own light—and still be aware of everything that is happening on this planet. Stand alone and release the sound of your voice out there. You are your own best teacher, and the more you centre your mind, the more the Laws of the Universe will reward you. This journey of enlightenment is yours and yours alone, so make your light bright.

Action springs not from thought,
But, from a readiness, for responsibility.
Dietrich Bonhoeffer

Chapter 11
The Masters Of Time

My life moved on with a miracle a moment. There was nothing but bliss; I had an endless smile and my laughter rang out all around the planet.

In 1988 I began to connect to my inner journey in earnest, with the teachings as to how I could understand the 'Masters of Time' that had walked before us. I could see them, through my vision world and when I asked for their names, I had extreme difficulties in understanding them. They would speak to me in riddles that I had to quickly work out, and then came the Sacred Alphabetical quotations to understand. At the same time, I was also learning to understand the Language of Numbers as to how they had collected together to pronounce a word and more importantly why they had collected in this way. All of this information predicted what would become our next thought!! Now that was something to remember.

It is amazing that the numerology that surrounds us is also embedded in our genes, where each section composes its inner sound. This sound is alphabetically echoed and is transferred throughout the wholeness as it harmonizes and rebalances each layer of consciousness. The Divinity of Numbers, which collects through the Sacred Alphabet, working through the same etheric levels and then beginning to facet a coherent behaviour, where it multiplies and releases each number which has been autonomically registered up into the unconscious mind (higher mind). It is through the acceptance of numbers that we are introduced up into the Sacred Geometry, which is a language of our higher education between our self and the Laws of the Universe.

I could sense that the Sacred Alphabet was connected to every cell in our body and as we phrased our thoughts, our body was busily re-phrasing our next thought! I realized that my intellectual awareness was introducing me to the metaphorical language that was automatically released from our genetic inheritance, when we had earned their recognition. This ancient language is embedded in our cellular structure. It is the language of the original blueprint, was the way it was introduced to me by my teacher Sharon, as to how I could accept the emotional responsibility that each thought represented.

I now realized that each time I listened to a metaphysical interpretation of a story that my heart beat changed, this story seemed to open up my DNA, which automatically rearranged my language, and then I could take note of how my language had changed. This influence seemed to take me into another mode of thinking, where I could investigate another challenge which seemed to place itself before me! Life was never dull, it just kept rolling forward.

Each one of these Masters of time was representing one of my personalities or genes that I had inherited. Why did they always speak to me in a religious language? What had that got to do with me? I had been informed by my teachers that I would learn to understand the alternative step up into Jacob's ladder, (as to how we alter the native within) one rung at a time, for me to understand the mathematical and numbers inheritance. Also, to how we are gifted through the connective of the consciousness, to initiate us into our next collection of the eternal inheritance that awaits us all. I was at the beginning stages of my education at this time and I knew that it was a step by step discovery into these hidden realms of humanities earnings.

Once again, I felt the need to speak with my father, who was my first teacher and I tried to explain my journey to him; he mentioned the words *metaphor*, *metaphorical*, and *metaphysics*, and the more I understood my teachings the more I realized I was metabolically retracing my own *matter of physics*. My physics was donated to me as a gift to my inheritance from my forefathers and mothers, now that was something to be thankful for!

I began nourishing myself through my own thinking. My father informed me to believe in myself and take one small step forward with every thought I had and to know that God was standing beside me all the way. This last thought kept me sane over the forthcoming years as I crawled and stumbled my way forward.

I took an interest in the art of the Psychometrical worlds which is where we step up into the beginning of understanding this indelible hidden language that is automatically scribed in our cells. I learnt to see through the veils of consciousness which is called "trekking the psychometric consciousness"—that is, where we learn to measure the psyche.

The pictures came from the creation of my inner language and would become my vision worlds; they are an extension that is formatted from the inner lenses of our eyes opening up through the core of the iris, where this language becomes our seeing, as it is reflected back up into the unconscious mind (higher mind), where we also have the opportunity to view the soul's truth of the matter. Remember also, that our eyes are exposed parts of our brain. All of which, is identical to how we receive the language of our dreams. This sacred energy collects at the top of the bridge of the nose. Maybe now you can understand the ancient myths where, when we step onto the road less traveled, we earn these sacred writings when we cross the bridge (of the nose) to the other side!

As usual I began to hesitate in the beginning, what if I gave the wrong explanation; or what if it was just my imagination? This inner explanation could be distorted so easily if I wasn't assertive enough in myself? Wow!! How to be able to be in charge of my mind and in charge of my thinking at the same time? Now that thought was well worth thinking about!

I asked my teacher at that time how to begin? "It is all very simple, just close your eyes and visualize the clouds in the sky and just wait," she said. So, in all my innocence I did just that! I watched as these huge cumulus clouds rolled around on my inner screen and waited... and waited and I waited... I knew that if I opened my eyes, I would lose the pictures that were forming in my mind and I would have to start all over again. I just had to continue to trust and believe in these natural laws at first and then myself. So, I continued refocusing and stilling the mind and with all of the patience I could muster, I waited.

I could sense that my teacher was now standing in front of me as I could hear her breathing, her breath seemed to get longer and longer and I felt my body relaxing and my own breath working in with hers; all of a sudden, the clouds started to part and a huge ray of light began to push itself through the center of the clouds. Of course, I could not open my eyes now, even if the house was on fire. Wow!! The light was so bright and the rays had the strength of gold in them that I had never seen in my outer worlds. The clouds began to rise up into the air and I followed the rays down to the ground and an old dirt track appeared right in the middle of my picture.

Now remember, before we are aware of this existence, we referred to these pictures as our imagination, so let us move onwards and upwards to interpret this word as the 'image inside my nation'. Sounds better when it comes from the right hemisphere of the brain, don't you think? It takes ones thinking through to its next level! The left hemisphere automatically detracts from this thinking, as it does not want to accept the consequences, which is the final result or outcome of the inner language.

In my vision the track stretched itself far back into the distant mountains and walking along this track and coming towards me was an old man shuffling along with an old black dog ambling beside him. I could even see the white whiskers around both of their mouths. The old man had piercing black eyes and was dressed in a shabby dark coat with a red rose on his left lapel and old grey serge trousers and scruffy boots with the laces undone. He had old black leather gloves on his hands that had all the finger stalls cut back to half their size and gnarled hooked finger nails that were protruding out of them. I noticed that there was a tree on the left side of the track and a small bright white house away back in the distance with a large tree on the right-hand side, of the road. A few small boulders were on the road and larger ones lying beside it, but nothing else was in the picture.

My God! I thought, what had happened to the beautiful rays of light I had just been witnessing. My teacher felt my hesitation and called me back to the moment. Before I opened my eyes, I wanted to see the landscape once more. Where had the light gone, I wondered. I was viewing everything through a distortion that was beginning to create the overtones of sepia layering over the landscape. In the distance this little white house shone with a small single beam of sunlight down onto it and a large tree to the right of the house seemed to be tinged in a soft golden glow. Those bright rays that had expanded my vision in the beginning were disappearing fast. Behind the house, in the distance were dark steep mountains and it looked like a thunderstorm was approaching? I looked at the clouds and thought yes, rain was on the way and I had about fifteen minutes before it came down. I looked along the road again and way back in the distance I saw a woman approaching me with a halo of light around her head and I waited for her to come closer and when she did, I realized that I was looking into the eyes of my teacher. At the same time, she was calling me back softly into the room. All of these experiences seemed to take forever and yet it had all happened in just a couple of minutes.

I opened my eyes to see my teacher, who had a soft smile on her face and her eyes had this misty expression as she asked me what I had seen. I gave her my explanation and she proceeded to explain the metaphysics of the story. We began with the clouds and what they are here for. Clouds build up and collect around energy grids that suffice one another, where they are collected and attracted to one another through the same mind. Clouds represent our behavioral patterns through the sacred divine language. They represent the make-up of the human brain; where our thoughts automatically collect to fortify to be at peace with one another. They are like our own personalities or genes conversing with one another. And they are making us aware of the next possible moment and act like a buffer zone between the moment and our future. If we have an inner turmoil going on in our mind, then the clouds attract each other in confrontation. If they are small, light and feathery then we have an easy mind, it is where our fear is in abeyance as to what is happening around us. That is why to this day, when I step outside in the morning, I check what the sky is informing me of my day ahead.

If we take our attention to Indo-Asia, which believe it or not, is the most metaphysically advanced section on this planet, as they have already accomplished the inner language, long before we had even become aware of it! This land is even mentioned in The Revelation of St John the Divine (Book of Revelations), Revelation 1:4 where St. John talks to us of the seven churches which are in Asia and from the seven Spirits which are before his throne. Thousands of years ago, this area incorporated the land mass right down to Turkey, where it is now referred to as Asia Minor.

The words written in this amazing last book of the Bible explains to the reader, the Sacred Path of Shamanism, which is the metaphysical journey, that each human has the opportunity to discover when their mathematics have equalized and they have reached the end of their third dimensional mind/antenna; all of this information links us back into the codes of Egyptology. It is where you are deemed ready to evolve into the next advanced educated level of humanities earnings, or as Egyptology explains to prepare yourself for the afterlife right here on the earth! I have recently finished explaining my interpretation in an eBook format, *Decoding the Revelations of Saint John the Divine* please enjoy the read, as I bring the codes of Egyptology and the intelligence of the Bible together.

Isn't it amazing that the codes of Egypt, once deciphered, are explaining the codes of the evolution of the human nervous system, were explained to us thousands of years ago? And here we are today so further advanced, still trying to understand our original story. Oh, what a wonderful world we live in!

You will notice in Tiananmen Square just outside the gates of the 'Purple Forbidden City' in Beijing; their totem poles (traditional Chinese ceremonial columns) are there for the entire world to see. They are introducing you to the original heavenly language that you will be stepping into as you enter the Old City. Each one of the 9,999.5 rooms are explaining the personalities (aspects of self) that we are able to collect and bring forth to achieve our entrance up into the Royal Order of the unconscious mind. Three quarters of the way up the totem pole (also known as the pole of the DNA, or totem of humanity), are the clouds which are representing the doorway into the heavenly kingdoms. The heavenly clouds are manifesting as your ideas, as your lesser Gods earn their way up to the area situated in your brain.

I have explained in my previous material written on the Biblical agenda, when we understand the correct language, our Holy Book was first written in; that your body up to the beginning of your neck is the earth and your head is represented as the heavenly realms. As explained by my Chinese guide Chen, each of these Chinese totem poles are representing your spinal column; which is the journey the intelligence of your DNA must traverse through to the brain of each person. The cloud section represents the seven vertebrae in our neck area, the end of our third dimensional mind. And when you become aware of this section of the body intellectually, you have the seven sacred steps explained in Egyptology, which are also represented as the seven bands of peace, or the seven churches of Asia as explained in The Revelation of St John the Divine (Book of Revelations). These churches are represented as books, or seals, which are sealed on the back and can be opened when your intellectual awareness has evolved through this hidden or unknown intellect where you are at the doorway of being able to enter up into your unconscious mind (higher mind).

Now once again, we come back to the story—my vision. Then next came the light that broke through the clouds and this experience is the introduction into the wisdom of the Egyptian language and knowledge explaining our journey into unconscious mind of the Atem Rah (Atum Rah); which is the highest form of eclecticism, we have had passed down to us. Or another explanation is the noble strength we are able to accomplish within ourselves.

So, as you are now aware, the scene collected itself, the curtains parted and the spotlights (the rays of light) came down to the stage. The landscape appeared and the stage began to take the shape, as to how I could tune into my mind, and also as to how I would accept and continue to receive the information, that was being shown to me. The old road appeared which represented the past knowledge of our previous generations, or the past influences we have already walked, throughout to attain our own evolution. This information is also the pathway of our own DNA. The next appearance was the scruffily dressed old man with his old black dog.

Here we begin to understand how our intellect is setting the scene for what is ahead. The old man represents the father figure we all have to confront. In other words, he represents the Beast, please remember, that the beast is the one who can only live and survive from feeding himself on his past. Once he has connected to you, his survival depends on him trying to stop you from attaining your future and the battle of the wits continues.

Why? If there is something that we have not understood correctly, he then appears before us, to remind us that before we can move on, we must sort out our mind to allow the next positive thought to appear. Another explanation is through the myth of King Arthur known to us as the Merlin figure; he represents the magician we all still have entrapped within ourselves.

Every human at one stage during their life will have to confront the old man. I can quote a thousand stories that I have been given from my students as they recall how he interfered with them, when they set out to walk and talk this magical mystery of life. He walks into your life when your mathematics has aligned to a given position as he thinks he is there to create your next venture in your life. Most of you who have prepared yourself for your next evolutionary step, whether it be through your education, a business exploration or when you want to make an important decision in your life; you will be held up by the old man, as you step out of your old kingdoms into your next. He is there to test you; even down to his dress code and that evolves into another story. The old coat denotes his thinking; his garment that he wears is comfortable and from his past; so, he feels that there is no need to go on with his life.

He also had a beautiful red rose in the left lapel, which denotes that he is wearing a reflection of his soul outside of himself. We can very easily become confused and think to ourselves that he cannot be all that bad. Through the sacred codes of the body language, if the rose had been in the right lapel, I would have received a different interpretation. The right side of our body denotes our inner thinking; the left side is how we wish to present ourselves to others. His scruffy boots with the laces undone, denote that he is representing the past understanding that we have not yet brought together at this stage of our education and also that his thinking had not yet been accredited for, through the earnings of his soul.

His hands were covered with old leather gloves with the fingers poking out of them. Each finger stall was ragged at the ends. It was as though he had deliberately pulled them off the glove until they gave way. Also, his nails were long and dirty and were corded. This denoted that he has protected his own action and has kept himself buried and living back in his past. In other words, he has still not evolved up into his own higher wisdom and is waiting and ready to bleed your information off you. He has not tidied up his own act as yet and tries to interfere with your wisdom. And what can we do when we meet him? Thank him and honor him for his interest in you; and then get back to your next positive thought, he will soon disappear.

As each new experience was presented to me, numerous times I was presented with the old man, before I found my inner strength. I remember the first time I was invited to give a lecture and of course I said yes! Home I went choosing my subject carefully writing things down, crossing them out and rewriting the same things always choosing a different avenue to see if my words sounded any better. The day finally arrived and with my heart jammed up in my throat, choking my breath and tongue, I walked in the door and there he was. He tried to draw me into a conversation which began to interfere with my mind. He was taking me away from my plan, as I had primed myself up and was ready to start. My heart felt like it was beating so fast, that my throat could not form my words. I could not allow him to step in to interrupt what I had created for myself. I finally found the energy to excuse myself and asked him to take a seat where he sat down at the back of the room and I walked on stage and began my talk. The moment I refocused my mind, I found that my words came freely and as my lecture began, I felt myself relax and thanked myself for not forgetting my lines and I looked up and noticed that he had left the room. I knew then that I had passed my first test!

Our fingernails are composed mainly of keratin, which is a hardened form of protein made from dead cells and are to be kept short; they are here to protect the tips of the fingers and to serve as a barrier against injury. The longer our fingernails become, the more we try to place our control over others. Note in the Asiatic Continent how the old Emperors and men of renown had their long nails; they represent the inner daggers or swords and it automatically sets a fear amongst those that still feel intimidated, all through them not understanding who they are. Our fear cannot recede when it is continually threatened by someone of higher exaltation who thinks they have already accomplished their own royal behavior.

Now let us return back to the vision. The tree on the left side of the track represents my tree of knowledge. This tree represents the beginning of my journey where I will come to terms with my ego, through it learning to understand itself. My ego represents the logic side of my creation, and the little white house, with the larger tree surrounding it in the distance on the right denotes the third brain, which is where I will futuristically learn to walk towards, to release the knowledge of my higher intellectual mind.

The old black dog represents the ancient loyalty of the animal kingdom of the species; every matter of species is an energy that has evolved on this planet and is registered and recorded within the human brain as an emotion or to be more precise, an energy in motion; throughout the collective consciousness, which has been automatically placed at our disposal. When we have collected this matter, it replaces our fear; and we are well on the way to discovering our freedom.

Take notice of those around you, as to what sort of dog they have connected too. Dogs are all representing the emotion loyalty and yet there are many different breeds. Why has the person connected to a certain breed of dog? What is the personality of self, that is in abeyance in the person that they have a need to attract this animal to them… what is not balanced in their own lives that they must keep this species amongst their midst? No, do not become offended to understand these hidden laws that we will all wake up too, as we learn to open up, to acknowledge our inner mathematics. We know now that metaphorically every animal is connected to the second layer of our brain that we have earned and until we have the belief in ourselves to trust and rely on our own thoughts, we automatically reach out for other thoughts of same mind to sustain us. As I have mentioned previously, please remember that the human psyche is a reflection of every other species that has previously evolved on this wonderful planet; we are all connected.

Every species that has evolved has its own mathematical vibration or series of numbers which create its own set of laws that must be obeyed by their thoughts, throughout their evolution. Through their thinking their ideas become the tools we can use to alter our inheritance, as to how our psyche is able to create these personalities that we are able to rely on, which is added to the intelligence of our forefathers that are embedded in our genes. We will learn to become every species that has evolved on this planet, as each species represents an emotion that is here to assist us at some time during our life.

How we begin to understand the pre-birthing of our personalities (aspects of self) is through the messages passed down through the Myths, be they Greek, Mayan, Asiatic, Arabic or the earlier gestations of humanity, who understood that their courage came through, as their personalities gained their own strength and were declared by them, as their lesser Gods. These lesser Gods began by vying for their own control; also they were responsible for the training of the lesser personalities. Their journey was to release the twelve strands of their DNA; to exalt the combined intelligence up into the heavenly kingdom at the crown of the head where they could take their place in the mathematical equation or unconscious mind (higher mind). Similar stories to the evolution of the "Twelve Tribes of Israel" explained in the beginning of the Bible.

Finally, back to the story. The dark mountains represent the battles that are still ahead for me to overcome through releasing my own fear. My fear has been passed down to me through my parents and grandparents and great grandparents etc; these fears have been collected and have become a catacomb of my DNA.

I would like to explain this word with much more eloquence. We are aware that the 'catacombs' are subterranean cemeteries of those who walked before us. These bodies of higher cast or knowledgeable humans were placed into niches into the walls under the Cathedrals around Rome and other areas, where the energy of their intellect would protect the ones who served in the Cathedrals. Now let us move on to another famous word that I have included in this information and that is the word—catalyst. The Macmillan Encyclopedia nicely explains this word; "the acceleration of a chemical reaction by a substance (catalyst) that is not itself consumed in the reaction." Virtually every reaction must overcome an energy barrier and here is the point I wish to make; "as the molecules of the reactants rearrange to form the products or thoughts." The catalyst allows the reaction to proceed via a different lower energy pathway.

Now let us repeat this word again, catacombs. Can you now understand how the fears of our past generations are locked away in these subterranean cemeteries of our DNA? And it is only through us repeating ourselves over and over again that we can release those past yearnings that our forefathers and mothers had, for us to reveal our next possible moment; otherwise, we follow on exactly the same life path as our parents and there is no progress for us to look up to. Through not facing up to your responsibilities of your own self acclaim; you have automatically passed them on to your next generation. The onus is all up to you! We all require a substantial release to create an adjustment that our previous sixty-four generations held themselves back for, through their innocence of not being able to understand their thoughts at that time. Every human has this inner Shaman, and will become the initiate, when they are ready to believe in themselves! Thank you for reading this story.

Just a little story about Crow. When I was correlating with the Masters of Time, the crows and another species of birds—which we refer to as Apostle birds, as they collect and fly in groups of twelve—liked to fly inside my dwelling and be with me while I was working; they wanted to connect with my energy. The Apostle birds would become entangled in my hair when they were flying around, and, finally I shouted out to God, "Enough is enough!" So the birdseed came with the next delivery of groceries, and it helped ease the situation by keeping most of them outside the door. Once I had explained the situation to Crow, he stood silently at the door, as if he were a sentinel, and stopped the others from entering into the room.

When I placed out my food scraps along with some seed, I began to become aware that Crow has this uncanny habit of walking around a group of birds, checking to ensure that the share of nourishment each bird received was balanced and harmonized between them. If not, he would march into the circle of birds and give the greedy ones a beating. His wings would encircle that greedy bird, and his feet would march over the bird very quickly; the greedy one was then sent out to the edge of the circle. Crow did not hurt the bird; but the guilty bird was very quickly reminded of its manners, and I watched as the other birds surrendered to Crow's bidding. Through their deference, they soon realized who the boss was! Crow did not eat until the others had had their fill. Crow had earned the role of the keeper of the sacred laws; through the sun shining on his iridescent black feathers, he completed the colours of the rainbow, shining like an opal and blinding the others.

Man cannot discover new oceans unless he has earned his own courage to lose sight of the shore.
Anon

Chapter 12
Opening The Heart And Decoding Ancient Egyptian Metaphysical Codes

It was at this stage in my life where my interests were becoming more absorbed into the metaphysical worlds, since we had bought into the restaurant business down by the ocean. My journey in the outback had come to an end. Again, we created another chronic experience of working twenty-four hours per day. There was no time for ourselves, we were open twenty hours per day, seven days per week and this went on year after year, and it was at this time that my husband and I were deciding to separate.

I was finding it harder to pay too much attention to the restaurant, my new worlds were becoming more important and my mind was focused on so many other things. I could not sleep at night and I started grouping and lighting candles and adding aromatherapy around the house. There was apple and cinnamon in the kitchen, lime and lemon in the bathroom and magnolia and sandalwood in the lounge room and ylang ylang in our bedroom. This was all just a little too much for my husband who had partnered me for over thirty-five years; his whole world was being turned upside down. 'What is wrong with the perfume I buy you every anniversary? This is irritating my senses,' was his remark. I placed a Christmas wreath on the wall which permanently stayed there with a sign underneath 'Peace on earth will come to stay, when we live Christmas every day.' I loved it and I knew it was a little out of the ordinary and drew many comments from people who entered the room. It was as though I had gone back into my childhood, and some members of the family were becoming embarrassed with my behavior. My teacher explained to me that I had not gone backwards; I had entered into a new realm of knowledge and was innocently exploring the fields where I would need to rephrase my power and strength to support me in the future.

I knew I could not stop this inner excitement of understanding a world that I had never known about, which was being explained to me in my current reality. I allowed myself to be gently pulled away. I had been sitting on my suitcase for over ten years and I could not find the inner strength to close the latches. To be honest the time to talk had gone; we had just outgrown one another. He found it hard to accept my new growth, so I mentally asked for someone to come in and take over from my position in the restaurant that would know what to do and was experienced with the general public and I was answered within twenty minutes. This gave me the freedom to continue with my studies and extend my time on my research. The woman who took over my position became the next partner in his life and 'all's well that ends well'.

I moved out and was given an apartment by my friend only fifty meters from the ocean. At first, I cried myself to sleep every night. I had never slept alone before. I had left my childhood home as a young woman and had my own family quickly after. So, there was always someone to attend to. I heard every rattle and creak in the apartment. My whole world was being turned upside down. I could even hear the conversation that the neighbors next door were sharing with one another at their table. Their TV annoyed me, as it was so loud. "Get used to it" I would tell myself, "this is what you wanted!"

My next education began in earnest, I became a devoted student and as I grew into accepting my teachings, new teachers were presented to me. They just appeared at my front door! I seemed to have a permanent metaphorical stairway placed in front of me and I thoroughly enjoyed stepping up into other worlds; which were always waiting for me. There was a total of seven years of strenuous teachings, where I was led into the underworld, the book of gates, the book of the dead, the Netherworld, the Duat, the hidden Kingdoms or whatever name you wish to refer to it, plus the Bible. What began to amaze me was that they were all representing the same story, only the names were changed. I soon realized that we must go through our own darkness before we attain our own light! And we all know by now that our light is our own intelligence; the more we believe in ourselves, the brighter we become, for us to realize that our light reflects out to those who do not know.

Another important test was reading the Bible backwards which gave me confirmation to accept all of this information. It took me four years to file my education into the inner pantry of my mind and place labels on each one of my experiences, where I could teach and explain the science and physics of God, now known to us as the Natural Laws of the Universe. It was in that darkness that I learned about the consciousness of 'Being Human' and how this energy collects and mirrors back to us our thoughts, through the mathematics of every other human. We call it the Collective Consciousness or let me bring it back inside you and with the greatest respect to every human being, being human, and call it God, which when decoded denotes to the—Greatest Oracle of the Divine.

It is in here where we begin the journey of the awakening into understanding and becoming this divine intelligence, as we learn to unclasp the seven seals in the book of—The Revelations of St John the Divine—which lifts us up towards the new city of light into the language of the unconscious mind (higher mind). I found that during my training, I was learning to understand the ancient Phoenician alphabet with its twenty-two symbols or characters, which is still referred to as the universal language on the planet. All other written languages stem from this one, so it is said. It is the first and the last language, as it is the language that is created through the unconscious mind (higher mind) and it is threaded and embedded within every one of us. If we care to look into the ancient past, we can see all of the information that we need to excel ourselves, is embedded in every cell. Once these seals have been opened, it is the first step into forming our syllables which sound the same in every language. That is why I have no difficulties in listening to another language and understanding their meaning.

As the ancient language of the Hopi Indian Elders has informed us through their stories, "We are the ones, we have been waiting for." Oh, so true, while we are waiting in expectation for our guardian angel to fly into the window of our mind and appear before us, we soon realize through the commitment we are making to our new growth, that the angels are within us, watching every mathematical movement of our thoughts, for us to accept and acknowledge ourselves.

This can only be achieved once we have surpassed the reawakening of the heart area, metaphysically known as the Ancient Egyptian Amanea (Amarna) period and the journey by the Pharaoh Arkenaton through the Egyptian Principles. Akhenaton through measuring his own mind up into the heavenly energy—or the crown of the head—had opened his heart to himself and was a complete manifestation of God. Akhenaton went through his night—or netherworld—in order to find his own light, and he had earned his balanced mind. The Aramaic language has pronounced Akhenaton as 'Ayanatun' or 'EA-nat-on'. 'EA's' nation of light.

Let us return to the hieroglyphs that were brought forward for us to earn our own Royalty, once our heart has been opened to our self. Each crown that is worn on the head throughout Egyptology begins to form itself as each story presented to me began to unfold itself. I relate these stories to our own personalities (aspects of self), that are accepting their new state of grace; where they are learning to believe totally in themselves. They must traverse up through their inner education to earn their freedom, all the time gathering and fortifying their own strength. Once they move beyond their education up towards and through the heart area, we note the stories of Egyptology begin to change. Also, the colors on the crowns change, through the divine inheritance we are introduced to the colors of gold and royal blue. This is the doorway to the unconscious or divine mind.

For us to earn our first crown, we commence with the Ancient Egyptian Nemes crown (archeologists believe that it was not a metal crown but a stiffened headcloth/headdress and symbolized the pharaoh's power, but we are referring to it metaphysically). The gold funeral mask of Tutankhamen (also spelled Tutankhamun and Tutankhamen) was used to cover his head and shoulders for protections as well as safe entry into the afterlife. Around the face of the mask is a blue and gold Nemes headdress with a cobra and a vulture sitting on top of the brow. There's an inscription on his shoulders as well as the back of his head which is a spell (from the Egyptian Book of the Dead) first seen on masks in the Middle Kingdom and a long braid like appearance on the back of the mask.

The Nemes crown, blue and gold stripes (representing the left and right hemispheres of the brain), metaphysically informs us of our inner alphabet (the words we would use, when we are busily thinking our thoughts) that is embedded into our DNA. This language is finally breaking free of the restrictions that we have placed around it owing to the fear of believing in self. In our fear we act like a child, or become child-like, as we do not have enough belief in self to this point. As our freedom emerges, we then begin to understand the changes that naturally occur to our spoken language, which automatically reverberate to open us up to the next educated level of our mind.

And, if we take a look at the mask that was placed over the young king's head, viewing it from the rear, the headdress depicted on the mask is collected around the back of the neck, and we see how the braid is bound symbolically to represent our spinal column; also the strands of our DNA, as to how it traverses up into the higher mind.

On the brow area of Tutankhamen's mask are the cobra and vulture rising from the forehead. The cobra represents Lower Egypt and the vulture, Upper Egypt. The double crown represented the unification of the two regions of Egypt.

The cobra, the Uraeus (representation of a sacred serpent as an emblem of supreme power) is a symbol for the goddess Wadjet. She was one of the earliest Egyptian deities and was often depicted as a cobra. Metaphysically the serpent (cobra), emerging from the forehead is announcing the strength we bring forth from our ego (left hemisphere of the brain) conforming to its own state of grace. We tune into our ego as it learns to earn its own respect, to venture up into the heavenly kingdoms to release itself from its own bondage.

The vulture represents Upper Egypt. This is a representation of the emotional mind, (right hemisphere of the brain), and is a symbol for the goddess Nekhebet It is here, where we understand we have earned the right to enter into the doorway of the heavenly kingdoms, where the Lesser Gods are earning the right to become one. We are very much aware of the sanctification the vulture represents through our totem inheritance. It must make sure the soul has left the body it will devour, before it steps forward to eat.

Tutankhamen's mask symbols of the cobra (serpent) and vulture (Lower and Upper Egypt) metaphysically symbolises the ego (consciousness—left brain) and emotional (subconscious—right brain) being in balance which escalates and lifts us up into our heavenly kingdom—or unconscious mind (higher mind)—which is where we begin to enter into the Divine Intelligence where we can release our free will. The kingdoms of Upper and Lower Egypt must balance themselves continuously.

Balance is a condensed energy equalizing itself; if we are not in this power zone, the Laws of the Universe will not hear us, and, if it cannot hear us, it cannot work for us. We are on this life quest to create a balance within ourselves. We create an emotional intelligence through understanding our ego or our fear, not through trying to be intelligent emotionally. By placing our feelings first before we speak, and then we try to feel those thoughts we have in our mind; we will be surprised at the result of our own judicious wisdom. Remember this: knowledge knows, and wisdom achieves.

The next evolutionary step is how we evolve into our emotional intelligence, and the right brain has the claim to this fame; it sits on that throne. This is the Divine Myth of Isis. In the word Isis, there are two syllables: 'Is-is' Decoded, this word means 'Through the Relationship of the Intelligence of the Soul'. That means that we have to find this relationship within ourselves in order to balance both brains.

To further explain the ancient Egyptian journey of opening the heart, ancient Egyptian royalty wore different crowns/headdresses and the metaphysical passage can be decoded through the hieroglyphs:

As per previous information for us to earn our first crown we commence with the ancient Egyptian Nemes crown. The Nemes crown, blue and gold stripes (representing the left and right hemispheres of the brain), metaphysically informs us of our inner alphabet (the words we would use, when we are busily thinking our thoughts) that is embedded into our DNA.

We then venture up into the crown of the Uraeus also known as the Wadjet crown, (The Uraeus is a symbol for the goddess Wadjet) which is the next step of the Nemes Crown with the serpent coming out of the forehead announcing the strength we bring forth from our ego conforming to its own state of grace. We tune into our ego as it learns to earn its own respect, to venture up into the heavenly kingdoms to release itself from its own bondage.

Our next educated step is to venture up into the Royal Academy through the ancient Egyptian crown known as the Hemhem crown. The symbolic interpretation behind this crown was to boast the power of the Pharaoh. The Hemhem crown was a more elaborate version of the Atef crown; because of this, it was sometimes referred as the triple Atef crown. This crown was originally noted in the Temple of Kom Ombo near Aswan; it began with two Uraei cobra figures on the crown which is informing us to accept that the ego is protected to secure the passage of the person to whom the story was about, as we traversed or broadened our journey up into the heavenly kingdoms.

Also, through the sacred codes, the ego was earning the right to form a relationship with itself to bring both left and right hemispheres of the brain into becoming a balanced mind. The more our DNA opened to reveal our next education the Uraeus fortified us with their security.

As we continue on our journey, we become more aware of the next crown, known as the Khepresh crown, notably again worn by Akhenaton. Not only was the Khepresh portrayed in its most common form with the uraeus serpent, but it was represented in more complex versions as well. When representations of the Khepresh are painted, the colour is blue. The wearer of the Khepresh crown, furthermore, connects the king/pharaoh to his ancestor kings/pharaohs, portraying wearing the crown as the living heir of kingship from a line of deceased kings/pharaohs. The shape of the crown can be described as the crown rising from the core of the helmet, which is explaining to us how our mind is reshaping our tenure, through our intelligence rising up towards the crown of our head. The Khepresh is often called the 'war crown' because it was work so often in representations of battle scenes. Metaphysically this is transcribed as the inner war we all have to claim, to gain our next evolutionary step of intellect, often referred to as Armageddon or the armor of Gideon.

Once this has been earned, we note how the feminine mind steps in to initiate us into the Royal Vulture Crown, which is the crown of the emotional mind, representing the right hemisphere of the brain. It is here, where we understand we have earned the right to enter into the doorway of the heavenly kingdoms, where the Lesser Gods are earning the right to become one. We are very much aware of the sanctification the Vulture represents through our totem inheritance. It must make sure the soul has left the body it will devour, before it steps forward to eat, whereas an animal will attack and tear at will. We see this crown as the balanced mind, where we are free from insulting our self or others. Finally, after many years, I had been brought back to the beginning of my journey, to receive the answer to my question as to why the language spoken to me was in a religious context! It all has to do with the opening of the heart! Thank you for reading this story.

This very important step of opening the heart is where we are given the eternal promise of stepping up into the mental nature of the mathematical kingdoms, whether Biblical or through the Myths of the past, as they are all explaining the same story, which can only be attained when the mind is able to feel a sense of freedom and live in its own silence. All of this information creates a record or a concordance of our thoughts and sets the scene for the mathematics of our mind to assist us, as we enter up into the Divine Eternal Wisdom.

We achieve this outcome in our third dimensional reality naturally, when our mind is reposed, by releasing our thoughts towards a sleeping state. It is only when the ego is resting, that the subconscious mind has the opportunity to walk our thoughts through into the perpetuity of the unconscious energy (higher energy). Also, known to us as the fourth dimension, it is in this space where we earn the right to become free of the restrictions of our ego; that the mathematics will continue to work on our behalf.

I did not want to hold myself back; I yearned for the next dimensional education of my new found reality. It had taken me many years to be able to release myself from my old ways; for me to find the courage to create a sense of reality, which would encourage me to achieve and expand my inner education. These codes had always been there, standing by for their precise moment to release themselves. It was only when one has reached a certain level of mathematical attainment through learning to balance both hemispheres of the brain, that we become aware of our own progress. Some refer to this state of grace as lucid dreaming, which is where we are able to live in both worlds as both the left and the right brain have the opportunity to work in unison with one another. It is not through allowing the ego to keep on creating excuses for its own blind behavior, by locking the right hemisphere back down. The more we ask of ourselves; the more silent we become while we search for the answers. It is only through us achieving this silence that we will release the unconscious (higher) language back to ourselves. My internal conversations were beginning to open up within me and I liked the communication. My longing to meet my God within was becoming a new love affair that I wanted to participate in.

My teacher Helen arrived at my door one day, she had come to see my new dwelling; she was most impressed with my interior designing. I had just boiled the kettle as she knocked on my door, so her cup of tea was delivered straight away and we sat down viewing the magnificence of the ocean. I tried to explain to her what was happening in my body and informed her that I was afraid of dying before I had completed my education.

This was the first time she had been to my home, as she normally did not enter or attend our private lives. Teachers are in our life to teach their information; they are not here for us to grasp, or to hang on to for support. The decisions we make to our education are totally under our own control. If we make a mistake; then, so be it? We yearn—to learn—to earn our marks at the end of the year. There is no judgment or reprimand. I asked her for advice from the other side? Could they please explain to me what was happening to my body or was there more responsibility for me to uphold.

She looked at me and gently closed her eyes. She started to take her deep breaths that I was now becoming accustomed to and I watched as her body started to sit in an upright position and her spine became more aligned and her words came forth quietly and with reverence as she said to me "No, no you are not about to die, as you term the word, not yet! You are dying to your old ways, there are things that you no longer need; you have already experienced many of them and have held on to them to support you; you have a position of importance not only to yourself, but also to others to whom you will help in the future to teach them how to release their fears; to fill them with a confidence that will abound in them. You are about to partake of extreme spiritual experiences; they are only for you, not for anyone around you. You will receive spiritual messages. You will be asked to make great sacrifices and you must keep your levels of awareness aligned and balanced where they must always be free of congestion. This means that the more silent you become within yourself, the more you will understand and accept what will be placed in front of you. Learn always, to be in a focused mind. Do not allow the clouds to gather and block your view to the horizon. Are you first willing to listen, and secondly hear yourself, to accept my words? You will always be looked after, and your temperament will alter as you commit to yourself; and this will change your thoughts for always."

After all of these years I was beginning to finally grasp this language of metaphysics. "What were these spiritual messages?" I asked her. My mind naturally thought of a letter, I was to receive or maybe someone would give me a book to read or even a further thought came in that they would be from her. This expose` happened many times during my life over the next few years, although I was always brought back to recall my father's words, that the first step was the hardest. It did not matter how large or how small it was, just believe in yourself and step forward. "Follow your nose, he would say to me, keep your eyes focused in front of you and always remember that your nose knows." I brought my attention back to hear Helen say to me, "I personally cannot speak" she replied, "this is between you and the sacred universal laws of God (Laws of the Universe); you have asked for advice from the other side and these are the messages I am receiving." I thanked Helen for the information and she left. All in all, she had only been there around ten minutes. It seemed to me that it was all over before it began. I had to sit down and think about the words she spoke to me and after assessing everything she had said, it was the same as always, I was still left in the dark! Deep down I knew I had to birth the courage that had been trapped within me, for me to go on.

My teachers Helen and Sharon have recently passed on to their next alignment; I had been given their blessing to know that I was now ready to walk these worlds of understanding, as to how the metaphysical language interprets and reproduces itself throughout and into our everyday language.

*Blessed is he that readeth,
and they hear the words of this prophecy,
and keep those things which are written therein:
for the time is at hand.
Revelations 1:3*

Chapter 13
Expanded Consciousness

I continued on my quest of learning and further reflection to the power of thought. As we think our thoughts to ourselves, the Universe also answers our thoughts, through the people we meet or through the members of our own family, by mirroring back the consequences of our thinking. We are what you see.

As an individual the way to analyse yourself is by looking at your own reflection in others. For example, you may have a family member or colleague that you dislike. What is it about that person that you find irritating? If you are very honest with yourself, that irritation is a reflection of something that you are not aware of about yourself. This Spiritual journey is one of looking into yourself through the mirrors that the Laws of the Universe gift back to you.

The next time you are thinking about something, open your eyes, look around, and you will see the reflection of that thought coming back at you. The people walking past you will reflect the answer to that thought back to you. In which way was the wind rustling the tree outside, was it coming from the east or the west, or was it the north or the south? In what direction was the wind asking you to pay attention? Which part of the Medicine Wheel had your first thought? The bird flying up in the air, was it coming from the right or the left? The car driving past your window, what colour was it; who was at the wheel? Was it male or female? How many times did that dog bark? Always, your totem energy is working with you. Please remember, the Laws of the Universe are always serving every one of you.

In Shamanism, we call this process 'trekking', and my first experience of this was when my teacher, Helena, came into my life. Helena came to teach me silence, and this was the first introduction to understanding my Oracle. She could only stay for a few minutes on that particular day, and she asked that we go outside. I followed her to the outside table and sat down to face her.

"Now don't take your eyes off me," she said. "I have a piece of paper here, and I want you to write me a story about what you have just seen." I looked down at the table. "No! Do not look down, just look at me and write, and I will give you two minutes to give me half a page." "What?" I said. "I haven't seen anything." "Okay, so I will make it easier on you. Please close your eyes and don't open them; now begin to speak and release what is already stored in your unconscious mind," she said. I had to learn to see through the veils, and we call this "trekking the psychometric consciousness"—that is, where we learn to measure the psyche. To recall my mind, I had to go back to where I had stepped outside the door. I hesitated at first, because I was afraid to trust this unknown; I was not prepared for this experiment—I thought that she had arrived just to tell me another story.

So, I slowly searched through my memory to find something to begin with, and I found that my thoughts began to open up my inner screen. With my eyes tightly closed, I looked right and left, and then I said, "There is a young man walking down the road on my right; he is coming towards me. There is nothing to my left. In front of me there is a woman with two small children—or maybe it is one child and a dog—walking across to the right-hand side of the road." I was so proud of myself!

"Good!" Helena said. "Now go deeper into the unconscious mind; I want to know what the young man who was walking towards you is wearing. Can you see the colours of his clothes?" I searched my mind again. "Yes, he has on a green T-shirt, I think, and there is a symbol on the front of it. He has long dark hair, dark shorts, and thongs on his feet." Again, I was so proud of my memory. "Excellent," she said. "One more question. Can you see the emblem on the front of his T-shirt? What is it?" I searched again, and burst out laughing. "Yes! It is written in large white letters, and it says 'Shit Happens!'" We both laughed. I had passed the test.

I had to step up into and through the Metaphysical language to condone the physical, in order to be able to reveal to you all these hidden messages. I began to trust the wisdom of my thoughts. This is where we begin to look through the eye of the God within, and know that we are all entitled to collect this inner intelligence.

The clothes that you put on each day will also give you an answer or message through their colours. Look around at what colour clothing others have on, and read the reflections of your own thoughts. Do they have a moustache or beard? What colour is their hair? All this information is introducing you into the thought you have in the moment. Yes, it takes time. Little by little, you are learning to connect into the ultra-consciousness. I watched over the years as each student grew into his/her freedom through understanding these codes, and it was a joy to behold each of their smiles and intelligence becoming broader and lighter. All these species and events are revealing to you the mathematics of the Collective Consciousness.

These are the messages that the Collective Consciousness releases to your higher mind, and they transfer back to your thoughts, before you have consciously thought them. It's the language of the Soul, in cohabitation with the thought that you have in the moment. These are the cloaks of many colours. When the Soul—or your Higher Self—introduces you into each moment, your right hemisphere or subconscious self is accepting and adjusting that current thought. If you are in your left hemisphere or conscious self, you are totally unaware of this concurrent occurrence. The memory strands are of no consequence as it has not repeated itself enough for your ego to be able to rely upon the moment. When you are not in attention to yourself, you automatically reach for what you feel like wearing—preferably, something comfortable. Usually, you do not think too much about what clothes you put on each day, so your Higher Self chooses them for you in order to remind you of what you are not doing about yourself. Your Higher Self is asking you to look at your thinking, and the colours it chooses will show you where your mind is at. Now, armed with this knowledge, you have the possibility to think before you dress, and to think about your day before it starts. What is your agenda? Whom do you wish to impress? What outcome do you wish to achieve and receive?

An explanation of how colours represent themselves back to you follows.

Wearing something *green* will spark an awareness of jealousy in someone who is close to you. Did you know that? Let us discuss the individual colours in detail.

Light Green: Represents emotions; i.e., to feel yourself emotionally. So your Higher Self is saying, "Give love to yourself before you start your day."

Dark Green: Means that your Higher Self is asking you to bring through the power of your emotions. It is asking you to use more energy, as it is waiting to serve you.

Light Blue: Is the colour of communication, so your Higher Self wishes you to speak more clearly. Be careful of the pastel shades, because they are an excuse to hide behind. Light blue is the colour of the throat, so a man who wears a blue tie will always be able to communicate better.

Dark Blue: Is conservative; it is reflecting a balanced strength.

Blue-Grey: Means you must balance the speech of your higher mind.

Turquoise: Represents the heavens and the waters; the reflection of the sky sharing itself with the abundance of the Collective. The waters represent the consciousness, and the consciousness is situated in the lower part of the body. The learning process starts from the kidney section of the body. To wear turquoise is a healing for the kidney section. This colour heals your feelings and reminds you of your own Soul energy.

Pink: Is the only colour we use to heal our self; it rewards the emotions of the inner child.

Red: Means sexual power—whether you wear it, or see someone coming towards you wearing it—you are being asked to bring through your sexual power with strength; remember this is for your ego to know it is supported and is not ignored. After all, our journey is for the ego to ascend! It is the beginning of balancing both brains. Start fresh. Create new beginnings.

Dark Red: Is also power; extra power to control and help you prosper in your thinking.

Orange: Calms the yearning; it is the sexual flow. It is a prosperous announcement. This allowance comes from the Soul regenerating the flow of what you do not understand about your own capabilities.

Brown: Is also connected to sex. Your Higher Self is telling you that you have your head on backwards. We wear brown when we are not surrendering to self; instead, we are forced to surrender to others.

White: Represents innocence and purity. No matter what colour a human is on an outer level, the inner level of pureness and innocence vibrates through the Soul levels through the discovery of white. The brighter the white is, it then becomes opaque, and this light reflects through your aura.

Black: Represents the power of the ego self. It is also a reminder to others that you are representing your own responsibility; you do not need others. Remember that little black dress hanging in your wardrobe, ladies?

Deep Purple: Is very powerful. In the Bible it represents the building of the Temple, or the building of one's mind. Your Higher Self is telling you to speak your words with more conviction. The colour purple is the germination of new ideas through the third eye. Deep purple is the vibration that you use to construct your mind into a focused point. Others are aware of you when you are in purple, and they stand aside.

Gold and Silver: Also fit into this category. Gold is the controller of the ego, and silver is the expanse of your emotions.

Loud Mixed Colours: Give you the opportunity to make excuses for yourself. For example: Wearing two colours is okay. Three colours mean: "I am a little bit scattered today." Four colours: "Oh my God! I'm in chaos! I can't think at all today." People who are above you in their mind will turn away from you when you mix too many colours; the only person you attract is someone who is beneath your station.

The energy of the weave of the fabric will either close you off or open you up. A closed weave will constrict your aura. Patterns in fabric give you the opportunity to change your mind, rather than clarify yourself.

For further explanation of hair colour, hair types, and symbols in your life, please consult my book *Decoding the Mind of God*.

I continued with expanding my consciousness (trekking the psychometric consciousness), and two weeks later Helena returned and was pleased with my progress. My conscious energy was outside my restaurant as I was working inside; I was observing everything through my third eye. I did not have to go outside to view that Helena was about to walk past, how many people were in the street, or what color car would drive past my front door. Helena informed me "You are entering into the world of freedom; where you are beginning to understand what silence really means!"

The Shaman is well on the way to receive a balanced and sensitive mind; the more balanced, the more the mathematics sensitizes the mind, where it can sense the reality of its view. Through our initiations, our body becomes sensitive to the light, which is created through the vibrations of every cell opening up. Why? These vibrations must come up through the heart to enter into our eternalness. Your order of merit, releases this ancient energy up firstly into the Hypothalamus gland. The Hypothalamus gland is that sleeping Master at the back of your skull; this gland collects each thought, then transfers the energy over to the Pituitary gland, so that these extra sensitive feelings maybe emitted throughout your body. Thoughts that have not been digested correctly (thought through to the end) prefer to stay behind, until they can find the strength to believe in themselves. As each cell is revitalized to expand more light-this light then stimulates our intellect to surge forward which releases our natural endorphins, that will take over to heal those memories that have been bogged down and have lost their way.

The Shaman is well on the way to receive a balanced and sensitive mind; the more balanced, the more the mathematics sensitizes the mind, where it can sense the reality of its view. Through our initiations, our body becomes sensitive to the light, which is created through the vibrations of every cell opening up. Why? These vibrations must come up through the heart to enter.
Omni

Chapter 14
Visitors From The Next Dimension Of Time

My next education began in earnest, in order to introduce me into the world of pneumatic waves of consciousness, which I already had begun to gather around me. I was learning to understand the process of how we achieve and accomplish the intelligence to enter up into the unconscious mind (higher mind). To be able to transform our consciousness into the Divine Intelligence of the Universe, we have to 'cross over the bridge to the other side', as the old saying goes. This is the language of the Shamanic Principles, and it is the last test of treachery that we must exude from our previous third-dimensional existence. The Shaman has to walk through hell to enter into heaven.

I knew Beings of Light were revisiting me when I noticed a heart appear on the trunk of my paw-paw (papaya) tree just outside my bedroom window. Each morning another heart appeared on the trunk until thirty three hearts had been seared into the trunk. I never saw how they appeared, they were just there! I extolled to my friends how these amazing phenomena just appeared and my friends made it a point to come every day to count them. We had some great conversations regarding ideas of how they could appear on the trunk.

I started to feel very fatigued and spent more time in my room; my body started to break down and I had difficulties walking, I kept on losing my balance. At first, I began to panic. I remember one day I yelled out, "That's it! I'm finished. It's all over, before it began. Oh well, you gave it your best shot. You did what you believed was the right thing for you to do."

On the thirty third day the visitors from the next dimension of time, revisited and have been with me ever since that time. They have never left my side. It is as though a portal of time had been opened just wide enough for me to slip into, where the information cabinet had been placed before me and as long as I calibrated everything through the vibration and tune of numbers, the mathematics could assist me in attaining the truth of all matter!

At that moment, I began recalling the words that a Chinese philosopher whom I had met over twenty years previously in 1979; when I had taken an interest in Chinese Medicine. He informed me, that I would have no more contact with the earth from the end of 1999. "There are no more biorhythms to work with you," he said. And of course, I had never heard of the word, biorhythms, therefore at that time, it was of no interest to me.

But, his words from that time sprang back through my head while I was going through this experience. I still had another ten years to go before my predicted death. Had my experiences into this heightened intelligence shortened my life time span? At least I had progressed this far! Every day my body collapsed a little more, until I could not get out of bed and my friends would assist me into a dining room chair. Now what to do? Do I go back into the marriage and start again? No, and I would not go and see a doctor. I had become cynical "What the hell did they know or understand about my extreme difficulties and more interestingly how could they understand me? If I tried to explain my life to them, I would have been put into a straight jacket and locked away!" I said to myself. Anyway, by now, some of the local doctors were taking an interest in my teachings and were becoming my students as they were interested in learning to understand meditation and other courses of Neuro-Linguistic Programming, Kinesiology, and they were interested in 'Energy' work, that seemed to be a great release to the stressed mind. There seemed to be a thousand other courses that I had been taught by my teachers in which I could now explain.

I had to trust, and at that time I believed that God permanently had his arms wrapped around me and would hold my hands until I had finished this education. I rang all of my children and told them how much I loved them and requested that they did not judge me on what I had committed myself to do.

On the morning of the thirty third day of this experience, the only part of my body that I could move was my right shoulder and the paralysis seemed to have taken over where I thought that God had forgotten me. I was sitting on a dining room chair and my friends by this time had fastened me into the chair with my father's old silken dressing gown cord. You know the one that was a royal blue color with a gold thread melded into it, with the tassels on the end? I thought to myself that this was very appropriate as this was the 'Royal Cord'. It could not become any worse; I thought to myself that I was finished. My speech became slurred and I noticed I was dribbling out of the corners of my mouth. I began to shake and convulse and the pain around my heart was horrific.

All of a sudden a bright image appeared before me. The image was bright shiny iridescent gold and white and was about two meters in diameter. I watched as it appeared to come through the closed front door where it moved to stand in front of me; the light assumed a definite form of a tall Pharaoh through the substance that surrounded it. He bowed to me and I acknowledged as best I could. The light was so bright that I had to squint to see the garment he was wearing—full regalia of the Pharaoh. He communicated to me with compassion and love. Slowly he moved closer until we were touching one another and my skin started to tingle and buzz as if an electrical current was coursing through every vein in my body and then he seemed to disappear inside of me. I was frozen to my chair but kept up my trust and belief that God was watching all that was eventuating. Always the small child within me had to find her own contentment.

My body twitched and moved as though there were two people walking around one another, inside me. My friends, who could not see as far into the consciousness as I could, watched the golden aura disappear. I was surprised when my friend Joy said to me "Where did that light go?" I was so pleased that someone else had seen it. "Inside of me and goodness knows what's going to happen next" I finally replied. The top of my head started to buzz and crack, whether through the excitement or my fear jumping to attention, and the pain around my heart became so intense that I was trying to utter the words "good-bye" to my friends. I heard my back crack loudly two or three times around the heart area and also around the back of my head. "Just go with the flow" I thought, "if he is here to take you home then what a trip we will have together. Wow, going home with a Pharaoh, everyone else just dies" I exclaimed to myself.

I waited in anticipation as to what would come next. I could hear a rumble around my stomach area and it moved down to around the lower intestines. After a moment or two the feeling started to travel even lower and seemed to go through the vaginal area and down into the top of my thighs.

I wanted to open my mouth but there were no words to speak. After a few seconds the feeling came again, and I knew that this time there were words to be spoken. I opened my mouth and waited; and a soft melodious voice came up through my body, which seemed to travel from my thighs to my throat asking me if I was comfortable with him (I call him a 'male energy' as he spoke to me in a low, melodious, masculine voice). "Yes, if everything is as it should be," was my reply. "What did you say," said my friend and I replied to her, "He's talking to me inside my head and he has a beautiful voice." "Well, tell him to talk to me, if we are here to care for you then we should know what the dickens is going on?" Joy replied.

I felt a smile appear on my face and it was as though I was in limbo and had no control of the situation. A sensation travelled up my spine, through my internal organs, tickled my throat and inside my mouth, and then words developed; "Good morning to all of you, my name is Men-Et-Rah." My voice had totally changed and the words I spoke were his words with a deep masculine sound; very pleasant to hear and my mouth tasted of so many different gases and metals. Some of them tasted earthy, others were very strong, like helium, others left a bitter taste on my mouth and tongue and then there were other tastes that seemed to come out through my teeth. "Have no fear" was my thought, "just go with the flow." My friends were stunned! "Are you all right, girl, are you still there? Hello to you sir, and what have you done with my friend?" was Joy's reply.

"For our lady to continue to take her next educated step, there are a few adjustments as to how we can help her change her frequencies and these will correlate with the rest of her institutional mind. We have come to help her open her heart, for her to attune and receive this next atonement (at-one-ment) to add to her educational process," he said to my friend. He seemed to speak in an old English biblical language. At that time, I could not talk or interrupt this melodious voice, so the essence continued to explain to my friends the resonance of the next order to come. He asked for them to sit down while I was being prepared for the changes to take place in my body. He spoke many words through me and sometimes I had difficulties to hear what he said. I was trying desperately hard to see if God was on standby and holding my hand as I tried to regain my composure to think for myself. Was this the extreme spiritual messages I was to receive? Again, these inner conversations were beginning to ignite me. God seemed to be coming closer, where I felt the Pharaoh's breath easing mine. I knew in that moment that I would be of service to the oneness for the rest of my life.

The more advanced we become, the more we move through multiple worlds in our mind.
Omni

Chapter 15
Extreme Spiritual Messages

I settled back in my chair and continued to be available to this Being of Light when all of a sudden, my mind opened up to view amazing pictures being reflected to me in magnificent iridescent colors. (When our third eye expands, we see everything layer by layer; viewing this through the brain coerces and magnifies our inner sight. The images we see from this eye are reflected up into the forehead). I recall that the first vision to appear was a bubbling mass of the earth similar to hot springs and boiling mud pools that release pressure from underneath the earth. The alchemy was stifling hot and smelt of Sulphur in my nose. Amid all of this I watched as the vision changed to a spectacle of gems creating themselves under the earth. They were huge and I watched as their gases swirled around them to create the color of the stones. I particularly noted how they collected their alchemy through the energy of the surrounding area, as to how their clarity built up, and their energetic resonance became clearer and more pronounced. I watched as the opal gained its perfection through one drip at a time seeping its way underground through the shale, over thousands of years. They were all the bi-products that resulted through the alchemy of the earth. It was as though they were formed through an upheaval that had been designated from the residue of the earth's energy. All of which would serve as an added value to repatriate the earth. I watched as they seemed to spread themselves around the earth; it was as though each one had a special purpose to fulfill on behalf of the collective. The gems seemed to be an anchor that held the planet together.

I have often reflected back to this part of my journey as to how we use these elements (gems) for the crown, we will ultimately wear. For us to accomplish something we have to dig deep into our psyche, for it to be accomplished and be reimbursed back to us, in its splendor. The Collective Consciousness inherits and creates the life force of every species. It is explaining an inner language; every species is autonomously connected through their inherited mind—or DNA—in order to review the life force of the previous generations. In humans, the information is embedded in our glandular (endocrine) systems; it filters through to the pineal gland, where it becomes the crown we wear. As the crown of our head aligns and opens up into the crown of the Universe, we are permanently in an etheric domain of intelligence.

I realized years later, that this particular vision of the gems building their energetic resonance metaphorically demonstrated the human embryonic development that would serve human evolution, which is also created through an upheaval of our thinking. The photographic memory that is autonomically registered in every cell in our body holds all the records of evolution and conciliation. These are the Laws of Self of our inner universe, and they reflect the Laws of the Universe. They hold and support us through every moment of time that we have endured as a species. All of which gives our intelligence the opportunity to advance us into becoming a greater species.

The next vision to appear at this time with the Being of Light was the Grass and Tree tribes that revealed their energetic energy. Iridescent pictures explained how their root system developed and why their branches and leaves had to form through a geometrical mathematical resonance for the emotional responsibility of the planet to create itself and grow. I saw how the evolution of the trees formed into their own geometrical shapes and which one became the most powerful of the species. I noticed how many of the trees needed sustenance from one another; they had to collect and create a forest of themselves to survive. In time, they seeded their own energy and as their seeds ripened, they dropped on to the earth's floor, to repeat themselves to multiply. They found their strength through collectively banding their electromagnetic fields with one another. The shimmer from one tree announces itself to the others, and they follow suit. Others sent forth roots under the surface of the earth in a lateral circumference where I noticed that once they had sustained themselves, they broke free of their restraint and poked their head above the earth.

As I was watched the different species of trees, I noticed how the grasses evolved and how certain grass seeds were attracted to the alchemy of certain trees. They required sustenance off one another at the outset of growth until they could collect and build their own colonies or stands to support themselves. There was a huge network weaving its web under the ground. I thought I was viewing the architectural plans in the Council Chambers of a village as it grew to become its own city. The trees and grass all had their own systems and realized that they were as important as one another. It was a huge net of intelligence collecting itself. I noted how once the leaves had evolved into their own geometrical/mathematical shape, that they became the pages of their own personal inner library.

Some were strong and others were weak, some were tall and others were short. It reminded me of a giant carpet being woven by the amazing universal laws and brought together and draped across the floor of the planet. They all had a specified reason for being here! It was a mind-blowing experience to be shown this splendor in all of its glory.

Other species of trees had gained their own strength to support themselves and they stood alone, where they could gather and collect into their own concubine equation. (Remember, that a concubine is an emotional thought that surrenders willingly to become a sacrifice to support the elder of the tribe!) How similar this was also to human kind. Some could endow their own company, where others who were not as strong, relied on one another. One tree was the country dweller, where the forest is referred to as the city dweller. I seemed to have been placed into a time warp through the fascination of evolution. I was watching the second stage of the correlation of our nervous system showing me how the branches of our tree of knowledge began reaching up throughout the body; up they came to broadening our channels to support our inner library which was embedded in each cell to become our education system.

Years later, through discovering the codes of Egyptology, I realized that the whole story of Egypt is explaining to us, the story of the evolution of our central nervous system! Much more is explained in detail in my eBook, *Decoding the Revelations of St John the Divine*.

To continue on with my story. I watched as the worm crawled up out of the ocean and moved under the earth, how, over time it pushed itself up out of the earth and collected its outer spine, which through its emotional instability became its first garment; its shawl or its shell. The more they collected their own consciousness they had an urge to release themselves from the ground and reach upwards towards the light. I could now begin to understand the gathering of the first brain collecting itself in humanities earnings.

I watched how prehistoric animals came into my view and lumbered towards me and way back in the distance behind them, appeared the birds, which flew as they also learned to fly above the tree tops. They were huge and as my inner sight filled; more pictures of different species of animals were brought to my attention. I watched as the first animals began to recede in height and realized that they had finally reached the end of the antenna of their DNA (reached a state of attainment). Over time they receded in shape and stature, as they were swept back into their past, as each new species stepped forward to take its place until they became minute forms of how they originally evolved. I watched how the complete Collective of the Consciousness developed itself. (The Laws of the Universe is the Soul Energy of Collective Consciousness; it is a mathematical program of all that is).

These pictures/visions reflected back to me years later when I was being escorted through the underground cities in the mountain region of Turkey. People had lived there for thousands of years; they were short in stature owing to their confinement of the light. The labyrinthine complex of corridors was finely chiseled out of the region's soft volcanic tock with low ceilings where sometimes even I had to stoop to walk through. It was when the people earned the courage to walk out of their own darkness and live in the light that they began to change their own dictation (inner language and thoughts); where their dichotomy autonomically enhanced and opened up their DNA.

I noted with the picture/visions I was viewing that the second brain (first is the left hemisphere, second is the right hemisphere of the brain) was being prepared for us to inherit. At this time, I thought of Noah building his ark! We were beginning to attract our multitude of personalities (aspects of self), that had been passed down to us from the twelve tribes of Israel (twelve strands of the DNA), as each species represented the complete alchemy of the creatures on earth. Do you remember the story? The animals were collected one male and one female and of the clean beasts we were asked to collect seven. It all had to do with the seven vertebrae that attached itself to the base of our skull. All of which is in relationship to the seven sacred seals, as we step away from our earthly body and evolve up into our heavenly kingdoms, which represent the unconscious mind (higher mind). The seven sacred seals unfurl for us as we release and live by our inner language as written in the 'The Revelation of Saint John the Divine' (Book of Revelations).

As we are the last species to inherit the earth, we need to understand why we are formed in God's likeness. Our animal mind was beginning to awaken through our desire of being tempted, we were inheriting our free will; we were given a choice to search for our own divine purpose and equation. Our mathematical system was at work busily collecting our future inheritance.

All of which, reminds me of the Sphinx and its purpose to be here; it alerts us to the animal body of what I personally assume could be the ancient loyalty, the dog; or could it be the lion which represents our ego, or maybe it was the lynx, the cat is decoded as our detachment, which was changed to the sphinx, with the head of the human where we can venture upwards through the opening of the seven seals, which are the bones of our neck, also known as the seven sacred steps or the seven bands of peace throughout Egyptology, as mentioned previously, to release the fear that habitually refrains us from stepping forward.

The metaphorical stories foretold in the ancient kingdoms are informing us that the Sphinx was previously known as the God Harmarchiiss; through the codes, this denotes as 'Ha-Rha-Mha-Chi-Iss', and it explains to us how we 'heavenly ascend to release the restrictions of our mind; through mastering self'; all through the relationship we earn from our mathematical intelligence that is embedded throughout these seven seals. I also believe that originally there was a moat that surrounded the Sphinx where the water was pumped in from the Nile which represented the ocean of consciousness. If you look at the body today you can see how the water marks are moving up the animal not eroding from above. This figure of the Sphinx was informing the people that while they had the bodily mind of the animal, the consciousness was always there to protect them.

I watched the bird kingdom through time automatically learning to fly higher; exchange their bat like wing structure into developing feathers. They had to evolve from a leathery membrane (similar to the evolution of the bats) to be able to birth their feathers. Why? Some were born with elongated arms, where they had the ability to lift themselves up and out of their gravity fields and fly above the earth as they did not have a lymphatic system to deter them. Through their intellectual evolution becoming greater and more expansive than the other animals, many did not require a lymphatic system, as they did not need it, so their gravity fields were free to externalize and the rest of their species could take to the air. The more advanced had earned their future intelligence, through their divine inheritance advancing on its self, which had evolved through their sonic sound becoming more mathematically aware. Those that had the limited attention span of their DNA were kept closer to the ground, as their bone structure was not applicable to fly. Lymph nodes are only present in some aquatic species such as ducks, geese and swans. Also, birds rely on the mitochondria they produce to provide the energy for each cell to work. The most important information for us to realize is that birds purify the energy produced for the survival of each cell, which eternally balances them; hence, their long age.

On this metaphysical journey as we become overloaded with knowledge (or over think things) we place a strain on our body.

So many of us find that our lymphatic system collapses during our own evolution, through us being earth bound, as we were not born with the geometrical bone structure to fly; we note that our skin begins to droop under the arms to compensate for our bodies becoming heavy. All this is in relationship to how our lymphatic system functions. The lymphatic system is extremely important in its function as a heavenly outpost, watching and securing us as we earn the acceptance of mastering our self. Our lymph regenerates itself through us returning—or nurturing—our energetic thoughts back through our body. Do you remember the heart and the feather being measured through the codes of Egyptology? (By the way my Masters of Time explained to me that sipping lemon juice in water will help rejuvenate the lymphatic system).

Throughout the stories of my Shamanic training, the turkey is represented as the earth shaman—or the first initiation into entering up into the angelic realms—and it represents the power of the pituitary gland, which has its responsibility right here in this moment to reimburse the earth. When turkeys use force to empower their wings to scrape along the ground, the sound is like that of a drum; they are sending out a vibration to attract the lower, or earthly, kingdoms to pay attention to their tone. Through the Shamanic Law this bird represents the worlds of our possibilities. It cannot fly a great distance, as its evolution is still caught up in its primal evolution; it is still here to remind us all that we have the possibility to fly. It represents to me, the beginning of the angelic realms!

Through the falcon's stillness of mind, it gathers its own responsibility and creates for itself a perfect hologram, where it can see through all the layers of Consciousness. Look at the bird, and you will see that it is able to fly and hold itself in abeyance, while in its stillness, in order for it to be able to mathematically set its prey. All this depends on the power and use of its wings.

Now we can begin to understand why the bird kingdom knows what we are thinking long before we have brought our sentences together, as they live totally in the layers of the unconsciousness ether and rely on their sonar to show them the way. Also, why in the world of mystery, the angels have wings. The angelic realms were now entering my psyche and showing me the evolution of their wings; once again I was entering up into the divine mathematics of our evolution. All of these pictures were explaining to me how our personalities were growing into their receivership, where our master glandular system took control of each situation that had to be earned, to allow the mathematics to inherit their next lesson.

The consciousness was massing itself together and had to work harder to produce the right conditions for the next one to inherit.

Even the chickens were as big as horses. I noticed how the supreme consciousness was creating the species and feeding off itself, through rearranging the next species inherited thinking to become lighter and brighter. Do you feel like a glass of water? I know I do, the words are just falling out as I recall this amazing event that occurred through me, to what now seemed like a million lifetimes ago.

Just a side note about the bat. King Tutankhamen from the Egyptian philosophies and Lord Pacal of the Mayan philosophies, both were unearthed for us to become aware of the bats that had been placed over their mouth. These bats are symbolically representing the metaphysical language of the heavenly kingdoms referred to by some as the 'afterlife', through their initiation of accomplishing their supreme intelligence, through opening up their inner sight and sound, which is where we learn to speak from the unconscious mind. I became aware that the supreme consciousness buffered my worlds of learning, where I knew I was protected and shielded from harm. My fear was no longer visible. If we notice, the bat always hangs upside down! So too do we, when we have mastered the path of ascension!

Through the pictures I was viewing, I thought to myself, the responsibility always falls onto the shoulders of the last to inherit. I noticed the claws, hooves, pads and paws of the feet developing each species. I watched how animals went out to forage for their feed, where they could peck at the earth for the seeds that could not burrow into the earth, chew on the grasses and rip off the tops of trees and I watched how those lacking in their own security could devour those less fortunate than themselves. It was totally coded through the mathematics of the laws, as to how they had to be obeyed.

I watched the feet of the birds developing, most with claws, some webbed, and which ones had spurs on the back of their claws for their own defense because they could not fly and why. I did not realize that it was their fear that kept the webbed feet birds near the water where they felt safe to be able to use the water as an escape plan.

I observed how bird beaks changed into different shapes and became smaller through their evolution educating itself. More importantly I saw how they confused the other species with their colors appearing throughout their feathers. They were trying to disguise their weaknesses through trying to deceive the others. I watched as the larger birds were able to diminish the resilience of the smaller ones. Again, I noted that this was the way things had to be for the species to continue. I saw the older species becoming smaller, where they receded further into the background as the new species of the Collective Consciousness expanded itself and more birds appeared on the planet. Each new species that developed deprived the ancient ones of their limits of expediency, through adding advancement to their own DNA. How could they progress if they had reached a zenith of their own understanding or how could they act out what they had not yet earned?

I noticed which animals became carnivorous; and the reasons why this had to be so. Their fear could and would not abate. The only way they knew how to survive was through their need to force themselves onto others and try to control them. They nourished themselves on their own envy. They ate smaller quantities of food as the meat sustained them and strengthened them to help them evolve their ego. Humanity does the same when they are in doubt of taking their next step! There, had to be a replacement and this replacement had to be more formidable, to fill us with awe, which would surge forward to create our inner strength to release in us our inner harmonization and balance. In other words, we had to learn right from wrong.

I was then taken into the ocean where I was introduced to a totally new world of thought. We are now more aware that water can support memory as well as energy, so much more work to be done here. What fascinated me was to see how they had the opportunity to create their own sex through the energy that massed around them. Everything must balance itself out, is their motto. To keep each species evolving there must be an equal mathematical balance of emotions and ego. Each species seemed to be able to place themselves into a state of altered consciousness very quickly. How come they were so far ahead of us? One minute they were swimming around and the next they had placed themselves into a sleeping state, where the oxygen seemed to collect and press into their bodies to be used as required. Their fields of energy were supporting every thought they understood through their own correlation. It was as though they could create their own air bag which surrounded them. Is this what we refer to as the soul energy? Was I being shown the creation of their unconscious mind? We have a fair way to go to be as Collective as they are I thought to myself. I have since worked with this energy over the years and now understand that this is how our own unconscious mind works to supplement our own benefit, while we are yearning to understand their truth, and during the process, we have learned to accept our self! The human foetus is exactly the same; upon gestation each pregnancy is a derivative of the female body, which autonomically changes to accommodate and answer to the DNA of the mother's mind.

I remember being shown the beginnings of the human body creating itself in the womb and what fascinated me was how the face of the developing human seemed to change its shape as it developed into many different fish, to reflect what has already been accomplished and seeded into our genes.

Our brain is the mirror of the Collective Consciousness. It was as though God had placed a mask over the child as a form of protection. Many years later, I have been shown a video of this same process that has now been captured on film. So, I wasn't mad or crazy at the time, after all. I now realise that these pictures that I was given at that time were showing me the advanced development of our supreme consciousness, that we have named our unconscious mind.

How did these events of totality occur in our consciousness? How had the ocean benefited more than the land? Why didn't the same thing happen to the animals and the birds on the land as well? If it had in some species, then they were few and far between. What did our gravity fields have to do with connecting us to the earth through all of this? Was this the reasoning behind the two super powers that we have named the left and right hemispheres of our brain? Was the left hemisphere the earth energy and the right brain the oceanic energy? We are aware that in the ocean, the species are living in their foetal conditioning of time, which accompanies and influences any forthcoming event. I have since learned that through this allowance and more importantly through accepting all of this information, it makes change easier.

On the earth, the species must learn to walk upright, supporting themselves, learning to balance within the gravity fields; there is work involved in this process. The birds have learned to trust themselves, not totally committed to working with gravity alone, for the birds to walk upright; they rely on their own forces to interact with gravity which allows them to fly freely. Was it up to the bird energy to bring both water and land species together, as we learned to open our heart to ourselves? I believed this to be so and time gave me the answer as I understood the codex instilled in my DNA. Was this the reason why the oceanic species could change the development of their membrane moment by moment? As time went on from this experience, I realized that the oceanic evolution of the earth, begins above our heart area all the way up to the base of our neck. In other words, it is the last outpost before we journey into the heavenly realms.

There was so much happening in my mind at that time of my journey and I hope to recall it all to bring this through as I continue on with this story. My brain seemed to go click, click, click! Each picture seemed like an old movie introducing itself to me one frame at a time.

I tried to pay more attention to the words that were coming out of my mouth. I forced my eyes open, which took me a tremendous amount of energy to find. I turned my head and looked over to my friends who were standing in the room with looks of amazement on their faces and I heard my friend scream "What's happened to your eyes. You have no colour in your eyes; your irises have disappeared out of them. You look as though you are blind," My friends turned away from me in horror. I could vaguely see my friends; they had a misty mauve ring around each one of them. This misty ring I have understood now as time has moved on for me was their aura, their energy, their soul's force field or as I explain it now through my teachings; I was viewing them through the layers of my unconscious mind.

This voice within (Being of Light), explained to my friends, that my frequencies were being remunerated and that I would return to normal when the adjustments had released and equalized throughout both hemispheres of my brain. Little did I realize at that time, that I had entered into the divine language of releasing futuristic information that I knew I had the possibilities to earn.

And then I was introduced up into the final level, where I was being slowly familiarized into the species of the insect population and to the reasoning they have evolved on the planet.

It was at this level that I was introduced to the geometric symbols which appeared to me in their viewing, as most insects are designed to work through the layers of the energetic sound waves. This was a slow process, as the background pictures were of a totally different structure. As the insect appeared in my vision, the background seemed to waver and move in unison with the insect; it was as though the insect could carry a section of the Collective Consciousness along with it as a support team, and that it would become a benefit to assist the insect. At that time, it seemed to me, that the more advanced we become, the more the Universe supports our thoughts, just the same as our own cellular structure supports us the same way, when we have found our inner silence. I have now come to realize that the insect population has evolved through their expediency of their learned evolution, up and into the levels equivalent to our unconscious mind (highest mind), as they are both one and the same.

Through time, insects have been able to eclectically (multi-facet) design their mind, all through the focus of their intention; which has created their inner freedom! They vibrate to the sonic range, through the Collective Consciousness becoming their sonar fields to assist them, when they are tracking their food and nourishment. We as humans also have the ability to create an inner freedom for ourselves. Our intellectual light manifests only when the mind is focused. When the ego (or conscious mind) releases, through learning to trust itself, and is in silence, it is then collected into the subconscious (or emotional mind), as the emotional mind automatically trusts the next level, which is the unconscious mind (or Higher Self). You cannot doubt yourself for a moment! We are being introduced up into our blue blood, or the Order of Royalty, that we can attain through our thinking; we can earn this intelligence through learning to trust in our own self-worth.

Again, I digress a moment as I remember when we first purchased our property up North in the tropics of Australia, and we had built up quite a menagerie, I was taking a bucket of food scraps to the feed the chickens, when I side-stepped a cow pat (also called cattle droppings, or cattle poo/dung) and saw a large beetle, known as a dung beetle, rolling a ball around inside the cow pat. I watched in awe as the ball grew in size, and then the beetle burrowed underneath the dung ball and lifted it off the cow pat. The beetle then rolled the ball and lumbered off towards home; when he had difficulties urging the ball forward, he placed it on his back and shuffled off over the hump and then continued to roll. I watched as another beetle took its place on the cow pat and the same thing happened. I asked the locals about the beetles. I was informed that the dung beetles play a critical role in Australia's grazing ecosystems. By burying dung in the soil, beetles improve the flow of water, nutrients and carbon into the root zones of pastures. Furthermore, fortunately, dung beetles compete with flies for dung and the dung beetle can be so efficient that a cow pat is buried in as little as a day or two. This means that fly larvae, do not have time to develop, so the fly life cycle is halted in its tracks.

From then on, I looked at this little insect with respect! In the following years throughout my training, this same story has appeared in my vision world many times over, to assist me during the growth of my journey. Is this why the dung beetle symbol (scarab) was used in ancient Egyptian hieroglyphs and made into amulets? We now understand that through the Ancient Egyptian religion the scarab was also a symbol of protection, immortality, transformation as well a symbol of the enduring human soul, whence its frequent appearance, often with wings spread, in funerary art.

The majority of insects do not have lungs; they have respiratory systems that are extremely simple to empower themselves. They survive on the etheric combustible energy that is produced throughout the Collective Consciousness. They see only in circles and spirals, which is how their mathematics tunes into the solid geometrical substance of the planet, by honing in to the energy surrounding them. Everything is delivered to them as geometrical sonar energy; they use the shapes that they sense in the Collective Consciousness, as their sound vibrates to higher frequencies. The mosquito works on the same principle when it lands on the human skin. The blocked energy that reflects out from the human, releases a positive reaction to the insect. The insect lands near the irritation and pokes its proboscis (adaptation of the mouthparts) into the skin to release the heat from our body. Other insects release their urine onto the negative patch, and of course the acid in their urine burns our skin and we come up in welts!

The pictures/visions I was receiving was just like watching a 3D movie. It displayed the auric field of the cellular structure; this is also delivered to us from the Divine Inheritance (DNA). It is through the stillness of the mind that we are drawn up towards the next layer (higher mind), which links us into the etheric worlds of the human brain. Embedded in our cellular structure is the evolution of everything that has been, is, and will be. To further explain this concept: our thoughts are heard right around this planet. The Collective Consciousness sonically registers them. By sonically I mean by sonic sound: When we raise the level of our thinking and therefore vibration, is where we begin to harmonize our thoughts with the potential of "the all" the unseen, where the level of our thought creates and manifests into physical reality, matching the experience. First, our thoughts collect within our own auric force field, which then equates with the outer Collective Consciousness, where, depending on your intuition, we all have the opportunity to unconsciously hear others thinking. We call this 'telepathic communication'. I am explaining to you the principles of Egyptian law and philosophy, which have been carved on the temple walls for us. This represents an intelligence of a higher wisdom for us to walk or work towards. This is the buzz, the hum, the overtones, that the collective vibration of the insects are totally connected to, through the unconscious or telepathic energy which is layered, and as we expedite our intellect, this action autonomically draws us up into new territory.

My goodness, I have just realized that this same story has been introduced to you in Chapter 7: where I explained how the Elder from the Pitjanjatjarra tribe called the rest of the tribe to the camp! That was in 1987! As previously explained the Aboriginal people are still connected to the unconscious energy. It is as though I had to begin with these wonderful people back in Coober Pedy for me to open a mind map, to the way they explained their spoken language to me. It was six years later that I was to receive my transmission from the Pharaoh regarding the insect population, through the Channels of Consciousness.

This sequence also reminds me of the shades of the worlds that Van Gogh was honing into through his balanced mind, as he noticed different sequences in his vision worlds, and thus produced his star systems, for us in his paintings. It was at this level that my mouth filled up with the taste of gold. I could feel it throughout my teeth and gums, my alchemy was reaching up to a peak of its own perfection that we create through eclectically learning to rebalance our mind.

I took particular notice of the next equation as to how the insect population created their colonies through the mathematics that each species had evolved into. They were such tiny creatures who had condensed their energy into so much power through time. Their mathematics had delivered them into their own species through the generations of their ethereal emotions that they had collectively inherited. I realized that we as human still had a long way to go.

I never took things for granted any more, I was fascinated with how insects used the four elements to create the inner workings of the beehives, the air conditioning of the termites, the insects who relied on the trees for their dwelling, those that bred on the water and then there were those who relied on the air for their continuation etc., they had earned their intellect through having relied only on their own microscopic worlds. Their DNA has completely enhanced itself! They owed their survival rate to the combustible energy that they have evolved into, as well as their ability to sense through their holographic make-up of their eyes, which is how their repetitiousness produced the facets for them to telepathically hone into their food supply; this is also identical to how our third eye teleports the information and is able to communicate with us.

In this moment as I write this chapter, I recall a memory from a long time ago of a bite from a small meat ant on my big toe—the pain went up into the crown of my head and I felt like I had jumped through the roof. That small injection of concentrated toxin stayed with me for weeks. So, next time you are injected by a mosquito, bitten by an ant, buzzed by a fly or stung by a bee, they are the reflections of your thinking. Every consequence in your life is through the results of your thinking; all of it mirrors back to you, every moment of every day.

I began to realize that I was coming to the end of this transmission as the inside of my skull was ablaze with tiny blue flashing lights which moved in different directions as my thoughts danced their way throughout my brain. Slowly, oh, so slowly, I brought myself back and gently opened my eyes only to hear my friend say, "Now you have the shape of a cross in each eye, at least they look better than before."

I closed my eyes again and felt at peace with myself for the first time in years. It seemed that all of the information I had been jamming down my throat to try and accept had finally found its place. This warmth seemed to seep into every cell in my body and I felt at home. I knew now the gentleness of God and his plan, as well as the ancient laws and how they guide us home (higher thinking). This gentle loving Being of Light thanked me for my commitment to this experience and quietly withdrew from me. My friends noticed the glow around me again and watched as it moved towards the door and disappeared from our view.

I could not believe that this experience had happened to me. Was this my mathematics working on my behalf, or did I consciously create this event and where the dickens had it come from? And more to the point, what had I lead myself into? I asked to be taken to bed where I slept for twenty-four hours and when I woke up; I was a brand - new being. My body was so light, I seemed to float and I watched as my movements became more collective over the next few days. I came to realize that I had totally reinvested in myself.

I never felt troubled and whenever I was asked a question, I always had an answer. I looked at the world differently from that point on, as I realized that every species of the whole planet had been selectively designed to invest itself in both you and me. Through the worlds of Shamanism each species that has evolved on this planet is recorded into our cellular memory. I found that I could clap my hands and thank the fly for its presence and ask it to leave my dwelling and within thirty seconds it had! I finally understood the dichotomy of how the mathematics of our genes (DNA) had collected each memory for us to evolve into accepting the responsibility of every living thing.

And the next precious step of my journey continued.

Aim for the highest, there is room at the top.
My grandmother's saying

Chapter 16
The Mathematics At The Time Of Your Birth Created A Cosmic Program

On the day you were born, the mathematics at the time of your birth created a cosmic program which was unknown to you. This is your Life Program. Your Life Program was created through your parents DNA, which provided the basic principles for you to become you; it is the first gift given or passed on to you from your parents. Your life program keeps on creating itself through each of your thoughts building upon the other, and the transformation continues until you have taken your last breath.

This Life Program is connected to your inner library (our DNA), which is the make-up of the Soul Energy. That Soul Energy force field grows in strength and opens you up into your Higher—or heavenly—Self. Your Higher Self follows you through every thought you think, always encouraging you to create and expand your thinking. Metaphorically the Bible is the story of your Life Program: **B**asic **I**nformation **B**efore **L**eaving **E**arth, in other words, until you have evolved intellectually enough to take the journey to reconnect to your Soul. We now understand that you can't walk away from it, as it has been finitely measured to play out its role, long before you birthed for the continuance of your inherited DNA

This information has been gifted to us by the knowledge of knowing by the ancient ones who walked before us, which is explained through their stories. This includes the Mayan Principles, Egyptian Philosophies, Indo-Asiatic Principles, Greek Myths, through to the Roman Empire, who announced themselves in the Latin Language, as it introduced us up into the biblical agenda. I now understand through decoding my last book 'Decoding the Revelation of Saint John the Divine' (Book of Revelations), that the earth is your body, up to your neck! As we earn our intelligence, we are learning to leave the earth, which evokes us up into the layers of the language of the heavenly kingdoms. It becomes an inner calling in our self. This opens up your genetic memory, where it has the opportunity to disentangle and reorganize itself, to the current value of your thinking.

To expand this: To understand our self through the lines of what we refer to as our "meridians", which are the energy of the unconscious mind (higher mind) relating to the responses created throughout our nervous systems. We cannot see these meridians with the naked eye. They are the autonomic responses of language that flow up through our body from our toes, throughout the trunk and connecting through the heart, where they then flow down through your arms and reconnect back up to the yoke, or collarbone, where we carry and 'shoulder' our responsibilities, and then entering up into the temple area of self. As it is written in the Bible, this area is known as the 'earth'! Now we begin to add to this information. It is in the neck area where the body begins to enter into the unconscious territory of the mind. These meridians then have to work their way through the glandular system of the neck, reaching up into the glands at the base of the brain. This is our heavenly home, so we are both the earth and the heavens at the same time! You have entered into the home of the sonic sound.

Further expanding this concept: As we are intellectually prepared to leave the earth, we must enter up into the last book of the Bible—The Revelations of St John the Divine—where we take the exalted seven steps of unfolding the clasp on the back of the seven books or seven seals or seven churches, which are in Asia, these are represented by the seven vertebrae in the neck. This area of the body is also known in Egyptology as the seven bands of peace, for us to journey up into the heavenly kingdoms or explained through Egyptology, as the afterlife. This is the story that Egypt left for us to understand as we open up the seven sacred seals, where we bring the creation of our central nervous system to our attention.

You can't stand still or keep walking away from yourself. This Life Program will keep on reminding you of how it has to regain its own momentum to benefit not only the intelligence of self; it is also for the intellectual benefit that is able to metaphysically spread itself around of the whole planet!

Go back to the teachings in my volume of nine books explaining the insights in 'Decoding the Mind of God,' where I explained how the Elders of our first Tribes were all named Urt or Urth, which was brought down through our intellectual knowledge to be called the earth. Hence the name that the Elders of the Tribes were given and addressed by the tribe, was always the same.

What are we learning here about ourselves? Within your own imagination, you have created a conversation of what you wish to create and endure; through this endurance you have the opportunity to foster and grow to release your own special creation. Can you see how we have reversed the previous sentence, to bring the sentence back into its own continuum? Of course, it will work! It is only when we stumble enough and become lethargic through this endeavor, that we begin to question ourselves.

We wonder why things are not panning out the way we wanted, when doubt stepped in to our dictionary and believe me; we use this word quite a lot, for us to note that our plan didn't work. How many times have you begun a sentence with "I doubt if I can or I doubt if I will have the time" etc. It is this autonomic response that sets the scene of mathematics in motion and when someone steps before you to help you understand, it has the power to present to you a new opportunity where you can return that belief back to yourself. I will repeat myself once more and inform you that the most important event in your life; is the thought you have in your mind right now.

Watch how the next person to cross your path has an answer to the question you are having difficulties in accomplishing. The answer is always there right in front of your nose, everything we need is always in plain sight!! Is it a positive thought or a doubtful thought, which one do you think is benefiting you? Now you are beginning to understand the journey of the Sharman through the endless possibilities that you release from within yourself.

I have watched as many attended my seminars, where I was explaining to them, their 'truth of attraction' and I have watched them squirm and cough in their seats, as they became uncomfortable with the words I was speaking, I have asked many to remove themselves from the room and go out and make a cup of tea or coffee and relax, while the other students wrote their thoughts down. A few of them had the confidence to go out of the room and then there were others who made themselves sit through the information that was being delivered to them. They were the inheritors.

As my Teaching Academy could seat around 230 students in the ball room, as well as accommodate and house around thirty-five students from other lands who attended the schools that I delivered, there was many a time when I was awoken to one of the new students who had welts and burn marks surrounding different areas of their face, arms, chest or legs. Each area denoted a different reaction to their bodily organs, which were over reacting and wanted to work against the teachings, thanks to their fear not wanting to subside, through its own insecurity. So out came the Aloe Vera and Vitamin E oil, which was swathed over their skin. Their genetic engineering was nowhere to be seen, as it could not collect itself. Their rashes subsided over the next couple of days. It all happened through the repetitive endurance as to how they were accepting the information; through the high energy of the conversation and communication that they had felt they were ready to accept. Their fear had stood to attention and as always, it is the sixth sense or skin, which is the first one to register their thoughts and suffer.

Remember there is never a mistake! A mis-take is a gift we have earned! A gift in the old language was first interpreted as poison! Today we have named it—the cause of our actions. Our higher intelligence is within us, and is in abeyance to us all, until it can release its own light. It is the mathematical measurement of our psyche reverberating into our soul and as our soul expands through this new found belief we have in self; we are moving up into the unconscious energy of our mind, which tunes you into your Palace of Worth, and when these words are decoded, it is explaining our Place of Words, which is known to us metaphysically as your place of worthiness. Hence the saying "Come around to my place?"

The Greek Prophet Homer wrote of his experiences in 'The Iliad' which is a series of poems dedicated to the God within and then 'The Odyssey'. Odysseus was given twelve ships (one for each strand of the DNA) and those ships represent the temple of how we earn our freedom to sail into the consciousness. The consciousness represents the worlds of thoughts instilled in our brain. Homer explains the relationship to our own inner working domain perfectly in his epic poem, the 'Odyssey'; I pronounce the word 'Odyssey' as the 'Ode to Zeus' and also as the 'ode to see'. Remember that the word seeing means 'to look through'. Odysseus encounters nine islands; metaphysically in sacred numerology is the life cycle of 3 x 3 = 9, which is explaining the three Gods, El-An-Ea, who have finally earned their freedom, where they could become the one.

The water is used as an example through the ancient myths; symbolically, it represents the deep, dark section of our consciousness. It is hidden under the ground, which is where we are relying on our past to fulfil us. This is why most of the tales that came from long ago usually tell us about someone in a ship crossing the ocean, such as in the Greek epic poems of Homer. Homer interprets through the codes as the HI- (Ho) MER- (ocean of consciousness.)

We can now begin to understand the Principles that have been handed down to us from the Land of Egypt, where we have earned the knowledge to bring through the next level of intelligence that is already carved for us on the walls? The hieroglyphic intelligence is still not yet fully understood in its correct interpretation. We must remember that it has been scribed to us through the heavenly divine language, just the same as the Bible has been brought through the mythical agenda, where it is only accepted by a small handful of the billions of people on the earth.

I recall a spiritual experience when I was out in the desert in Central Queensland, finely tuning myself into accepting the divinity of the early Phoenician language of the unconscious equation. I was so stressed to do things the right way, back in the mid-eighties, and early nineties, that I felt myself on the brink of the universe and unable to think sensibly any more. At this time, I had three 'space - ships' or glyphs of light that would come and hover over my tin shed, and then move off towards the Turkeys Nest, which was a circular dam not too far away from the main house. We create these dams on the rise of a hill, in the outback, so that the water can be gravity fed down to the house for the bathing, washing and if we were lucky, also to water the vegetable patch and the rose garden. When we noticed the blades of the windmill spinning in the wind, we could afford to take a few seconds longer in the shower to scrub our senses clean. The water would be pumped into the dam through the power of the windmill when the wind was available. I knew that I could take a few hours of reprieve, when the three spaceships landed by the water. If they continued over to the mountain, I knew I still had not completed the lessons correctly that I had been given. So back over this inner journey I would go until I had corrected the hiccups that I was in the process of creating.

I was learning to watch every sign of movement around me. Where was the wind and in which direction was it coming from, and in which direction was it going? Was it North or South or maybe it was East or West? I would look up at the sky and read the direction the clouds were taking. (The meanings of the different directions are: North: Message from above. East: Message from within. South: Message from the past. West: Dichotomy; where we bring the energy of both brains into harmonizing with one another). I would often think, thank goodness nobody was watching me or listening to my thoughts or they would think I was going crazy. "Go back to your training in the desert all of those years ago with your Kurdaitcha man!" I would say out loud to myself. As I observed I would ask myself how many trees swayed in that breeze? Why only some of them, why not all of them at the same time? What was the wind trying to explain and teach me? If there were five trees standing in a row and three of them were moving in the breeze, then what happened to the breeze that should have connected to the other two trees, I wondered. I thought to myself, why had the wind been diverted and more importantly, how was I to read and understand the message that I was in the process of receiving?

Slowly I learned to bring these sacred messages into fruition; to earn the freedom (5 trees) of this thought, my mind, (3 trees) had not yet formed a relationship to the thought (2 trees) of bringing the mathematics together to empower the exercise to move on; that is why those two trees were not connecting to the other three. So back into the equation I would go and extend my knowing until I got it right, then I would run out and check the trees again.

This went on hour after hour, day after day, month after month, year after year. I would ask myself what did that insect want with me and how could I communicate with it? Did it want to bite me or was it trying to deliver a message to me? Why did it land on my right shoulder; what was the difference to landing on my right side and what did it mean if it landed on my left shoulder? I decided to watch closely, to where the insect landed on my body as it moved through the reliance of its unconscious energy, honing in on mine. Was it reading the vibration of my cells or was it reading the energetic responses of my nervous system, as my glands heralded down the truth of my thinking?

I began to realize I was tuning into the energetic responses of the atmosphere; I was watching the mathematics of these amazing Laws of the Universe release themselves. They were also showing me where my energy was collecting itself and through the previous thoughts not having been digested correctly, they were collecting and massing together on their own behalf. My goodness if this is all true, then we still have not evolved up to the wisdom of the intelligence of insects or the birds as yet, in our own evolution, I remember thinking to myself. I thought we were supposed to be the highest evolution on this doorstep of God's home, which we call the planet earth. How come they could hear my thoughts and to know my thinking; and how come it knew the outcome of my thinking before I had even finished the thought I had in my mind? I thought. What was it sensing when I wasn't thinking? Oh Wow, these energetic responses were so powerful, they were something outside the box!!!

Was I tuning into the mathematical laws, through another aspect of higher consciousness? Is this what it is all about? I was beginning to tap into the unconscious mind or what is now referred to as the Collective Consciousness (also known as the supra or universal consciousness) of the planet and through time, I found I was working up here in the phi of the mathematics of the planet. Remember, I have previously mentioned that the insect tunes into our sonic sound through its own combustible inheritance.

I came to realize that I was watching how the Collective Consciousness was autonomically tuned into my thoughts to retaliate to each sentence I created, as to how my thinking within was already aware of what and how I thought, long before I did! The words of Einstein in one of his famous quotes remarked: "The harmony of natural law reveals an intelligence of such superiority that, compared with it, all the systematic thinking and acting of human beings is an utterly insignificant reflection." Oh, these words kept me going for years and so true!

I remember when I first began the education regarding our teeth and their soul's purpose. I remember an old friend of the family could not eat cold food, as his teeth created so much pain when he tried to chew or swallow each mouthful of a cold drink. I needed to understand why the pain was echoed throughout his body. How did our sensory perception collect to alert us to the fact, that there was a discrepancy in our thinking for us to collect our dues?

Where had we gone wrong, what had teeth to do with our thinking. I went over this sequence so many times for me to find the answer to bust this code wide open! I already knew what emotional thought each tooth in our head was responsible for; which was all connected to how we rephrased the vowels of our inner alphabet! My surprise came when I realized that the words he had prepared in his mind, were being falsified by his thoughts to get him out of a predicament that he was not prepared to speak on behalf of! In other words, he was either lying to himself, or lying to the person he was speaking to, and his teeth had to step in to take over the sentence that he was hesitant to speak. Now do you understand my teachings that there is never an accident, every thought we think, is all connected to the occidental, which when decoded is informing us of how we earn our truth through bringing our thoughts together.

My goodness! The magnificence and wonder of this place we call home! My heart filled with awe and respect of every living thing! We were all one! Is this the way it had always been? My bow to the universe each morning when I awake has now become an automatic reaction through me! My DNA is in attendance to the DNA of the planet and of course I have a perfect day! As I ask, I receive!

My dictionary began to change, I realized that I was tuning into the genetic engineering of the planet, for me to know how it did relate to every human. Over the next few years, I came to accept this information, as I was being shown how this same transference of energy was also the genetic engineering of how the genes in our body have collected over the previous generations, to assist us in our understanding of this immense knowledge. The mathematics of the human body and the Laws of the Universe are identical to one another. They tune in and work together as one mind.

Remember there is never a mistake! A mis-take is a gift we have earned!

The Truth is incontrovertible.
Malice may Attack it
And Ignorance may Deride it,
But in the end, there it is...
Sir Winston Churchill

Chapter 17
We Are The Ones, We Have Been Waiting For

How does one feel compassion for the journey of self discovery? I did have cancer years ago, which had eradicated its self through me learning to rearrange my thinking. Had I been compassionate, with myself since this event without me knowing it? Had I deliberately ignored myself so often during my life? I thought I had always been compassionate, to others who were worse off than me and had volunteered for years to assist them. This time it was for me and me alone; that put a different slant on the picture!

I continued to learn to silence my mind for me to achieve a new found state of grace. I was finally realizing the extent of the Collective Consciousness in all its wisdom, where I could and would, accept the mathematical reality of its truth. Were we all magnetized into this ethereal energy?

How could this wonder of the Divine Energy present itself to me every minute of my day and still be in charge of everyone and everything else at the same time? I found that I was entering up into the worlds of telepathic inheritance; these realms or cosmic laws override every thought we are capable of thinking. It amazed me to think that these laws had the answer to our thoughts before we had even finished thinking it! I was only an Adept Shaman in training at that time and yet I knew I had to stay focused on my path to see this commitment I had so blatantly made through to its completion. Everything was instantaneously passed on to me.

How many birds are in that flock passing overhead? If they were coming from my right side, I knew that I was about to hear the angels (which are the bird tribes) speak. They were about to deliver an incoming message that could rearrange my thinking into a positive outcome. If they came from my left side, I realized that my thoughts had not been completely finalized and there was a much higher level of attainment waiting for me to add to these thoughts of the moment, in my mind. I knew I had to count the birds in mid-flight, to know why they flew past me in this moment. "What the dickens was that thought I just had begun with in my mind, and how important was it for me to receive the results of my thinking?"

I would say out loud as the questions reverberated in my mind. The number of them was an added answer to my thoughts. I had to convert the numbers into the ancient languages before we had invented the alphabet to realize the conversation and messages, they were delivering to me. These levels of attainment continued to grow as each new section added to the equation. Here I was in the outback all alone, having a conversation with the bird tribes who knew what I was thinking long before I could finish my thoughts.

And then there was the murmuration of thousands of the small grass parrots and budgerigars swirling and becoming at one with the universe. As I walked out into the paddock and watched their magical display, they would swoop around me and spiral up above my head, and fly up until they had just about disappeared, which would change my thinking instantly. I was receiving an instant cleanse. I realized they had become one mind and were all using their telepathic enhancement where instantaneously they were able to use the same thought to balance and harmonize their minds. In other words, during this ritual, they were repairing and healing themselves.

This finite energy is the world available to us as we enter up into the unconscious mind; it could not deceive or retract; it only knew the truth. I had been taught that all birds represent an emotion in connection to our heart, they are our introduction into the divine equation; and if we are having difficulties in equating with them as they cross our path, we will have difficulties in enabling ourselves to finalize our thoughts. This is all a part of God's original plan. No, there was still no dice thrown to make it all happen!

I realized that each new thought I had was an introduction into expanding and awakening another code! "What was the emotion that these species represented to us here on the planet? Why were they so important to us? Had I committed myself to take this step by step, introduction into the Collective Consciousness?" I had to go on, to find out as I had been taught that everything that has already evolved was representing a personality that had been superseded within my genes, as to how I could understand and release my thoughts to free this almighty stress that I was prone to ignore or overly protect.

Wow! How the dickens could I keep on remembering all of this information. I had begun to understand that the little birds meant flighty childish thinking when they crossed my path and seemed to be the first step into us earning our integrity. And yet they were built for endurance; was this why the larger of the bird species, could see further, whereas the little ones required a lesser area to survive? Why did the larger birds need to devour the little ones to replace in themselves what they were lacking? In the spring time, I had watched how the hawk could swoop down and pluck the baby out of the air as it was being taught how to fly. And the bigger the birds became, the more powerful the emotional explanation was heralded back to me. What was the difference between the species, why were they colored the way they were? How come crow appeared before me, every time I began to create a thought and how come I knew by the number of his caws, as to how I could interpret his answer that he was releasing back to me and add it to my equation? He was always right!

I remember the owner of the land where I had been placed to complete my shamanic training, informing me that since I had come into the area that the bird life had multiplied by thousands, he said it was a pleasure to wake up with their sound each morning. He was the caretaker and owner of 540 square kilometers of land; we formed a symbiotic relationship with one another over time as our respect for one another grew.

I realized that the Collective Consciousness was revealing to me the symbolic structure of these sacred codes that were written for us to understand and accept as we opened up our intelligence through our DNA releasing itself. I was awakening the 144,000 personalities (aspects of self) that are embedded in mine and your DNA; they are the opportunities that I have been given to use, to exercise my free will. I could read the clouds and faces would sometimes appear before floating away. "No, don't move away from me and wind please stop blowing so hard, I have to find time to digest all of this information, I needed time to think!" I would state to the Universe.

"Give me a break" was my cry to God. "What did you say God, I can't hear you, the wind has picked up and the trees are rustling so fast I can't hear myself think?" "What do you mean I am trying to turn too many pages at the same time? I know you are always with me, just let me do it slower, and what do you mean it's up to me?" I recall at that point in time a fly landed on my right arm and then traveled to my right eye and then landed on my heart. To enter into the language of the fly; he was answering my thoughts of the moment, he was giving me confidence to become aware that my spiritual action (arm) would awaken my positive seeing (eye) through me opening up and entering into my thoughts through my heart. Wow this magnetic force field was worth remembering. I was just returning back into where I had come from! Crow flew over coming from the right to the left and cawed twice and then flew in a circle above my head and when I looked up, there was eagle soaring in a spiral going higher and higher and it did not flap its wings once. Now you work this one out! "What do you mean you want me to reverse all of these messages and I will begin to understand what you have spoken to me?'"

Oh Yes! Those daunting days return for me to explain to you the truth of how these natural laws of the collective consciousness is eternally working twenty-four hours per day for every single one of us. This is God at work! These are the natural laws that release from his hands through his action, at work!! And all of this information is identical to the intellectual knowledge of how our brain works with, for, and on behalf of us. There is never an accident! There is an occidental response from the collective consciousness that is always present to answer and respond to the mathematics of our mind.

Now let us all have a pause and have a glass of water to flush the cells and stop them creating so much mucus. When we become afraid of ourselves, the mucus gathers and spins in an anti-clockwise direction and this creates the fat cell and when other cells become aware of this singular cell, others rush to sympathize with it and because its energy is so much stronger, through its own stubbornness walking backwards on itself, it soon over powers many of the others, and more fat cells appear! And the old thoughts linger and cling on. No wonder we have been born with a memory bank to keep reminding us to store what we have already completed!

Every one of you are living this Shamanic existence whether you are aware of it or not. Allow me to bring back a few sentences I have previously written, that relate to what I am explaining to you. The young man who plays football and then meets the woman who he feels will become his partner in life; and then all of a sudden, he realizes that there is not so much time spent on his game as he used to be able to commit too. Does he give it all up or can he still be an acquaintance with friends, through his sport? They marry and then the wife begins to become aware that the weekends are hers, not ours. The warrior has his commitments to practice, to keep his body supple and flexible. It is hard for both parties to relate to one another in a peaceful situation when it continually goes on and on. The time taken to his commitment is around three quarters of one year and when the children come along; it is mother who becomes the grass widow.

Then there is the business executive who marries himself to the company he works for, so he has two relationships to contend with.

The house must be kept quiet when Dad is working in his office to finish off a project after coming home at the end of the day. He has made a commitment and this must be carried out. There is the doctor who is woken at all hours of the night and is called away. He has studied for all of those years to carry his enquiring mind forward. Then there is the mother who has a position in the boardroom and then comes home at the end of the day, to suffice the family. We have to switch off, to switch on and then reverse it every day. There are children to rear, meals to prepare, cleaning to be done, washing and ironing to look after. You see, I also had a position in my office of trust and also had to look after the family, which are my emotional personalities at the end of the day. There were times when I was very stressed out, through the consequential life that I and them; were creating for ourselves.

I remember the day when leaning over the counter at work feeling so tired, I thought that I would love someone to do my washing and ironing to make things a little easier. In that exact moment, a woman walked into the shop and asked if she could place a sign on the notice board we had in the shop. I looked at her sign that stated she was available to take on washing and ironing. She still had two children at home and offered to pick up the washing and deliver it for a small fee. Instantaneous it was! And that day I began to see a difference in me! It was not too long after that another woman walked in with a note for the board who wanted to do some housework for four hours per week and of course I began to realize that because I had honored myself, the money would automatically come to pay for the services I needed to make our life more manageable. I began to acknowledge that when I said the words "Thank you" it was an ending and when I said "Please" it was a new beginning.

Maybe now, you can begin to understand the commitment that I had made firstly to myself, and then I began to include my Universal Laws and the Laws of the Universe into my plan, all of those years ago. I had no one to share with, only myself and the heavens. I learned very quickly in the beginning to give thanks for what I had received and this made my life much easier to contend with.

Hopefully you can now understand that we are all being faced with responsibilities throughout our life and sometimes the experiences go well beyond our own boundaries; this is all due to the consequences that we have automatically created for ourselves. We can't blame anyone else; we are in complete control of our own mind; and if not, why aren't we. This is where we are being measured mathematically through both the Collective Consciousness and God (this **G**reatest

Oracle of the **D**ivine) through our self-worth, on every level of our intellect, which becomes our intellectual light, and then we can begin to accept that every member of humanity is on the path to become the Shaman. There is an answer to everything, if only we could believe and trust in ourselves, to allow it to stand before us. As the Hopi Indian Nation have informed us. "We are the ones; we have been waiting for."

Through the worlds of Shamanism each species that has evolved on this planet is recorded into our cellular memory.
Omni

Chapter 18
The Language Of The Shamanic Principles

Through the worlds of Shamanism each species that has evolved on this planet is recorded into our cellular memory. Our thinking began with the world of trees, where we yearned to stand upright. In the form of the human body, the tree species are embedded in the feet and lower legs. The tree's opposite was attracted and became the worm. The worm came out of the oceans of consciousness to invest in the ground where its strength grew through the importance of self, and then it evolved into the serpent, where it took its place above the ground.

The Animal Kingdom then took its place in our evolution where we learned to understand ourselves, and this understanding became the collective of our left brain. The taller we stood, the more our consciousness expanded towards the heavens. This second collection of evolution is situated from the knees to the naval.

The next step up the evolutionary ladder presented itself to us through the Bird Kingdom, which is collected and gathered from the naval to the heart. We begin to earn the strength of our heart when we enter into this kingdom, through entering into and opening up our right brain. These are the worlds of our emotions or our 'energy in motion'. We had evolved and grown through our confidence expanding, where our education entered our mind and we began to believe in this new form of self. We noticed a change in our emotional behavior as we traversed up through our spine with an expanded language and calmer approach to living each moment.

From the heart we move up into the chest area to the throat, which creates the third section and this is the evolution of the ocean. The species of the oceans help us to release the intelligence of the unconscious mind (higher mind). It silently works on our behalf.

From the throat or the base of the brain we enter into the unconscious mind and this is the world of the insect. The insect has evolved to reduce and replace the irritations to the exalted mind. From here we have the power to hone into the potentiality of our sonar or sonic sound, which is the inner ear, to correct the 'mathematics' of our conscious and subconscious minds. Insects rely on their sonar, as they do not eat matter; they remove and digest only the juices. They represent the alchemy that we produce in the brain; these are resonances that we collate through the two holes in the roof of our mouth.

Now let us hear the above story again with an example from each kingdom: As the tree grows, it moves up and throughout our system. The oak tree in the Shamanic world stands for wisdom and is the Elder of the Tribe. Through all kinds of weather, the strength of its roots and trunk do not waver in the winds. It is the last tree to release its foliage in the autumn and the last in the spring to release the new. Through the winter months the oak tree hangs on to many of its old leaves and those leaves represent the pages of our DNA, our inner library. It never let's go of its past until the new leaf, which has evolved into the strength to create its own shadow, emerges. We need this balanced growth to enable us to rest our minds in times of doubt. This solid tree helps to create the inner strength that we need to present our thoughts up into our pituitary gland. This gland twists and moves through the storms we create in our mind. It has the responsibility of our intuition, to equate each of our thoughts and process them into either the left or right hemisphere of the brain before they settle into our memory banks.

Next progressions, we note the animal becomes our ego. The wolf likes to work with the pack, not against it. He represents the pathways of the 'Ancient Loyalty' of our evolution, which is the belief in the knowledge that we have gained so far, through those who have walked before us. We all need our loyalty to sustain ourselves with; this is the confidence that we achieve through our belief in self. We have named wolf, through the gift of Shamanism, the 'Inner Teacher'. He is the one who still holds the old codes that we have the ability to endow ourselves with. These codes are the sustenance that we feed to our ego, to create our possibilities to remain focused on what we are setting out to achieve.

The bird evolution lifts us up into our angelic nature through the opening of the heart. The dove is the shamanic principle to the heart. The dove represents the codes of shamanism as it relates to the gift one gives oneself. Another inference in many cultures is the tiny hummingbird. It is a complete miracle that can create forty strokes of its wings in a single second. Its colour creates its own luminous light through the arching of its responsibilities, which also creates a humming sound that is automatically attracted to our unconscious mind (higher mind). It lives on the essence of flowers, which is the ultimate code of angelic resonance at this time in our evolution. The hummingbird makes its nest by combining its own spittle with spider webs, which both come into the divine equation of self. Hummingbird multiplies its energy to such an extent that while flying it completes its task in seconds, not minutes. Through its swiftness, the Collective Consciousness attracts itself to the energy it creates; therefore, it lives in perpetual energy in motion. It is known through the Laws of Shamanism as the 'Carrier of the Web of Consciousness'.

Then we move deeper into the Collective Consciousness of the ocean. The manta ray represents the oracle of harmonic convergence of all the species of the ocean. Symbolically, the ocean represents the divinity that we earn through the Collective Consciousness. Once we are balanced and free, the oracle awaits our proprietary earnings and is automatically opened to serve us all. As he flows through the ocean, manta ray acts in the likeness of the 'Government Overlord' and as such, is available to be in the right position at the right time. He does not step outside of his own boundary and is always in balance with his mind. He lives in the centre of the ocean and uses the equatorial energy to become one. Manta ray harmonizes and gathers all information on appropriate matters through serving one master, himself. He is continuously checking and cross checking that all things are running smoothly. He swims just below the surface of the water; therefore, he is in charge of every situation and is continually respecting each scene that is presented to him. As a consequence, he will succeed in all aspects.

We then enter into the worlds of our unconscious mind. The bee is adding to the evolution of all insects, where the mathematics is now changing into the algebraic and geometrical equations. Bee is extremely powerful. Its sting is created from its collected alchemy, which can become a hindrance to others. Poison is released from the unconscious mind and rids the self of insecurities. Like ant and fly, bee hones in on energy and collects only the essence of all things. Bee is an insect of pure mathematics, which conforms into the geometry in our lives. Symbolically this is one of the highest orders that we can achieve. The bee has the wisdom to create the nectar of the Gods and its honey is needed by all the insect population to harmonize and balance their own survival. Sweetness repairs the injustice of our thinking.

The brain is much greater in matter and holds limitless opportunities to benefit our future. The more we accept our own intellect; the more we add to what we can achieve. Each step of evolution is opening us up to extra responsibilities of self and as we move forward, we must accept the reasoning as to why they evolved in the first place.

Through the 'Totem' energy of all, the ancient species that have evolved before us, represent an emotional inheritance that we can rely on to sustain our moment. They will become the beneficial intelligence when our mind is in the fields of doubt.

As we release the Shamanic Principles from within, Metaphysics describes how every myth was an inner kingdom that each human could find within themselves. Through the Collective Consciousness, we connect unconsciously with every story that has ever been written, spoken, and collected mathematically. There are three worlds that we live in, and, as we leave one world, we are brought up into the next one. Hence, the explanation of the three-dimensional mind, which is represented by the names of the three Metaphysical Gods: 'EL', 'AN', 'EA'. Interpreted through the matter of physics—or the Metaphysical language—these three names are here to remind us that we can attain Everlasting Life, Accepting and Nourishing, and Energising our Ascension. All this is similar to how we introduced our self into our spoken word, which was released to us through our DNA.

If you feel you already know the information from reading my other books, please breeze through these next few paragraphs. In the beginning, there is the story of the God 'EL' (Everlasting Life), which represents the home of our ego in relationship to our sexual encounters. These encounters are our basic structure of searching for a placement of our own responsibilities, and, when someone bows before us and does our bidding, we acquaint our earnings through the word control. This is the first doorway to where we connect to our lungs of consciousness, which is where we understand the breath of our inner worlds.

We know, through the codes of body language that the upper inner thighs are referred to as the 'lungs of Consciousness'—or where we learn to breathe the Breath of God. We are named humanity, ('HU' through the codes); this is the interpretation of the symbolic reference to the scribes of Egypt. At first, the scribes are kneeling down, but, in later hieroglyphs, they are standing up, usually with their right foot forward, in reference to our emotional mind. Always look for the hidden body language. We slowly release the codes that are embedded in our legs as we are urged to move forward through the autonomic responses of the unconscious mind. It is fascinating to note that the language of the past is ensconced in every cell of every human; also, it relates to our modern language, no matter how it is pronounced. As it has collected in the ancient Arabic language, so it has been rephrased and spoken in our modern-day speech.

Our brain begins just above our hip area; it traverses up the spine, not down. That is why the brain and our DNA coincide in unison with one another. They are a compatible working team snuggled up inside our vertebrae. It is here where we begin to announce our desires through the initiation of us releasing the species of the Animal kingdoms. The ancient code of everything that has evolved is still present in this section of our body. This area of the upper inner thighs is Shamanic-ally known to us as 'the lungs of consciousness'. It is known throughout the divine language as where we begin to breathe the breath of our God within. It is where we are being initiated to our higher forms of intellect, which is known throughout the myths as the first God EL, denoting—Ever Lasting—which is explaining to us the continuation of our species.

Our next evolution is into the God 'AN' (Accepting and Nourishing), where we have understood our primordial earlier worlds through collecting our intelligence and accepting the possibilities of harvesting the seeds we have already sown (our thoughts and deeds). You have entered up into your education system, which is your inner university. Automatically, this subconscious awakening brings the information up to your heart, which opens you up into a belief that you can accomplish anything your mind desires. This is where we shape our characters, and these characters become our personalities (aspects of self), which work with each other to become our support team. They are known throughout the myth as the 'lesser Gods'. The dove is the Shamanic symbol of the heart; which is known throughout the codex strain as the gift one gives oneself! This species is informing us always to honor our self! I love to hear them first thing in the morning, cooing to remind me to thank myself for the day ahead. Have you noticed the stain glass window in St. Peter's Basilica in Rome, where the dove is rising towards the light? This area of the Vatican is explaining the heart.

The bird kingdoms, which equate with the lower section of our right brain; there are many tribes of birds that cannot fly; turkey, emu, ostrich, chicken, kiwi, cassowary to name a few. In my mind they are the angelic realms that have kept themselves at bay to equate with the first and second dimensional mind. It is as though they are an introduction to the birds of flight.

Now we relate to the birds that are free to fly, which is where we learn to open our heart to our self; it is up here in these higher realms of thought where we also birth into the angelic realms. Maybe you can recall the Egyptian hieroglyph of the weighing of the heart? We have named this area the doorway to understanding the language of our divinity. The higher our intelligence rises, we realize that our arms represent our wings, our fingers become the result of our flight feathers and since the beginning of time we have named the movement of our hands and fingers as, the language of the stars. We have the possibilities to accomplish this finite creation, through the courage we release of re-educating our self. All of which allows us to release this hidden God or inner Biblical language that every human has embedded within their cells.

The combination of this energy then traverses up to connect us into the highest form of intelligence—our unconsciousness mind—that is, to the Divinity of the God 'EA' (Energizing the Ascension). Through the earlier language, was pronounced 'He-ia' (Heavenly Energy of Intelligence Ascending). This is the last of the three prime Gods that we connect to, and it is the home of our heavenly kingdom, which is situated around the crown of the head. It is where we realize that we have the ability to reconnect back into the origin of our Soul.

When we take the Shamanic Metaphysical journey, we can explore the myths and ancient names through the Sacred Alphabetical codes to further explore the Metaphysical Gods: 'EL', 'AN', 'EA'.

Exploring the codes of the Collective Consciousness in regard to the Mayan Oracle, there is a temple near Mexico that many have called the Hall of Recognition (another reference is the Hall of Abundance). Through the Egyptian principles, this is known as the Akashic Records. It also has many other names through the different levels of languages and lands. That temple holds the codes—or the Akashic Records of the mathematical information of our past evolution. The Akasha ('Ark-Ash-Sha') is explained as the exemplification of the sheik, or the elder of the Tribe, which through the sacred coding, is the one who resurrects the self in order to exalt himself up into the inheritance of the higher mind. Throughout the Mayan Philosophies, the temple and buried at the base of the Pyramid, is the sarcophagus of the supposed sun God, Lord Pacal. Let us pronounce the word 'Pacal' correctly: 'Pha-Kha-EL'. Symbolically, this word represents the 'father of knowledge'. 'Pha-Kha-EL', through the Sacred Alphabet, interprets as, 'through the power of heavenly ascension my knowledge heavenly ascends through everlasting life'. This first God 'EL', through the records of the myth, is initiated into the Collective Consciousness from birth. This holds the knowledge of the first time, which is referred to, through the Shamanic resonance, as the 'God of yearning'.

A wonderful Merlin energy awakens within us on this journey of life, and it allows us to look at the world without judgement; we begin to see what our truth really is—the dances that we co-create behind the veils of how we interpret what we think. The word 'Merlin'—or, more correctly, as it was collected through the words 'Mer-EL-AN', once it was decoded—means that the Meer—or ocean of consciousness—of the God 'EL' opens up through intellectually nurturing the home of self, which is the mythical home of the God 'AN'. As we have intellectually progressed through time and accepted the codes, we then changed the pronunciation of the letter a to i. All this means that the 'oceans of consciousness' bring you everlasting life when you come home to the inn to rest.

Cairo was previously called 'EL-Kha-He-Rha', which, when decoded means 'through everlasting life our knowledge heavenly ascends through to the heavenly energy, and releases us up into heavenly ascension'. Wow! Many mentions of heaven here; three, to be exact: one for each level of God. Remember that the word -through- means 'seeing from within'. What a title! This is a grand commission for the people of Cairo to live up to and call home. Cairo is also referred to as the 'home of the Pyramids'. If we care to look from the right side of the head into the matter of the brain, we see the three glands: hypothalamus, pineal, and pituitary. These three glands are placed inside the brain in identical unison to the way that the Pyramids are placed in Egypt. They do not align through the left side of the head. Remember that the mind of the Universe is identical to the mind of the human body.

To my understanding, the smallest Pyramid is the small gland of the hypothalamus; the middle one is the pineal, which is slightly above the other two; and the largest, the pituitary, relates to the Great Pyramid of Chi-Ops. This is the story of the mythical Pharaoh, known through the codes as the unconscious Energy (Chi) of the Oracle, which is the Power of the Soul (OPS). In the Great Pyramid of Cheops there are two shafts that penetrate into what is known as the King's Chamber in a northerly and southerly direction. In the same analogy as the brain, through my estimation, I believe that, what is referred to as the King's Chamber is the home of the pineal gland. These two shafts are directing the energy flow into both the left and right hemisphere of the brain at the same time; as explained through the opening of the heart ceremony described in Egyptology, which occurs when the right brain has been freed by the restriction of the ego through releasing its hold or control over the mind. We also note that there are seven steps leading into the grand gallery, all of which reminds us of the seven vertebrae of the neck area, or the seven seals, as to how we have exonerated ourselves.

'AN': This hierarchical story is written on the walls of the temples in Egypt. The Torah is the 'Door of the Rah', and the Quran is the 'Core'—or, through the ancient language, the 'Kur (Healing through the Heart) of AN'. This symbolic intelligence represents what is already known to many cultures as the Middle Kingdom, where we must harmonize and balance our understanding and action of self. 'AN' is the second name of God that we earn. Let us remember that this is our relationship—or our connection—into accepting our truth. The past is inheriting itself, and we must cohere to it in order to free ourselves. Energy re-creates itself, and, if it is positive energy, it always extends itself. If we have not learned from the responses of our thinking, that thinking is returned for us to view all over again. This is the Universal Law reflecting back to us so that we may earn our truth. If it is a negative energy, it short-circuits itself and embeds itself deeper within. When you think through the highest scope of your intellect, the whole world hears you telepathically through the Collective Mind (the unconscious); you are transforming (trance-forming) the memory of the Collective Inheritance that is heard by every human. Your bandwidth collects with other bandwidths of same energy, and this energy creates a manifestation within itself. These are the electromagnetic fields being automatically drawn and arching towards one another. When they have the opportunity to cross one another, they collectively release the energy to dispose of negativity. It creates a new thoroughfare; it clarifies the old in order to allow for the new, which is interpreted through our alphabetical speech or language. That language then filters throughout the airwaves, coinciding with other likeminded thinkers, and they begin to connect and vibrate with one another.

Another explanation for the word Kilimanjaro—or 'Kilim-AN-Jaro'—is that the word Kilim means 'hand-woven', so, through your own action, you weave your words. 'AN' is the God of the Middle Kingdom, where you learn to harmonize yourself; Jaro is an ancient word from the Ethiopian language that means 'our Oracle'. So this powerful word is explaining to you that, as you weave your words through harmonizing your mind, you release your own Oracle.

The Metaphysical God and the world of 'AN' opens up and gathers the emotional feelings that release up through our heart, which begins to create the action of our angelic resonance; that is where we begin the path of our Divinity, which was previously known as our Divine Unity, and, through opening our heart to ourselves, we symbolically birth our wings. We return to Egypt, understanding that the hieroglyphs explain this awakening as the woman with her wings outstretched; she is named Ma'at, symbolically representing the mathematics of the mind. In other words, she is representing the one who has opened their heart to understand themselves.

The Old Testament explains that Solomon became the King of Israel. He was the second son of King David and his wife, Bathsheba. Let us look at the codes to understand this word 'Bathsheba'. The 'bat' sits at the base of the brain (the pituitary gland sits in the base of both hemispheres of the brain, nestled inside the sphenoid bone, which we know Metaphysically in the fourth dimension of reality, as the 'bat within', and which is also known as the 'mansion of the sonic sound. 'She' (or 'chi') we now know relates to our inner energy, and we know that the 'Bja' is the tribal strength that we carry in our bones—the storehouse where we inherit the fear that was trapped in our past generations, through their innocence of not understanding themselves. Metaphorically, Bathsheba represents the emotional balance of the inner screen, which is tucked away behind our forehead. Solomon had difficulty in paying the wages for building his Temple, so he had to raise the taxes—or the tithing—in order to accommodate the King of Tyre's commission. So, he had to believe more strongly in himself. He also paid three tons of his own gold (the results of his higher intelligence—or mind), in advance, so that the building could commence. After finding ruins under the site he had chosen, Solomon went in search of another. He chose a place called Mount Moriah—or was it Maria or Murea (the ancient land of Mu releasing the 'EA')? Maybe it could represent the Meer of 'EA', (which is the ocean of 'EA'). In other words, Solomon moved his plans from the left brain, where the old temple lay, to the right brain, which we know is responsible for our inner emotions. So, once again, we understand that the Temple of Solomon—or the Solo-Man"—has been brought inside the self; it is not a relic which was constructed from the past.

The ancient Egyptian Pharaoh named Akhenaton image has been defaced from many of the temple walls in Egypt through the Coptic interpretation of Christianity. At that time, they had not yet grown up enough to understand the levels of intellect that Akhenaton had evolved up into. It is up to the individual to add to his/her intelligence. He was the holiest man of all, through the writings on the wall; he became married to himself, and, when we look at the shape of his body, we see that he is symbolically representing half woman and half-man. Through him measuring his own mind up into the heavenly energy—or the crown of the head—he had opened his heart to himself and was a complete manifestation of God. 'Ark-he-nat-on' went through his night—or netherworld—in order to find his own light, and he had earned his balanced mind. The Aramaic language has pronounced Akhenaton as 'Ayanatun' or 'EA'-nat-on'. 'EA's nation of light'.

Take your time reading this chapter, it is heavy with information.

If necessary, please read it again and again to allow the words to register themselves throughout your mind. Two or three reads and you will find that you will understand each paragraph, as they will automatically open up the barriers of your innocence, for you to understand much more eloquently.

Extra-Terrestrial energy is automatically creating a future reality for you through the power and strength of your thinking.
Omni

Chapter 19
Vision World of Extra Terrestrial Energy

In my quest of knowledge, I discovered that no matter what happens in our life, it is all meant to be at that given time; it must happen. Our 'Vision World'—or our 'Vision Quest'—is where we become the source of our own knowing. We automatically become an outer auric field; all of which creates a vibration that collects our future on our behalf. The more we become that permanent mirror—or outer boundary of self—the higher we extend our intellect; that boundary is the light of your own creation, which is urged up to become the golden cap on our pyramid. It is the outer boundary that collects your strength. It must equalize with your inner thoughts.

The emotional species of the falcon represents the inner sight of self, which opens us up in order for us to be able to view through a wider perspective, broadening our peripheral vision. All this also symbolically reveals to us our imagination, and it also provides the codes for us to understand our dreams—or, through the Shamanic Principles, our 'Vision Worlds'. As we start to experience our intellectual flow, we will begin to open up our vision world.

I discovered that our next realm of self is utilizing Extra-Terrestrial Intelligence energy. This energy is automatically creating a future reality for each one of us through the power and strength of our thinking. It is a continuation of what we are doing right now, that is alive and living beyond our third-dimensional reality.

To understand the concept fully of Extra -Terrestrial Intelligence and the next step for humanity, let me explain in the term as 'Extra-Terrestrial Intelligence'—our evolution of consciousness. Remember we are extraordinary beings not only of this Earth but of our Universe.

It is said that we learned to open up the left brain over 6,000 years ago. As of 3,000 years ago, we began the awakening of the right brain, which led us into a closer understanding of our emotional behavior, through the form of religion; this, in time, brought forth the Age of Christianity. It was an evolutionary step up into the Collective Consciousness. The positive behavior of that evolution brought us forward to this point.

The next wave of consciousness is knocking on the door now, and so we begin again. Over the next 2,000 years, we will learn to bring the two brains together (left and right hemisphere of the brain); that balanced brain is called the unconscious mind (higher mind) and is what I refer to as Extra-Terrestrial Intelligence. It is through the understanding of the unconscious mind, which is also the mind of the Ancient Telepathic Inheritance—the Collective Consciousness that we will begin to accept the possibilities of our future inheritance. All this energy has released itself into the Collective Consciousness over millions of years, and it will be available to all of us as we unfold our DNA, which is our devoted inheritance.

The world of Extra-Terrestrial Intelligence reveals an automatic Universal Language that all of humanity is able to realize through its own potentiality, (state of being). The Laws of the Universal Law is the Soul Energy of Collective Consciousness; it is a mathematical program of all that is. The Laws of the Universe answers to our thinking in a balanced way, but it is not always in the way that we expect it to be! So, through balancing our mind, we uplift our emotions, and we become not only more aware of our intelligence but also emotionally aware—emotional intelligence. The whole planet has the opportunity of continually harmonizing and reflecting itself back to us, and this reflection is the mind, body, and Soul of all, the Collective Consciousness. Nothing is unexplainable; there is an answer to every question that we are capable of asking. The truth is out there.

As I searched for more answers and as my knowledge expanded, I experienced Extra-Terrestrial Intelligence. I was shown in my 'Vision World' spaceships of light and Extra-Terrestrial beings. Our inner language (mind chatter/thoughts) is a menagerie of egotistical and emotional thoughts that we are forever searching for within ourselves—we search for this in order to understand ourselves. This is the gift that the ancient ones left for us. For example, the hieroglyphs of Egypt are explaining the language of the unconscious recognition—of our unconscious mind, which is our Divine intellect—our highest realm of intellect. Paintings are displayed on the walls in many of the Ancient Egyptian tombs, where we see boats carried along by the High Priests. The number of High Priests supporting the boat informs us about the message; regardless, this boat was referred to as the 'Bja-Ark'! The Bja is referred to as 'the ego which is still trapped in our bone matter, asking questions'; the High Priests, are the metaphoric symbols of the glands around our throat area. As our intellect opens up, these boats evolve until they become our ship (body) to sail the consciousness. Once we have left our third-dimensional reality, we begin to create our own spaceship.

In reference to the Mayan civilization and the picture of a Mayan at the controls of a supposed—or metaphorical—spaceship is scribed through the metaphysical codes. It is an explanation of how our intelligence releases through the autonomic responses; that is, through the energy of how our Soul (unconscious mind) enables us to intellectually move forward. The intellect of the spaceship was left for us thousands of years ago, through the Mayan heritage. The Mayan Palenque code is similar to the Egyptian King Tutankhamen; they both represent the same states of consciousness, which are explained all the way through their emotional hierarchical languages. The Mayans explained through the left hemisphere of the brain, and the Egyptians explained through the right hemisphere. Symbolism is the doorway that creates our reality; everything we walk towards in our future has been repeated every day since human existence began! As we evolve into our own structure of intelligence, we all symbolically build and collect our 'ship of light'—and all of this pertains to the result of our inner education of a balanced mind through positive belief/thinking about self.

The Extra Terrestrials evolved as wisps of consciousness then into forms of alien like bodies when they were first brought to my notice and of course, I hesitated with this new understanding. The Extra Terrestrials came in many different shapes and sizes. Some of humanity have the ability to see them from an earlier age as I found out over the years, as you evolve intellectually and many of you see them in many different shapes. I learned to understand this specification of the energetic species through understanding the Earthly Treasures, Trees, Animal, Bird, Oceanic and Insect Worlds/Kingdoms.

The word faith, entered my vocabulary; firstly, it was faith in my teachers to know that they were explaining their teachings as they had been taught; they were placed before me for a reason to my seasons. I understood the faith I unearthed in myself, through the courage I found to see the journey through and more importantly faith in the natural laws that worked hand in hand with all that is, for me to believe that it was all part of the original plan for every one of us. The first Extra Terrestrials to visit me were the little ones from Chiron and the word 'Chi-rah-on' when it is decoded means: The energy releasing and ascending us up to the heavenly first City of Light. Remember that the word 'ON' is explained to us through the mythical stories as the 'First City of Light'.

Also, through the codes of the Sacred Alphabet this is decoded as the 'Oracle of Nurturing' us and the Chi is interpreted as our inner collection of energy. In many languages, the word Chi is pronounced as Qi, Ki or Key. When decoded is explaining that the key (Chi or Key) releases the 'First City of Light' (R-'On'). It is one of the first steps to the introduction up into the fourth dimension of our intellect. Chiron is introduced to us as the initiation to our child within; this child is symbolically represented as your next precious thought, while we are being initiated into the birthing of our next world of intellect. We have named this species of intellect as the 'Greys', and they are usually the first ones to introduce their equation to us. They are here to assess our inner vocabulary, they check on the inner merging of our intellect, as it expands through our cellular convergence with our thoughts, not necessarily by what we do. They are checking on our individual mathematical union (the way we are thinking) through the mathematical Laws of the Universe.

You see, thousands of years ago, we were beginning to pronounce these words that I am revealing to you now. They are still in fashion and being used somewhere on the planet every day and will remain for hundreds of years to come! The truth is never out of date, as it comes from the Oracle or the—aura—that is already impregnated in every one of our cells. Our Cosmic force field is our aura. Our aura is autonomically tuned into the energetic highway that has the information of the DNA of the total Collective Energy of the planet embedded into it, and that reflects our thinking back to us through our Cosmic attachment to self. Each one of us is the myth of Atlas holding up our own heaven. In other words, our aura is mathematically condensed with the wisdom of the sonic sound, which we refer to as the unconscious mind.

The next inheritance appeared and I evolved up into what is known as the Syrian connection, this area is situated around our solar plexus, also known as our education center, where we unite the verse in our new City of Light (intellect) also referred to as our—universe city—or university. These species of beings that I refer to were representing the business sector of the Collective Consciousness. They produce the corporate worlds, the planners, the organizers, industrial development, trade, transactions; how we gain our inner confidence by learning to think things through. This is our education department, where we begin to unite our verses (collect our wisdom and speak our truth—collect our 'ship of light'). The Syrian -Extra Terrestrial- Intelligence tuned me into the Collective Inheritance where I could understand and accept myself with more clarity, which allows me to accept that we are all one. I watched as my intellect released its next step, as it journeyed up into creating a much higher attainment from this new information, I was desperate to understand.

The higher we lift our mind, the more we collect this scientific matter, that is already available to us throughout our cellular memory, where our geometry and our physics, then come to the forefront, which improves our mathematics by stabilizing the etheric web we all weave. This added wave of Syrian consciousness gives us the ability to reverse our thoughts harmonically to balance and assist us in our hour of need.

And then my favorite Extra Terrestrial Intelligence group came from the star system of the Cetaceous energy. This particular energy group supports the oceanic species, especially those of dolphins and whales. This star system represents the worlds of conversation and communication. These beings explained to me how the mathematics of the cellular structure of the body work, and more importantly how to create the Sacred Fusion of Matter, to enable me to learn how to collect and move to reconstruct the energy through what is referred to as psychic surgery. This important energy relates to the mathematical inheritance we are able to release through our DNA.

My communication at that time was through the vibrations that I received running up and down my spine. As I accepted this information and harmonically tuned in, I could feel a special pulse and tone that grew within me and I knew it was mine. Now remember, they are explaining many different levels of the Collective Consciousness. They all relate to the language of communication that is embedded throughout our cells. Whales represent the intelligence of conversation and communication. I receive many a transmission from this time and space of the consciousness. In the beginning of my journey, they initiated me with the name of Om Mira, which was the largest star of this group, previously called the sea whale or monster of the deep. This area of consciousness has been announcing their intention, knowledge and wisdom to me for many years and are still explaining and supporting me to this day.

Throughout the Conductive Laws of the Shamanistic principles, we are asked to use the electromagnetic fields of 'Elephant' and 'Whale' quite frequently, as their sound waves travel completely around the planet, which adds to our gravitational fields. They are excellent collectors of eternal energy. We need them to fortify our strength; we do not need to eradicate them! Elephant, through the Laws of Totem Shamanic energy, represents 'Knowledge', and Whale is 'Conversation and Communication' as stated previously. Their sound vibrates to a very low frequency of around 2 megahertz, and it travels along the crust of the whole planet. Those sounds are collected throughout the electromagnetic fields, which are construed correctly to the given point through the contact of the vibrations coinciding or arching with one another.

Whales create fields of light energy that can be seen from great distances, even from satellites travelling in the outer Universe. That vibration collects, and then it is forced through the next field of energy until it completes a full circuit. That is why both species can speak to the other through their unconscious mind. They can hear each other's thoughts through the sonic sound that they produce, through the beat of their own heart. All species that vibrate to the same frequency can hear and understand this sonic sound.

I realized that this Extra -Terrestrial Intelligence energy was also connected to my inner library. This taught me how to design and release my free will. This energy enlightens each one of us to open our mouth to speak to others, and assist them to how they are able to advance their knowledge, once they had found the courage to change their belief in self. The more we trust in our communication with others, the more we are advanced into explaining and teaching with confidence, as we are now free to release more information from our inner dictionary. Through the Shamanistic principles, Dolphin symbolizes free will. The dolphin empowers his mind through his desire for his outer world to be as exuberant as he feels on an inner level. Dolphin is the teenager of consciousness; the young warrior who is out there to win any situation and who requires a harmonious mind in order to do so. They can empower their energy to suit any situation by opening themselves up to attracting the Collective Inheritance; which is freely available to us. Allow your thoughts to become free from entanglement, and watch as you release the power to collect a greater substance to your knowledge, which will create new skills that you can tap into and benefit from.

Lastly the beings from the Pleiades came into my life; they are an extension of the divine mathematics of the Collective Consciousness. In my book 'Decoding the Mind of God' (Book IX: Extra-Terrestrial Intelligence) I explain in detail how these beings presented their energy to me. The Pleiadeans (Pleiadians) represent the healing of one's self. They are symbolically represented by the seven stars of the constellation of the Pleiades. This is another interpretation of the Seven Seals that we learn to open throughout this journey of self-discovery. I ask that you to read my book 'Decoding the Revelation of Saint John the Divine' (Book of Revelations), to open yourself up to the secrets we reveal to our self as each seal unfolds its information to us right before our eyes. As it is in the stars, so it is on the earth. I loved these beings from the Pleiades, they were very tall, angelic and wispish, and when they walked, they shimmered ever so gently. It was their Soul energy reflecting back to us the intellectual light we could manifest from the belief we could release, when we had earned our free will and trust of self? It was at the end of their transmission years later that my name was extended to Omniaarelle (abbreviated 'Omni'); when interpreted, this name is encoded as a high balanced mind.

Now let me explain to you the next step of this wonderful consciousness. These four levels of etheric energies (Chiron, Syrian, Cetaceous, and Pleiades) are also referred to as the matrix of the physical body and is a step by step guide releasing you into your own intellect. These beings are representing your own central nervous system, where they collect at certain designated areas to become our glandular inheritance. Our lymphatic system is reliant on these subtle energies. I like to think of them as my relay stations that collect the energy and filter it through to other areas that need supporting or strengthening. They are shown to us as our new beginnings into the futuristic worlds that are still unknown to most of humanity at this time. The etheric energies represent to us the worlds of where we learn to understand the divine inner workings of our mind. So many of you immediately spring back into your old worlds of fear and shut down all your doors when they present themselves to you.

Spaceships of light are a manifestation of energy that freely releases itself through our consciousness where the energy holographically imprints with our unconscious mind (higher mind). In reference to the Mayan civilization and the picture of a Mayan at the controls of a supposed—or metaphorical—spaceship is scribed through the metaphysical codes. It is an explanation of how our intelligence releases through the autonomic responses; that is, through the energy of how our Soul (unconscious mind) enables us to intellectually move forward. Now to remind you of previously written, the intellect of the spaceship was left for us thousands of years ago, through the Mayan heritage. The Mayan Palenque code is similar to the Egyptian King Tutankhamen; they both represent the same states of consciousness, which are explained all the way through their emotional hierarchical languages. The Mayans explained through the left hemisphere of the brain, and the Egyptians explained through the right hemisphere. Symbolism is the doorway that creates our reality; everything we walk towards in our future has been repeated every day since human existence began! As we evolve into our own structure of intelligence, we all symbolically build and collect our 'ship of light'—and all of this pertains to the result of our higher mind education.

Take note that the great Pyramid in Egypt had four ships buried at each of its corners, which relate to the four directions or Medicine Wheel that we use. Those ships represent the temple of how we earn our freedom to sail into the consciousness. The consciousness represents the worlds of thoughts instilled in our brain. Again a reminder, do you see now more clearly, how Homer explained the journey aboard the ship in the 'Odyssey'? Maybe now you can bring together the story of how, once we face our self, the Extra-Terrestrial Intelligence of our mind begins to export itself back through the cellular recognition of our body.

The last Chinese empire, the Ch'ing Dynasty, came to an end in 1911, with the Empress Dowager, Phi Chi. When interpreted through the codes 'Phi Chi' means: the Balanced Energy. The unconscious mind had the last say as to this wonderful woman's wisdom unfolding throughout the history of China. She reigned in all her wisdom, and what a gift she left us—the legacy of the symbolism of the relationship of self! She had her workers build a beautifully decorated marble boat on the edge of the lake surrounding the Summer Palace; this boat serves to remind us all of the ship we will create within our self, which we will futuristically inherit as we glide our way through the consciousness of time. Once we move up the ladder of our own DNA, there is no room for blunders.

We owe a lot to the Indians who taught us how to count; without this knowledge; no worthwhile scientific discovery could have been made.
Albert Einstein

Chapter 20
Vision World For Healing

Another parable that presents itself to me is the time where I learned how to exemplify myself into the many symbiotic layers of the etheric Shaman; it was a fascinating education to be shown how I had to split my worlds of thought into categorizing how the emotions of each species of the planet were also energetically transferred into certain personalities (aspects of self), that we now understand to this day is autonomically embedded in every single human cell.

I became aware that I had inherited, through the healing arts and education of the Medicine Woman's journey, which personality (aspect of self) was the front runner of the moment. What was I feeling, touching, tasting, hearing and seeing? How had this personality (aspect of self) moved its way up the internal ladder of my DNA? This was where I began to understand how to read the thoughts behind the saying, of my energy attracting its own attention.

As my inner light expanded during a healing process, I came to understand that there were really only twelve of us on the planet; (written previously in other works), where these twelve strands of our DNA are continually relaying important messages to every one of our genes. Allow me to provide a quick refresher: Have you come across someone that is similar to someone you already know? When I was living in Germany a woman walking down the street looked the same as my friend Julie back in Australia. I investigated this phenomenon, and understood that a Julie could be found all over the planet—that the twelve strands that form the DNA—are everywhere—a global inheritance—that the whole planet is designed to reflect as 'one of the twelve strands of DNA'. Symbolically, we have twelve strands in our DNA, and those strands are coiled in a double helix and held together by the strands of emotion

The more euphoric my mind became, as my energy levels came to attention, the more the light expanded throughout my cells. I noticed that these personalities became quiet. Those that did not feel secure in themselves tried to pull me back to the safety harness of their past; as they want to argue and distort this new information with any excuse that comes to mind. And yet they quickly understood that the light reigned supreme! Once this is fully understood you can begin to understand how our personalities seemed to be at constant war with one another, as we strengthen our internal dialogue with each step we make. The Armageddon of self!

All is explained in the first four books of the New Testament as we watch the journey of the Twelve Apostles or Disciples who head out into the far reaches to attract the people who did not know themselves, to come and hear the Master speak! These metaphorical stories are representing our personalities who fall by the way; through their innocence they have no one to follow, and do not yet have the inner strength to enquire of themselves.

Another is the myth told in story form of King Arthur and the twelve Knights (twelve strands of our DNA) of the Round Table. The Round Table is, of course, inside our head: the table of atonement, or 'at-one-ment', is situated under the top of our skull. Each one of us is King Arthur instructing our court to come to order; so, we order thoughts to be quiet. So as King Arthur; we set our Knights in order at the Round Table.

I finally understood that everything began with the worlds of revealing the inner worlds of self. Once we had accomplished this world, we were then free to allow our intellect to show us the next evolutionary step, where we could move on and up to the next level of understanding!

I learned while living in the outback, how to understand the etheric layers that are the production company of our life force; they force themselves to the forefront of our mind to play out their roles, and I quickly came to realize that as I moved my hands over a client that was lying on the massage table for a healing, that it was my energy that was attracting his or her attention. I could feel the subtle light body movements under my hands as I began to see holographically through the layers of their confinement.

The client was in a prostate position and I was standing. Their gravity fields were dormant or if they were stressed, their higher self could step forward to take control, while I was connecting to the earth; therefore, I was always in control of my situations. There was no need to hurry as they had allowed this time for themselves. They had already called for their space in the universe. They knew how many hours it would take to drive to the station and how many hours to drive back home. My position had to be designed into the time that they had allotted for the healing. If their mind was satisfied with their journey and they could relax when they arrived and not be caught up into the previous hours, then everything collated so smoothly and time seemed to stand still for all of us, for the healing to occur. We were autonomically laced into the eternal time warp, where the universe looked after our nervous system as well as the nervous system of the wholeness.

My clients came from the outlying areas, many of them lived in semi-isolation; they relied on the telephone for contact, now the internet is adding to their communication. Once the word was out, that there was a healer on the station, the phone would ring and they would ask me for my time. Of course, they became a great experience for me to work with. Their confinement was a new sense of direction for me, as these people lived an isolated existence. Their blocked emotions of not feeling well, was holding them in abeyance; they were marking time, as they could not see their way out of their current situation. They required help in understanding how they had brought on their negative responses, through their own self - doubt.

These are the restrictions of how our thoughts collect and gather through the ignorance or innocence of our fear, which will always hold us back from releasing our inner truth.

As I focused and silenced my mind, I was taught to look for the animal that was waiting in the wings for me. Through my vision world, the animal presented itself to inform me of what the client needed to replace within themselves. Remember that each species of animal is an emotional responsibility that sometimes we are lacking in within our self! Through the clients jumbled thoughts, the species had used up its emotions and needed to be replenished. Remember in the beginning that I was being taken back to the original way we understood consciousness. Those animals/personalities (aspects of self) that we healers see in our vision worlds, when we are in consultation with the unconscious mind of our clients, are a hologram of the client's personalities—or emotions—that need attention in that moment. We mentally connect to this energy and we have the possibility of helping our client, to correct the flow of the personality within that is not aligning. Usually, it is one that has been through an existence of that client holding onto a suppressed emotional thought. Metaphorically in other words, their totem pole needed attention. Remember that our totem pole is representing our spinal column, which is representing our DNA and embedded in our DNA is the memory of every one of the previous species that has evolved before us. Also, I recall that this is the evolution to how the human brain was nourished during the process of gestation as we began to evolve into the human form. Originally the totem was claimed for the whole village or tribe and hopefully you can see through the Biblical resonances, as to how the books in the Old Testament are explaining exactly the same thing, only this time, it is to the individual person! Can you see how the ancient ways had to explain themselves to us in the first place? Once I had understood the tribal heritage as to how they had created the consciousness to collect mathematically, I learned to understand how the consciousness imploded on itself.

The animals and their emotional inheritance are written in my previous works. A quick reminder of certain sections of our body which are affected by the animal kingdoms is from the navel down to the upper thighs. From the navel up, we note the changes we have made throughout our education of our ego transforming itself into its higher realms. The animal within us has subsided into releasing its own contentment.

The next evolution is through the opening of our heart, this area is governed by the dove, which is the gift one gives oneself. As previously mentioned, all of this area is in relationship to the bird kingdoms, known to us as the angelic realms, where we can stretch out our wings as we learn to fly in the mind. Above the heart area; we enter into the species of the waters; if they were stagnant then they were from the lakes, usually these were the frogs, crocodiles, ducks and geese, a strong movement represented the ocean to the thyroid gland and from there our evolution left the earth and entered up into the holographic microcosm of the insect species. The insect species rely totally on the unconscious mind (higher mind), usually beginning with the bat. As the people continued to come for healing, it was a pleasure to note how the animals changed to become birds, or fish which alerted me to the fact that these innocent people were listening to themselves for the first time in their lives and also had a permanent smile on their faces!

*There is only one Collective Consciousness,
which is shown to us through many layers of our mind,
or the levels of our life experiences.*
Omni

Chapter 21
Discovering The 'Dark Night Of The Soul'

Let me take you back when I was living in a tin shed on a property in the Australian outback that had been revealed to me; it was far enough away from the homestead that I could live and work in detachment, but not so far away that I was totally isolated from all of humanity. There were times when my resources seemed to falter and I felt that everything that nature intended for us all seemed to turn against me. I felt so alone. It began with my thoughts becoming stagnant, it seemed that my family of personalities (aspect of self), were the first ones to vacate from my home, they represented my inner family; I had even started to name a few of them.

The more I understood the metaphysics of the bible, the more I realized how similar a large amount of the parables were explaining the same information as the Egyptian philosophies; and wondered how could they both be explaining the same story; these similar stories just had different names. I began to argue with myself, and wondered where I had gone wrong in revealing these ancient codes. How and where had I confused myself to such a detriment that I now doubted every thought I was releasing. I began to notice that the native animal kingdom stopped coming around my door; the birds stopped their pirouetting in the sky, and more importantly, eagle seemed to have disappeared. There was no-one available for me to communicate with, and I felt all alone.

My master systems began to close down; in other words, my glandular systems seemed to swell, and the irritating entities started to come in, I began to see rats rummaging across the floor and little mice seemed to appear out of nowhere; a snake would appear to crawl through the wall; spiders would drop from the ceiling; I could even see the sheen on their web as it refracted in the sunlight. I had to ask myself if they were here in reality or were, they a manifestation of my inner vision world? What the dickens could all of this represent? I knew that each one of these species represented an emotion of positive behavior, as well as create a negative reaction, in regards to the current thoughts collecting on our behalf in the moment.

How come I could see these horrible invisible worlds; where had

I gone wrong? I was beginning to understand how powerful the reflection of my fear could show itself to me. I felt small and very vulnerable. There were times when my new worlds of thought seemed to becoming smaller and greyer. I seemed to have been sucked down into a void where I had lost my inner light! I had to learn the difference between what the Masters of Time placed before me and how it could affect the escalating intellect of my glandular systems as to what each entity represented. To achieve my master hood, I had to bring the teachings into fruition; if there was fruit on the tree, and then the tree was adult enough to reproduce itself. No, it is not easy to believe in these worlds, when we are confined through our upbringing to stop fantasizing.

Another thought opened up; was this my ten plagues releasing themselves? Had I inherited these thoughts or were they automatically placed there to test me? Back into the bible I went to decipher the codes regarding the plagues, there is a short article written on my explanations titled 'Decoding the Ten Plagues of Egypt'. I had to keep reminding myself that the only energies I had to be accountable to, was the force of the natural laws. In trying to do everything right, I had completely forgotten about me!

I had to wake up to the fact that I was creating these excuses all by myself. I wasn't listening to my inner voice; I was looking for an easy way out! At that time, I did not know any better, and these were worlds of intellect beyond the recognition of my little world.

There were times when I thought I was being taken to other planets where grotesque creatures lived, I noticed the plan of their village, as to how they gave each of their own species the opportunity to be secular, especially in regards to their own housing chambers; they seemed to be so far ahead of the way we lived. Peace reigned between them, there was no war with one another; the only opposition was between certain species, and this was when their mind was depleted of the other species emotion, they needed to take the life of the others to refurbish and strengthen their own.

I began to realize that everything shown to me was already happening right here on the earth! These species had already evolved! They were supplementing our energy; their job was to correct our deficiency. We are created through their emotional inheritance, their energy; they are explaining to us, their inner worlds as to how they have evolved. Again, we see the gift that George Lucas explained in his series Star Wars, as we watched the species lining up at the bar to communicate to one another. The more respectful they were between each other, the more each one improved. This is the world of the human strain as well as the Laws of the Shamanic Kingdoms.

Until the subject that I was working on had come to a completion where I could fully understand the education intended, by reversing everything I knew back to the starting point; I was not free to comment! When I saw Aliens with big eyes, I understood and realized that they were the worlds of the insect species; they represented the unconscious mind as to how they survived and how they came into being.

This is also the gestation period of a four months old fetus. When we look at the gestation period of the transformation of the human body from the point of conception, we can see the shapes of the species evolving through us, which is where our stability conforms to these natural laws.

I kept on returning to the journey of how I understood the species of the ocean, as to how they collectively thought in shoals. I noticed a repeat to how I had to understand the murmur. There was no arguing, no one stepped in front of the other. I had to bring my personalities (aspects of self) together to fortify what I had learned. And there it was! I had doubted what I was receiving, it went against my upbringing! I wasn't in those worlds anymore; I was now walking into new territories. I stopped judging my discrepancies, I kept returning back into the section I was learning, I had the right to earn this information as I had done over the years before, if I kept myself on track!

To digress a moment, I recall a time in the outback when my mind was jammed up with unfinished business and I was so tired and exhausted and I felt that I had to put down my tools of trade and create a space of peace for myself. My sleeping patterns lasted only an hour or so, which gave way to exhaustion at the end of the day. I wanted these ugly lessons finished as quick as possible. But no, I would not listen and I kept pushing myself beyond my limits and then one morning I woke up with such a force and I said to myself, 'That is it! I have had enough of all of this nonsense; it's time for me to go back to civilization!' I was so angry that I could have slaughtered any etheric entity that crossed my path in that moment.

I got in my car, and with a cloud of dust billowing behind me, I drove along the dirt track to the front gate of the property, and the closer I got to the gate the heavier I put my foot flat to the floor on the accelerator, I was ready to roar over the cattle grid that was beside the front gate, when the car just jerked to a stop! My foot had not even touched the brakes. No, I had no control over any of it. I had one meter to go before I was on the cattle grid. I realized then, that once I drove over the cattle grid and through that gate, I would have undone the last seven years of my journey. Once you have made the commitment which you had previously earned; there was no stopping and if you did, then you had to start right back at the beginning and commence from day one again. There were no half measures with this education.

Extremely angry, I got out of the car, and then I thumped the doors, the bonnet, and kicked the tyres. In my rage, I then punched a tree and broke two knuckles. As I cursed, I tried to pick up large rocks to throw at the seven crows on the ground in front of me; they were all looking at me and were cawing loudly, to remind me that they represented the Sacred Law and my seven seals. My thinking was, that if I could not achieve results through the contentment that I felt I had deserved; then I was going to pack it all in and return back into my past and start all over again, walking down another avenue which had nothing to do with this stuff.

I had often wanted to study architecture, as my father had done. Yep! I could have a go at that; I knew I would be good at it! He had taught me divining, to understand the divination of the four elements, how and where to design and place a house on a block of land using a compass, I learned topography in studying the lay of the land, which way would the water flow when it rained, where to place the dam to hold the water, to register how far apart to plant the trees, to note which way the shadows would fall to keep the house cool in the heat of the day, etc., so many years of learning.

But here I was at screaming pitch at the front gate ready to wipe out the last seven years! Then I thought that with this kind of thinking, I am achieving absolutely nothing; other than abusing my own mind and body. My left hand had begun to swell and pain was starting to show itself to me and I remembered to thank the pain, I had created for myself.

I never went over the cattle grid and through the gate. I sat in my Toyota, had a good cry, wiped my tears and then reversed my little car back and turned around and limped back to the tin shed.

When I had regained my composure, I opened the shed door to let any possible breeze come through to release the energy that I had collected; to replace it with my light. And at that moment the wind roared through and picked up my clothing that represented the garments I wore and they swirled above my head and the wind blew them all out into the yard. I went out and had to run after them before they had been picked up by a whirly wind and spiraled away. I finally picked them up and brought them back inside my shed feeling hot, dusty and exhausted, and closed the doors and then sat on my bed to pick off the burrs that thought they had found a new home and apologized to the Universe for my outburst. There was total silence, but the moment I apologized to myself, the Universe applauded me. The most positive movement that I created during my angry outburst was to destroy the shadows that I had collected within me. I wrapped my hand up in a crepe bandage and started over again.

My mind had opened up enough for me to retrace the knowledge of the ancient intelligences. This inner knowledge was a permanent structure within me, this lesson was to teach me about the evolution of all of us, where I was busily learning to understand how the human brain had formed throughout the eternal fusion of energy attracting its own attention. I learned why each species is here on the planet through their consciousness and more importantly why these species had to mathematically seat their energy into the Collective Consciousness for us all to become who we are today.

We are not composed of a few of the selected species; the codes of the metaphysical language of Egypt explain to us that we are all of them. I began to understand the emotional value of the consciousness, and through understanding these ancient laws, I learned how our DNA is traced from the consciousness to traverse and release throughout our genetics, as to why we have become human. I began to enjoy once again the experience of going back through time to understand how we have evolved into what we have automatically inherited for our next thought.

I also realized that I had walked up Jacob's ladder or my own inherited DNA to know that I had reached the top of my spine. Slowly I returned back to normal, the visions disappeared and the sun and wind became my light and breath, the animals returned, the birds spiraled overhead, my world had returned to me.

The next educated step was to take the journey into the heavenly kingdoms. I now had to commence to unlock those seven books that were clasped on the back of each book; which would open the door into the afterlife as it was explained in Egypt, or as I like to explain it as the next educated step of our inherited intellect. Once this part of my journey was finished, I then had to sit down for a few months and file the information away correctly in my mind; it had to be correlated through the alphabet and collected mathematically. There were no excuses in understanding this reference to humanities earnings!

After having listened to thousands of you in over 100 countries, explaining to me your fears when this started to awaken within you, it did not matter what language you spoke, you all explained the same reference, as your source of information was identical to every other land and language spoken.

I began to realize that I had finally passed the test of the Ancient Lemurian consciousness of what had evolved before me and how it had all taken its position in my memory bank and had seated itself within me.

What we all need to understand is that when our mathematical matrix has earned its next step of intellect, these worlds are autonomically presented to us! It does not matter if you are on your inner journey or completely unaware of any of this powerful education, through our own embarrassment, we sometimes feel that we are losing the plot! We have no wish to share this information with anyone. When you begin to hear this inner voice, remember, it is an aspect of your eternal energy; at first, we become afraid of what we are hearing or viewing; it frightens most of us and we wonder where this voice is coming from. We all have this inner voice within us every moment of our life, it has been there to support, influence, and suggest other ideas on how we can reconnect to our own home within.

It is your Collective Consciousness being returned to you! Through the myths (my theology, my way of life, as it was first delivered to us) handed down to us as we earn them, it is referred to as the high priest or the scribe, the one who registers everything. The more you add to your own portfolio, the more you evolve intellectually to collect the information from the source, which releases the pressure and broadens your perspective of how your truth is revealed and fortified within you!

Maybe we can begin to understand the child who hears the voice of their angel. This voice is automatically released from their unconscious recognition of self to distill the fear they are on the way to creating; they have taken a quick trip up into their higher mind to find a release of their moment! They find a safety in numbers! I have heard the most amazing stories from many little ones, under seven years of age. Do you realize, we all have the same experiences! We, the adult have, referred to it as our imagination, and that is correct, as it comes from the source of the image we receive inside our nation! Sometimes the story slightly differs, in mid translation, according to your own levels of intellect, and yet we all end up at the same gate!

And then, there are those who spend their time and energy mystifying themselves, who preamble on and on about nothing! They are so busy creating their fantasies, that they are missing their own boat, through being cast out into the deeper waters and told to swim back to the shore; always waking up before they reached the shore, feeling totally exhausted.

I would like to bring to your attention a synopsis of my writings, as I reveal to you, how I was trained to exuberantly bring forth my understanding to earning the metaphysical reply to the language of the hidden word of the Collective Consciousness/God. In Ancient Egypt the hidden one was originally known as Amon Re, throughout the Egyptian Philosophies; who supposedly represented the light or the sun and the hidden God within. This is the intellectual light which is exuded from the pineal gland situated in our brain. When we understand these philosophies in the way they were first described to us; we will realize that their philosophy was initiating us into understanding how we are connected throughout, as to who we become, so that we could learn to accept the unconscious recognition of our self! Don't forget my other writings, that the story of Egypt is showing us through the codes of their temples, pyramids, obelisks, etc.; the evolution of our central nervous system, by travelling through our glandular systems.

We understand now, that this pineal (Pine–Al or oil) gland, also known as the third eye, is the symbol that the Egyptians created when explaining Amon Re. The pineal gland has what looks like an eye on top of the gland that can only look up! What is this eye looking up at? There is a gene above the eye that is of extreme importance, known to us during our training as the God Head, (now reverse it and what do you come up with? The Head of God). This was also referred to in the past as the Lighted One or the Hidden God. The shape of this powerful little gland resembles a pine cone from which it derived its name. The pineal gland is located in the epithalamus, near the center of the brain, between both the left and right hemispheres, fitting snugly into where the two halves of the thalamus join. It is the final adjudicator of our third dimensional mind, before we enter into the fourth dimension, which leads us into the doorway of our unconscious mind.

All of these stories are explaining the responsibility that both the left and right hemispheres of our brain must finally adhere too. This support naturally balances our thinking as to how the DNA releases our next positive advancement. Our advanced computer is ticking away through every thought we release. These thoughts are being placed in the correct formula where they have been brought together through the glandular system, up into the hypothalamus gland where our mathematics keeps adding and subtracting autonomically on our behalf. The information is then passed on to the master pituitary gland, to be delivered correctly to the appropriate sections of our left or right hemispheres according to our truth; if it is our truth then the information is passed on to the pineal gland, if not we will be haunted by our self through the detriment of our ego, to relive the same experience again, until our ego submits and we get it right! All of which allows the gland to automatically release the chemical substance melatonin, as its secretion is dictated by light. We know now that our light is our intellect mastering the thoughts of the moment, which creates an essence that realigns our alchemy, as well as to reimburse our nervous system.

I feel that this sacred area could be where our dreams manifest, as these two elements of this important gene known as the Head of God and the pineal gland come together to register our truth, to inform us through our vision worlds of the direction we are leading ourselves into!

All of this creates a void or space through time, where the cellular structure has the possibility to re-construe the mathematics of the two ventricles of the heart, which allows for a harmonious continuation to pulse in alignment with our thinking. This keeps our body focused in modulation, which allows the body to release added information or the next step of intellect through our DNA. As stated from the pituitary gland all positive thoughts known as our truth, are passed on to the pineal gland, which passes the information onto this powerful gene we have named, the Head of God. Please remember, the genes connected to our pineal, are hidden and protected in our folds, until we learn to reach in to search for ourselves. This is where we have the opportunity for all information to anoint and heal the rest of the body where everything is magnified into becoming our intellectual freedom. This is our alchemy at work.

The light is then released through our pineal gland and the measuring is complete! We really are a marvel, aren't we?

Also, at that time I was still focused on reading the Bible backwards, as I had been asked to do so many years ago by my teacher Sharon. It was as though I had to keep my threads of consciousness connected to one another to keep holding on to my sanity. I was also trying to accept the learning of how our sacred numerology collected the inner mathematics, for us to behold.

Another learning I received was how each language translated their version of this inner divine language that is available to us all; the majority of the languages sounded the same, where I found that I could always understand each spoken word through the unconscious recognition of where we store our etheric sounds of music. This section begins above our ears. More importantly, was to know how the language we speak today, is also explaining the vocabulary of how the ancient ones, deciphered their own.

I wanted to know how the Ancients had first understood their mythical legends and interpreted the same story, we use today. Who told them and how did they receive the information? Did they earn their messages the same way as I did!

Why were the names of people pronounced so differently in the past? How did this happen? These were the Philosophies of the Egyptian, Greek, Tibetan, Hindu, Mayan, Celtic, Chinese, Japanese, Aramaic and Aboriginal where I found after many years, that they were all explaining the same identical story. Was this the twelve tribes of Israel at work? Was this the twelve strands of our DNA combining as one, to show us that there is only one story?

I could now understand how I was brought up into accepting the extra-terrestrial pathways of the unconscious mind. It was all through how we pronounced the Divine Alphabet in our own language! It had to do with how we digested each thought we released. As I kept on accepting the divine inheritance, another species of intellect presented itself to me to show me how each language needed an emotion for us to keep connected to these ancient ways. The threads of life were continually expanding as they grew.

I was discovering the mathematics as to how the inner Divine Alphabet unfurled itself! You could read the similarities between their stories regarding their myths. Did they all meet at the crossroads of the Old Silk Road to concur with one another, as to what story would be spoken or written at a certain time? As each group heard the stories, some had their attention focused on the speaker; certain words ricocheted deep into the cortex of their own DNA, which opened when their thinking aligned with the words. Others, who were not yet ready, listened to the stories and found them difficult to recall. I am so glad that I have had the experience to sit at the crossroads and travel along the Old Silk Road! I linked myself back into those stories spoken in many languages, where they still suffice today.

The Aborigines of my land didn't travel that far and yet there was the same familiar story spoken in their language. How come their language was spoken similar to the sound of the Ethiopian and Ancient Egyptian languages? This metaphysical language or the matter of physics (same word) had a lot of explaining to do! Even down to the Biblical stories explained in our Bible today? Was it all through listening to others? Or could it have been that the stories are always available to be passed down to you when you have reached a certain zenith of your own intellect? Lots of questions were surfacing in my mind. I began to realize that as our intellect awakens and moves forward, our outer boundaries attract information further out into the consciousness. This broadens our intellect, which multiplies our speech; new words come through our reckoning, where we are able to explain our story more eloquently.

Many truths have been explained in my book 'Decoding the Mind of God' (Book VII: The Sacred Alphabet and Numerology). We have a Bible; the Europeans have a Bibliotheca. The Aborigines have a Bibolicea (decoded interprets as the bible of the sea) which are all, when deciphered explaining the inner library of the DNA. All are resonating to one another. These mythical stories and Biblical stories were all explaining the same story and this information began to collect itself thousands of years before our Bible was written! I began to notice that the more information I filed away in my mind, these stories were balancing themselves out with one another!

I knew I was on a winner. I thought I just had to do it right. Each step of the way I thought to myself to take my time as I was learning how to bring the ancient language of Babylon back together for all of us to understand. There is no need for us to babble on and on. This ancient information is still all here, it has never gone anywhere; it is heralded down to each generation as they earn their right to evolve into their next equation. Don't worry about the information becoming outdated! It never will be; it still has not been understood correctly up to this time. These stories have been collected through the excuses we have made and are still making, for our life to continue.

Over the years, I have succeeded in understanding what strength we need to find within ourselves to take the walk through the 'dark side of the Soul'. Our fear is right there embedded within, helping us create our own furor. Why? As I found out, there is only road, known as the road less travelled, one story!!

We cannot change the consciousness, although we certainly do try to rearrange it, as we forestall our next positive movement! It is there to keep us balanced through continually rearranging us; as it has already earned its truth; we are still on the battle fields trying to search for ours! We are facing our own Armageddon or our own 'Armour of Gideon' and once both hemispheres of our brain have become more eloquently balanced with each other, they will become one; only then will we know who we are!

Allow me to remind you that our brain has two hemispheres. These hemispheres are sectioned; they open up in mathematical stages as we unfold our own intellect to become one mind. And yet we are unaware of how these two hemispheres work together. Left hemisphere is connected to our ego, which asserts the lower half of our body; right hemisphere of our brain is connected to just below our heart area which delivers to our emotions; its position is to accompany the ego to balance our thoughts when the ego is in repose. And you all understand that the only reason we need sleep is to relax our ego, which allows the body to heal and repair itself!

It all depends on the pituitary gland as to how our thoughts are registered through the balancing of our thoughts, if we make the same mistake this gland tips each thought into the left hemisphere where we will live the same experience again, until we refrain. If the gland ascertains that we have moved forward in our collective thinking, where we do not have to invent our story, our thoughts are free to move forward into the right hemisphere of our brain.

Our aim is to bring our awareness into its superiority, where we are totally connected to our thinking each time, we create our sentences. It's just another step forward, which makes great waves to conduit our DNA into opening up our next step.

I was thrown into the 'dark night of the Soul' and through understanding the world of Shamanism, I found the strength to pull myself out into my own light. I felt I had received all the knowledge known to man, plus the future evolution for the next millennium, if only I could do it right. As the Shaman initiate, I knew that I was protected by the force of God; as I have accepted that the force of the natural laws is autonomically connected forever more to my Higher Self. The messages came home to me thick and fast, once I had surpassed these barriers that I had placed across my path. The old world of my tantrums, were looking so childlike that I soon taught them how to grow up. My twelve Apostles had collected themselves and were now free to go out and work on my educated behalf.

It is entirely possible that behind the perception of our senses, worlds are hidden of which we are totally unaware.
Albert Einstein

Chapter 22
Quest For Life

As each new generation comes along, we find that there is a percentage of humanity that has been selectively designed through their DNA to be the teachers of the future, through their understanding and interpretation of the Laws of the Universe. These words that I write for you now, will be accepted more widely in the future through this exalted information releasing itself back to you. You will learn to earn, how the universe has always communicated telepathically to you. What percentage? It all depends on the focused mind of the individual, and when they had reached that pivotal point of understanding and accepting themselves. Your mythology unfolds in you as you develop your intellect. It is a fractional experience of your self-worthiness, which is cocooned inside you—tucked away in your tribal law (family/ancestors).

We can listen to this Quest for Life, and understand where it belongs within us; then the challenge presents itself to us to learn to accept the Laws of the Universe and through this belief we are automatically realigning and releasing our past. We begin to release and become more receptive to hear our inner truth! Each one of us has our own truth and yet when the information is collected throughout the consciousness, it is mathematically measured for every human to receive at their own personal level.

The word quest means 'to search for the answers that you cannot find within yourself' The word question means 'to search for the spark of light that is the reply to what you have asked for'; you receive this reply through the unconscious mind (higher mind) within. Watch how your thoughts change as your Higher Self leads you in the direction that it has intended for you.

Let me explain this further. Let's understand this Spiritual Quest. You exist and you are here through and for the benefit of mankind. You must learn to think before you do; and, more importantly, you must understand before you act. This thinking world of yours is called your 'Essence', or your 'Self', and that self is here for you to realize the quest of your life. Remember that the word nowhere is 'now here'! If we can bring the past into the moment, we can learn to accept it; that moment then promotes through its inheritance the action which promotes our future. Through this acceptance of self, we bring both our understanding and action together, which creates an eclectic implosion that begins in our aura, the energy of our Soul. The word eclectic is the higher religious experience automatically forming itself throughout our body. It coincides with the unconscious mind and returns our future back to us. The Spiritual Quest is your life unfolding itself through you looking at you! That is the cycle of life. Everyone is doing this journey whether they are aware of it or not.

Our inner truth unfolds as it is reintroduced back into the sacredness of our divine self. It is held in abeyance for us to inherit, which is autonomically protected through the embedment that is deep within our DNA. We have a tendency to over protect ourselves, by burying something we do not fully understand, which at a certain stage affects our DNA. We learn to outgrow our past intellect as we balance our thoughts, where we have the ability to search and reach up to accept our next step.

Our life builds and collects the energy to support us as we learn to cohabitate with our higher mind and when things are not going according to our plans, everything seems to close down; it is as though nothing seems to work for us, until we come home to revisit our emotional responses.

The moment each one of us enters into this inner sanctum of intellect, where we take responsibility for our self, we have a yearning to face up to our own existence as to why we are really here! One of the first things to confront many of us is that we begin to notice the changes in our family life; the arguments begin to flutter throughout the rest of the family, where they begin to sense a feeling of insecurity. It is through the emotional changes that we are making to our new dedication of self, the family feel detached; it is as though we have cut them off, while we are learning to face up to our new internal law.

Therein, we are becoming more aware of a husband or wife who may object to our self education (emotional intelligence), or a parent who senses the loss of their child emotionally, and then there are our own children who are still dependent on us and do not want to face their emotional world alone. They need us for their protection, as they are also searching for this inner security on a different level and have not yet come to terms with the 'Order of their own Court'. This is where our heart begins to reshuffle our inner waves, to bring a sense of calmness to our body; as we learn to feel what the emotion love really means to our vocabulary as we think our new thoughts. They will soon settle down!

We begin to step up to face the next 'Tribal Law' (family/ancestors). If only we all could understand this area more collectively, we would begin to realize that our thinking is our foremost priority—it is what allows us to theorize and release the Soul's evolution for the whole family tribe. This is also instigated throughout the whole of humanity; we set the wheels in motion not only for our own family, but also for the town or village that we live in. When I am solving an issue from my past, the energy that surrounds that old thinking changes its vocabulary; in doing so it becomes the present and it is in this moment where it can move forward to chelate to my future. Once I came to terms with myself, it made my education seem so worthy to know that if I could search and research through my new understanding, I would earn the right to have my questions answered!

We walk into these parallel worlds blindly; we do not know what is ahead and we would not have a clue regarding our own future and yet in our newly released innocence, we learn to trust and the big one is to remember that there is a greater being who is walking within us when we open up our feelings to our self. We alter our thinking and over time we begin to sense and feel these invisible laws that bring us comfort, which is for us to know that we are not alone. We start to realize that no matter what our age, we have become a new child of the universe all over again.

Another point to remember is that these universal laws are always showing us what we cannot see within. Remember the words of Einstein when he quoted;" It is entirely possible that behind the perception of our senses, worlds are hidden of which we are totally unaware". These worlds were the doorways that I had to find the courage within to open, where I could read and more importantly understand the mentoring of that ancient language, that we have not yet understood or adhered to, is all but forgotten.

As my mind speeded up, I became aware of an instantaneous form of recognition with everything that I could see with my two eyes, everything I noticed told me a complete story, just as in that car driving past... its number plate... the numerology told me a story of this person behind the wheel...the shape of the driver... the colours of their hair and what clothes were they wearing...did they have colors, spots, stripes, or checks... were they wearing glasses... did they have a moustache or a beard... what part of themselves were they protecting. The bark of a dog... how many times did it bark... the birds in the sky... were they coming from the right or the left…. every scene is a collection to an answer of our thoughts. I realized that I was viewing the whole picture instantaneously, whereas before I was looking at, (left hemisphere) and seeing through (right hemisphere). So, I received one third through the ego and two thirds through the emotional factor. Now I could bring the complete picture together. Whatever thought we have in our mind is automatically being reflected back to us instantly. The world is our mirror, and it is always assessing our thinking.

Every glyph of light is a story within a story explaining that thought you have in your mind right now! This is referred to as the Universal body language answering to our universe. These are also the ancient codes to the Chinese language, which they have named cuneiform. The Chinese language is also based on explaining a story through one symbol; through the way that symbol is constructed. Please let us learn to understand the religion of science correctly or did it all begin with the science of religion?

To further explain the metaphysical glyph of light; it is the intellectual light from your thinking that is your creation, not necessarily what you do, but rather, how you think to do things. As your intelligence awakens (through the belief in self, positive talk to self and ceasing the constant chattering of the mind by staying in the moment), it is automatically lifted up into the next realm. This creates an automatic reaction in the nervous system, where your mind reflects a stimulated light to show you the way. As your confidence in you surges forward, your third eye begins to open and expand until it becomes a much larger vortex of light. It becomes the inner kaleidoscope which multiplies as each new facet finds its own reflection; this reflection creates a mirror image which yearns to release your truth to you. Your truth is the result of your past inheritance; this is not necessarily known to you on a conscious level, but it presents itself through the subconscious energies, which are the emotional responses of your forefathers and—mothers— the mosaic of the mind begins to create the missing pieces, which brings your life into attracting an abundance of energy. All of these pieces are then reflected throughout this light and are collected mathematically and brought up into the combustible energy of your unconscious mind. This light is a soft hue of blue, and it is permanently switched on to help you see through your darkness.

The Laws of the Universe are involved with you closely as you evolve up to the next step. These Laws do not come down to meet you. They invite you to enter up into their light where you receive the contentment which is called enlightenment to release your peace within. Being enlightened is when the Universe works for you; it is not you working for the Universe, so, through trusting the self, you become your own Master, and you guide your own light. This light is the intelligence of your Oracle.

This Laws of the Universe/God energy has been with us every moment of our existence, just waiting for us to wake up! These are the ploys we create, which are the layers of our make-up that creates our 'Oracle of Life.' It is the energy strands of our DNA, that have been protected by this energetic force that has been held within; that we have named our Soul. When we understand how these ploys work, the stage is set and the opportunity for the play is about to begin. These are the worlds of the human experiences that each "Shaman Initiate," must learn to understand.

The next step will always be a little bit harder than the one before. We yearn to go back to when we felt safe, but we also have to realize that we cannot rely on our past; on this journey, one must always be moving forward. We are the latest species to carry our consciousness for all to hear and, through our truth releasing itself we are creating the next evolution for humanity to bear. Be prepared for the next example that the Laws of the Universe/God places before you, as you will also be tested.

My father, who knew of the commitment that I had begun, explained it to me in this way:

When you feel yourself falter with the load you are carrying on your shoulders, stop, straighten up, and pause, and then take a smaller step forward. Do not bend backwards or sideways, as this pulls you out of balance, where that movement then becomes the creation of your next excuse. God has his own set of rules, and he does not measure us; we must make that our own responsibility within ourselves; we place that responsibility on our own shoulders; your load automatically created itself through the culmination of your thinking, and it is included in the Laws of the Universe. As you move forward, your heavy load will become lighter, and so the heaviness of the weight is no longer applicable to your moment. Your wisdom then has the opportunity to shine and ignite itself to show you the way.

The rain is a baptism from the Collective Consciousness/God, and it comes to cleanse us of the worries that we are so busy collecting.
Omni

Chapter 23
The Rainmaker

I have been asked so many times by my students to explain what the Rainmaker has to do with the quest. Is it important? Yes, it is! And do we all become one, and more importantly, how do we learn to understand its principles? Is it an education that we learn or do we earn the title? It is briefly mentioned throughout my other books, and it deserves to be mentioned here more in depth for you to understand the explanation of the word. We are often referred to by others as the 'Water Walkers' the ones who walk on the waters; please remember without water this planet would soon perish. There is no life force without it.

So why are we known as the Water Walkers or the Rainmaker? Let me explain to you that the higher we open up and extend our divine intellect, the more we unravel what is metaphysically known as the scribe within. The scribe is referred to through the Egyptian philosophies as the author, this is the little figure carved in the hieroglyphs that is either standing or is down on their knees writing their next thought on a tablet of clay. Symbolically it is known to us as the written word, as it is so often recorded and mentioned in the Bible. Now can you understand the Egyptian hieroglyphs a little more?

You will understand and accept the meaning of this word more clearly and eloquently, as you read and release the knowledge of the writings explaining John the Baptist and also the explanations of 'Decoding the Revelation St. John the Divine', in the last book of the Bible.

The written word or scribe as it was known at that time comes from the everlasting energy that is embedded in our cells, and this embedment creates the bone matter of the body, it is magnetically maturated throughout our body or is surrounding us by the electromagnetic fields of the universe and is responsible for keeping us gravitized. This allows us to be able to stand upright to walk on the planet, where our own cosmic force solidifies, as we have earned the protection of ourselves.

Our cells become adherent, which creates the density in our bones, as it is the core of the body, (just as the planet has its own core) which is explaining how the Ancient Egyptians referred to the 'Bja'. And if we take this pronunciation back into its Arabian beginning; we pronounce this word as Bea, which is decoded as the 'Balance of EA'. We see this symbolic reference thousands of times, when we read the hieroglyphs correctly, where they explain to us a different interpretation of the original story. As to how these words are pronounced in the English language depends on the land mass the curators of the time, came from.

Let's take a look at the new born child, until the child begins to walk, our babies crawl along on all fours, just like a loyal little animal. At this stage, they are relying on their second dimensional brain, where they learn to empower themselves through their little ego's enquiring attention, which allows them to surge forward.

Yes, there are new words being mentioned in these paragraphs, as I explain to you the importance of the mathematical resonance of these words. We are autonomically sized up mathematically, glyph by glyph (light by light, thought by thought) throughout the Laws of the Universe; as we reflect out our inner strength through every word that our family has inherited, which is recorded in the genetic make-up of our DNA. Our DNA is a mirror that reflects an illusion to our written word, from our bone matter. Remember that our brain begins in the middle of our back.

I remember leaving the outback for just a few days and I was so excited to be returning to my family to become mother again. It was so hot and dry, there was another drought and the rains had not found their way out into the centre as yet. The earth was red and brown and dry, not one blade of green grass could be seen for miles. As the wind blew, the dust was picked up and spirals of mini dust storms and the occasional tumbleweed were blowing across the road. My view had all but disappeared. As the dust cleared after one strong dust storm passed me by, I sensed that I had slowed the car down to a crawl as there was no view ahead. I looked across to the right side of the road and saw two emus walking along the fence line searching for something to place in their mouth. I pulled off the road and put on my hazard lights and watched as they picked up little stones and rolled them around their mouth to assist them into releasing their own saliva and then they spat them out and took another step forward and did exactly the same again. This is ridiculous I thought to myself that the innocent must always suffer! What could I do to help them!

I got out of my car and clapped my hands to the heavens 'Hear my call' I yelled above the winds and spat out the dust that quickly filled my mouth and I bowed to them. I called for the consciousness to alter the energy of the area and bring the rains; these ancient birds were in total sacrifice to the Universe, I honored the emus and thanked them for their persistence as they were trying to survive the harsh conditions. They looked up at me and did not move. I don't think they had the energy to do so. I then continued to drive towards the coast for another eight hours and when I finally arrived to my destination, I was driving into rain. It was a soft gentle rain. It brought tears to my eyes and I asked that it continue on for another few hundred kilometers to the west and bring life to the parched earth. My daughter informed me that the rain had just started five minutes before I arrived. Therefore, she knew that I was not too far down the road as it always rained just before I arrived.

Three days later the outback was in flood. They received a total of seven inches of rain. I knew that the emus would heal themselves and the farmers had enough water to grow their harvest hopefully for the next two years. My daughter cooked me the lightest of meals; took me shopping and my son worked on my car. I had to learn how to communicate with them again. They replaced the plugs, hoses and a new fan belt on my car for further travel. I had become mother once again, just for a few days. Ask and ye shall receive!

Of course, I knew that I would pay my penance when I had returned back on to the station, as I had to begin all over again and I knew that I now had the strength to do so. Through this commitment, the Shaman is also the one who has the responsibility to walk the earth and the heavens at the same time, through each one of us earning and releasing our inner light, which walks before us, the more advanced intellectually we become. The inner light is a mathematical reflection of the unconscious mind (higher mind), that is seen through every species. We learn to equate with every available responsibility that is mirrored and presented to us. Our position is to re-harmonize the energetic force that wills itself to interrupt through its cataclysmic energy, to redesign the divine energy, which can never be achieved or accomplished by us.

But there are many who certainly make a mess of things and as always it is someone down the ladder who has to suffer for their consequences. The Laws of the Universe state that the results for our actions will always rule!

Now back to the journey of the Rainmaker who is the one who has been gifted with the responsibility to wash and 'Baptize' the earth; through the truth that they have automatically earned. We are the carrier of the waters; we attract the rain to cleanse the earth whether it be the planet or our earthly body. As you have read in my other writings, once I understood the metaphysical writings of how the language of the Bible in the books of Genesis and Exodus were originally written, the earth is also referred to as our body up to our neck and the heavens are our head, known as our temple or heavenly mind.

If we go back through our own ancient wisdom and look at the previous diseases of the planet, we can understand the evolution of our knowledge. We can see how our light is becoming stronger, we are growing taller and our skin is becoming clearer and lighter, so we are all moving on and progressing intellectually. This can only happen through us understanding and accepting the ancient ways, where we can all autonomically inherit the future; which automatically becomes the next evolution to humanities earnings.

One may say the eternal mystery of the world is its comprehensibility.
Albert Einstein

Chapter 24
The Three Phases Of Surrender

You are your own Universal Law; and, as you think, so, too, you create. You are given this gift to be in charge of how your thoughts create your world. As you allow one thought to finish itself, the next one is waiting to release itself to you. Your next thought will wait patiently until you are silent enough to allow it come through. It doesn't matter how high or how far out there you go, another challenge will always be ahead of you. Your challenges never cease; the completion of one challenge allows the next one to come towards you. The difference is that the more you walk inside yourself, the smaller those challenges will become. As you grow through your own self-confidence, you will feel yourself becoming taller, as you release your inner light back out to the whole of humanity.

Once you understand what your own Universal Law is, keep yourself focused, and you will be able to fulfil all your **desires**. Life will bring you up, through the temperance of your Soul, and, when you can **define** this inner education, you will become the **Divine**.

The Laws of the Universe are involved with you closely as you evolve up to the next step. These Laws do not come down to meet you. They invite you to enter up into their light where you receive the contentment which is called enlightenment to release your peace within. Being enlightened is when the Universe works for you; it is not you working for the Universe, so, through trusting the self, you become your own Master, and you guide your own light.

In reference to the Laws of the Universe each one of us is eclectically designed towards every thought that has manifested itself throughout the universe. Those thoughts are available for you to receive; to stimulate your energy in motion. They create your life force, which releases a personality of self (aspect of self) that you have the opportunity to use in the moment. A personality of yours ignites its own vocabulary, it is a thought of self worth, and it has the opportunity to build upon itself for it to release the truth. It must obey the hidden laws correctly for it to succeed. As our inner truth connects into the universe, it manifests its own light. This light attracts other thoughts, who release their confidence to empower themselves to follow.

The Shaman within, appears before you through the truth that has collected on its own behalf when you in your exalted—state of grace—are mathematically aligned to become one. This is through your thoughts becoming coherent with one another through an inner state of perpetual silence. How does one reach a perpetual silence? This can only happen when our thoughts are compatible to one another, if there is no hesitation; our mind autonomically balances itself, through the unconscious recognition of our inner language. The Shaman walks between the séance of these worlds of thought, which are autonomically designed through the personalities agreeing to your mathematical alignment, as to how each thought releases their own truth. Once accomplished, we are free to walk in the atonement of self, which becomes the 'at-one-ment'.

A Shaman lives in loyal reverence to every species on the planet. We are here only to teach the teachers! The teacher of the future is the one who is prepared to redesign their mind. The rest of the people will follow on, until it becomes their turn! We have a deep respect for what we have accomplished and we freely live this principle gift, that we have reserved and revered for self; the energy of our written or spoken word automatically reaches out to those, who will themselves to continue on in same mind; where they are free to explain these codes with others.

The more advanced our intellect becomes, the more we learn to communicate through our collective worlds, which is how our words implode one after the other. Our five senses (sight, sound, smell, taste, and touch) open up as we begin to accept ourselves. These same five senses then begin to create a measurement which enables them to square with one another; very soon they created a resonance of mathematics which began to collect one sense with another, and they brought forth the distinction of what we refer to as the 'sixth sense', which is the entrance to the doorway into the unconscious mind. We have entered into a new world up here, where there are no excuses, no hesitations, no blemishes of thought, where we have the divine will to go on. Our heart is open forevermore. We are imitated as the High Priest/Priestess or Shaman. It does not matter what your field of expertise is, you can be the butcher, the baker or the candlestick maker, and it is when our thoughts become congruent with one another that the scene resets itself. All is revealed when our mathematics have proven to themselves (obtained a resonance), where our belief has equalized within our body. Again, you can see the three Gods EL, AN, EA at work. We can create our own geometrical light waves and our energy multiplies itself times three. This releases the endorphins throughout our glands and our brain waves begin to speed up our energy, where we earn the right to become invisible to time.

Through the codes of attaining the resonance, the Law of the Universe—this 'Hidden God'—states that, as you earn the right to evolve up into the High Priest or Shaman, you must go through the process of metaphysically dying three times; this is a natural surge to connect up into the Ascension Process. Through the Shamanic philosophies, we refer to this as 'rearranging the original mosaic of the DNA'. The Shamanic code can be interpreted and alerts us to the fact that we are being reminded of the three Gods EL, AN, EA. evolving into the one God/Higher Mind. It is explaining the codes of how the mathematics began to collect through the three different dimensions of our mind. This reflects on our inner dictionary and how it needs to be refreshed with added words. As explained in previous written works, every ninety days our cells metaphysically regurgitate and purge the old ways out to make way for the new. These are the codes that release to equate to the number 90. In reference to Sacred Numerology, 9 represents: My Death; to my old ways, through the education of my understanding and knowing all. 0 represents: My Soul; my Alpha and Omega.

Once the spiritual cleanse or the essence of your mathematics has been brought forward, the three levels of our mind become one. You are brought back together again until you are being assessed for the next equation that the Laws of the Universe have placed in front of you. During these three initiations you are being confronted to finish your old life to start rebuilding an added value to self, which alternates the old you into accepting the new you. This was a principle part of my Shamanic training that seemed to take forever. I had to bridge the codes together to equate and balance the next thought to come to me, not me try and push myself towards it. These are the earnings we are able to accomplish for ourselves.

Allow me to explain how this happened for the first time in my life where I had to learn to move with the flow of energy that was directed to and through me. There was no way I could stop it or interfere with the process. It was beyond my logic thinking, and was being delivered to me through the next reality, which at that time was beyond my control. Little did I realize back then that I had to mathematically earn this experience.

I awoke one fine morning feeling excited as to what would be the lesson for the day. For the last few months, I had been drawn into studying the ancient art of telepathic communication. That morning

I began teaching my 120 head of cattle that I was looking after, while the owner had a well-deserved holiday, by telepathically sending out a message to them, as to what they had to adhere too. I began by going down into the paddock where the cattle were grazing and I opened the gate for them to walk into the next paddock that had been resting over the previous three weeks which allowed the grass to grow stronger. I opened the gate and walked back towards the house, I stepped on to the veranda and sat on the steps and proceeded to direct the cattle to the gate where I wanted them to go without me having to follow one of them. Usually this was a huge task as they seemed to have a mind of their own and I was the idiot running all over the paddock. This was a huge test for me to see if my thoughts could carry through into the group mind. Many of them raised their heads and turned to look at me as I transcribed my message to them and they slowly moved towards the gate, munching the grass all of the way; they walked in the next paddock and then continued to reap the fresh grass of its moisture. All I had to do was to walk down and close the gate when the last one had walked through. I was elated with my progress and thanked them for their attendance to my words! While I was latching the gate, one young bull calf meandered across to me and stuck its head through the wires on the gate and proceeded to swallow my right arm. I laughed out loud as the lumps on its tongue and cheeks, tickled my arm nearly up to my elbow. If this was my salutation for job well done, I was elated! (Cattle represent the word 'contentment' through the Laws of Shamanism).

I was free to go into town earlier than expected now that the job was completed when this next occurrence happened. I drove into town and parked the car as close as I could to the supermarket, and walked in with my grocery list. I needed to buy herb seeds to change the flavor in my food. At that time, I was eating a lot of brown rice, as my teachers had asked me to pick the grasses that grew around the house, chop them finely and mix them with brown rice. I had to take note of the colors each flower produced as this introduced me into to what part of the body it was working with. What each taste was like? Some were bitter; others had a slight sweetness, or tasted of grain. There was a different alchemy to each weed's personal design where they cleansed certain thoughts that were lodged into the organs. At this stage of my education I never argued I just did what was asked of me.

Little did I know that I was being prepared for what was ahead! I finished my shopping and walked out into the heat of the day that hit me like a furnace after the cool of the air conditioning; I was walking past a small park towards my car when I felt dizzy and noticed that I was starting to lose my balance. In the park, there were some old tree trunks lying on the ground under the large gum trees, which were about three meters long that could be used as seats. I tottered across and sat down on one of the trunks and it felt as though both my arms had fallen off my body. I placed my grocery bags on the trunk beside me and then my legs felt as though they had taken off to find someone else to attach themselves too. I felt utterly useless and wondered what the dickens was happening and what I had to do now.

Without my limbs, I noticed that I could not move my body. I felt paralyzed. An old black dog with a grey whiskered face meandered up to me and then sat between my legs and started to look out over the landscape as though it was there to protect me. I knew then that whatever was happening I was safe in Gods arms; the ancient loyalty was with me. Slowly piece by piece my body seemed to separate and I watched as the pieces seemed to float outside in my aura. I looked down into my body and all was a thick white mist. And yet I knew that my body parts could not separate from my force field. The silence in my ears was building up to become a deafening roar.

The dog between my legs never moved and I couldn't; I could not walk, move my body, or communicate with any other human, so we sat there in anticipation to what was going to happen next. The thought jumped into my mind "Was I about to have a stroke?" "Not now for goodness sake, I have my milk and butter in the shopping bag." I was aware that I felt quite euphoric in my mind and watched as my aura started vibrating around my body parts where I noticed a pale blue colour swathing its way throughout my organs. They were being cleansed of all negativity and ever so slowly they came back into my body the same way as they left. I felt light and cleansed and slowly my thoughts returned and I became sane again.

The colours kept changing and became stronger inside me and my energy felt stronger during this time which seemed to have stood still for so long. My light body of truth was new and innocent. Metaphorically I felt like a magnificent white iridescent butterfly emerging from its cocoon as I slowly stretched my body on a twig to dry my wings. I looked across the park to see a middle-aged man dressed in white shirt and trousers, with long white hair pulled neatly back into a pony tail standing in the shade of the tree; I realized that a guardian had been present all of the time. We nodded to one another and I picked up my groceries and walked over and stowed the groceries in my car. I noticed the clock in the car and realized that two hours had disappeared. I walked back across the road to a restaurant and ordered a big mug of cappuccino to take away; for me to collect my thoughts for the long drive home. On returning home I stowed my groceries away and was quite surprised to note that the refrigerated food was still very cold, after all of that time.

I could now celebrate my new life that I knew was in the wings waiting for me. This experience changed my senses, they seemed to have magnified over night, and everything appeared brighter and more colourful; where each item I viewed became more pronounced. I seemed to be looking at the world in 3D, my hearing elevated to where I could hear the sound of a fly's wings change its circuitry system as it flew in a different direction. I thought I would be better prepared for a future occurrence and had my own ideas as to what was expected of me. The years had passed and my new discipline was now reigning supreme. I thought that I finally had my ego totally in my control. I taught myself how to value this commission I had been asked to commit myself too. I had been waiting in anticipation for the next occurrence to come to me and when it did, I was again taken completely by surprise! I was driving along a dirt road that was empty of cars behind me, to the side of me, also ahead of me for miles. I knew I had two more hours of driving before I reached my destination and was pleased with my efforts of my day as I would be there before nightfall came. So far it had been a twelve-hour drive.

I was heading deeper into the outback to take on a position for a few months on a cattle station while the owner of the house was recuperating from an accident. They were friends of my family and I felt comfortable at accepting the workload. I also knew that there would be a new education on its way for me to learn, written more extensively in my book 'Decoding the mind of God'.

I was driving into unknown territory and was casually looking at the aridness that was around me when I felt my body start to stiffen and my back became straight and I looked at my hands on the steering wheel to see my fingers starting to fade and disappear. They looked claw like; just like a bird of prey. Had I created this through so much concentration trying to keep the car on the road? I yelled to the universe; "No! No I am not tired, another two hours and I will have earned a good day!" When these experiences had appeared previously, I knew that I was being shown where my energy was becoming condensed. I had forgotten that I had already driven twelve hours that day and to be truthful to myself, I had also forgotten all about my first death!

A white dingo came out of the scrub on the left hand side of the road and proceeded to cross in front of me to the right. Once again, my panic subsided as I realized that whatever was ahead of me that God would be right beside me to take care of me. "Faith! Faith, have faith in yourself!" I screamed to myself. "Oh no, not now, I am behind the wheel of my car, I'm nearly there" I thought. I tried to bring my trusty little Toyota across to the left hand, side of the road so that I could park on the edge, and realized that the corrugation was too deep from all of the large semitrailers driving from station to station to carry the cattle. Their wheel span was around nine inches wider than my Toyota's, hence the corrugation. I had noticed a few kilometers back that I was having to drive with one set of wheels on one side of the car in the semi tracks and the other side of my car was up on a ridge about six inches higher so there was already a lean on the car. Needless to say, I had to slow right down until I found an area that was safe enough where I could pull over to the side of the road.

By this time my arms had almost totally disappeared up to my elbows and yet I knew that I still had complete control of the car. I pulled up in the shade of a stubby little tree and sat there dumfounded as to what had happened. "Why now, I am losing daylight hours?" And away we went again releasing all of body parts. This time I was much more confined and did not have too much room to move. The first thing I noticed was that the colours were a different shade of blue, sometimes they were a deeper purple or cerise; there were deeper shades of pink threaded throughout the mist and I realized that my aggression was being shown to me. I tried desperately to change my mind and remove my frustrations, and at the same time, in the back of my mind was the knowing that the daylight was fading fast. I did not have a bull bar or spot lights for added protection and did not like to drive in the dark as sometimes the cattle wandered onto the road; they did not seem to care that you were coming towards them. Once again time seemed to stand still for me, as this time honored, ritual was allowed to continue.

Slowly I came back into my body and I felt pleased that at last it was nearly over and I could honor the new me. I started the car and drove down the road. I had not been disturbed; there was no other vehicle in sight and I quickly came to the homestead gate. I drove on up to the house which took another hour and I poured myself out of the car in the last of the twilight. I seemed to have been placed in a time warp for the rest of my journey so that I could reach the homestead in the last of the daylight.

The head stockman came and asked me whether I would like to drive straight over to my quarters. You have asked for isolation so we have put you in a shed near the butcher's quarters where we carve up our meat. There is no odor as everything is placed in the walk-in cold room. Of course, I had just been dissected into quarters and it seemed very appropriate to me! I said yes that would be a good idea and finally I reached my new abode. Of course, I had to receive this second Passover as I was being prepared to begin a new life. I was moving deeper into the Shamanic territory where the education to earn my freedom was steeped in mathematics and geometry; it was the hardest I had ever encountered. The following day I seemed to collect all of my bearings where I could accept and salute myself.

My third and final initiation came again a few years later when I was lecturing throughout Europe. I had taken over an old Chateau, renovated around fifty rooms and had created my Academy. This time I was sitting in the men's smoking room with my feet up on the beautiful marble fireplace enjoying my solitude in front of the large open fire after delivering a solid four days of informative schooling to around eighty students to finalize our telepathic education. It was late Sunday evening, the students had finally gone, I looked out the window to see the snow swirling around outside my large windows and a silence spread over the room as I felt myself being sucked into a vacuum full of the most radiant colours.

It became more difficult each time to interfere with the process and what took me two hours to complete through the first death as I watched how my body took a full day and a half the second time and the final initiation into my third death took me many months to fully understand the possibilities that were available to me; my current values had to prioritize to become my 'Principle Apostles'. I began to realize that I had finally released my twelve tribes, which were the twelve strands of my DNA. From the Sunday afternoon until the Tuesday morning I sat there in all of my reverie completely unaware of my surroundings. My staff came Monday morning, did what they had to do and did not disturb me. They thought I was asleep and left me to my own devices. On Monday morning I awoke to the fire crackling in the grate and thought I must have dozed off for an hour or so. Little did I know that the previous day had slipped past as I retraced my mind, I felt like I had been sucked through a black hole where I had to rearrange my DNA and be regurgitated back out again. "Oh, the magnification and wonderment of the natural laws" I thought. I finally realized the importance of the number three. My three Gods, EL-AN-EA had finally become one! Each one had to release the experiences previously lived; to empty out its past to free them up to journey into their next inheritance. I had finally attracted all of my millions of cells that had been in abeyance to awaken, for them to coincide with each other to become one.

My excitement grew as I noticed that my seven seals were now open for the rest of my life. I knew that the rest of my time in the Chateau would be unhindered and the teachings for the next five years would continue.

Great spirits have always encountered violent opposition from mediocre minds.
Albert Einstein

Chapter 25
Changing The Alchemy Of Our Body

The next step of my education took me into the world of physics (the world of matter—of physics—becomes that of the Metaphysical), where I observed the freedom, I had earned as my mind opened up into my higher intelligence. This is where my energy became lighter and tuned me more acutely into the alchemy of my brain. The matter of physics, or the Metaphysical language, is all about earning our own responsibility to release each one of our thoughts; it is about exercising our inner and outer levels as one. I discovered through my thinking I was informing the cells of my body to be prepared for their next possible venture. I was finding it easier to understand how the mathematics of the Collective Consciousness cohabitated with my past experiences; as to how they were mentally brought to their own attention to release themselves. It was an ethereal feeling of self - worth.

The lessons/experiences are the same for those who have just died and passed over. Now you can understand how I wrote my story in the 'Decoding the Mind of God' (Book IV: Death). This knowledge allowed me to help my late husband and many others to adjust to their new frequencies as they entered into the next educated world.

Let us bring in some more information here. Through the Egyptian philosophies in the Egyptian Book of the Dead, we take note that the fifth plate has no written words; all we see is a single illustration of one Deity, who has ascended totally up into the unconscious mind (higher mind)—he is sitting on his throne above the consciousness, which is represented by water. Now we can see more clearly why there is no need for any text, as the illustration informs us of the freedom that he has earned!

It is up in this mathematical or geometric world, where you become aware that the frontal lobe of our brain was explained to me as the eye of refraction. As we are aware, the pineal gland coincides with the powerful gene situated in the frontal higher lobe (known as the Head of God or God Head). To 'refract' is explaining to us that it can bend, detour, change course or change direction, through the thoughts we are creating in the moment. Remember karma is delivered to us instantaneously, so the reflection we envisage is directed to us in answer to our thinking. The frontal lobe of our brain was also explained as the 'reflection' that is delivered to you from your third eye, to create the holographic images that we see. The images have the opportunity to magnify, where they can collect a like-minded energy which when faceted or harmonized, becomes balanced to complete the picture. My mind opened up to resurrect other portals of time that are standing by in abeyance.

An explanation about karma. The Universal Law answers to our thinking in a balanced way, but it is not always in the way that we expect it to be! Another name for it is karma, or the 'Kha-Rha-Mha', if we explain it correctly, for this goes back to the early language of the Armenians and the hieroglyphs of Egypt. If we pronounce it in its correctness, it is the cause and effect, or the accidental and occidental; it is the occidental that is the key to your wisdom. The occidental is the final outcome of the length of your stay on this planet. The occidental is the light that keeps this planet alive. Our accidents are what we have produced for ourselves through our thinking. The occidental is the explanation, or the derivative from the Laws of the Universe, as to how we have gathered and achieved the accident in the first place. It is not only what you have done to you; it is how the Laws of the Universe answer back to what you are doing to you. I like to refer to the occidental as the 'messenger', represented as the Pigeon throughout the Laws of Shamanism. With its sonic sound, it hones in on a catastrophic conclusion of thought, and then it delivers the message to our heavenly home, which is our brain.

Also, a reminder in reference to how karma collects on our behalf in the case of war. In 1918, during the First World War, we created a bird-like flu virus through the thoughts of the Collective Consciousness. This virus killed around 20 million people. That number does not include the deaths of that war's participants. In 1916, people began to notice polio, which ran rampant past the end of the Second World War. The word polio, when understood through the codes, means 'through the power of the Oracle, life's intelligence is the Oracle'. The crippling of the human body began, and, this time, around 50 million died. That does not include those during the war, either. This dis-ease is the result of a tithe from the Collective Consciousness for all of those men killing one another.

At the end of each day, I take my mind to the frontal lobe section of my brain and become still, I ask for my day to be shown to me. This is where I have the opportunity to correct my thoughts, so that everything can take its place in my memory bank and the experience can seat itself. These few paragraphs took many years of earning the intellect to bring the complete story together. We all begin by referring to this section of our brain/mind as our intuition, our inner teacher.

It is important to learn to be silent within yourself; for, that is when your inner self communicates to you in images through the light worlds. Those light worlds are the illumination of your true self. Being silent allows one to venture forward while standing still. This is the Shaman's vision. Only the truth comes through this world, never a distortion or lie. All of which allows us to create an enhancement to explore many other worlds, as the metaphysical pictures begin to collect or connect with one of our thoughts to create our next story. We become charismatic; which is explaining to us the Chinese belief through their language of the ancient cuneiform, just how simple it is to explain the intellectual wisdom of one picture that can explain a complete story!

The same occurs through the holographic imprint that is collecting on your behalf and is coming towards you. Now maybe you can see how the emptier the mind (silent from chatter) becomes, the more you are rewarded. Each one of those words release through your mathematical alignment to lift you up through opening up a different portal to the cells in your body; through this expansion into the power of quantum mechanics is where we are able to release the next spoken word. We can now understand how our mirrors of light autonomously transform into the next cell where our enlightenment becomes our everlasting life. At this point you are not aware of linear time, and what you think is taking an hour, is only taking you one minute to quantify.

The same goes for the evolution of the human brain. As your intelligence evolves, so, too, does your thinking expand—where your belief is your light, and your light becomes your strength; where your strength releases and becomes your success. This is the creation of the Etheric Web.

I was conducting a seminar and watched my students who grouped in five around a table where I gave them a series of words to create ten paragraphs to form an article, each person spoke their thoughts and the others listened intently to the conversation. They began hesitantly until their fear subsided. It did not take them too long to trust one another where they could hear one another quantifying their thoughts into becoming one mind.

Their conversation opened up their own personal DNA where they surprised themselves as they all connected to the same sentence with a smile at the end result! Their stories were a joy to hear and laughter reigned supreme at the end of this experience. Please practice this exercise with yourself! You will be amazed at the result! The same experience is happening in the business world, or medical laboratory or a research center as the scientists delve into their new world to find solutions to their issues, also included in this arena are the players of a football game. I refer to this as the journey of our success creating its self, where time becomes irrelevant.

As time moved forward, I soon realized that it does not pay me to think too much, as it clutters the mind. If I could place myself into this void, I could inherit the mathematics of those unknown worlds of intellectual light. You can't just think a thought and then start to apply it. Each thought makes itself relevant to release the next thought, which autonomically attracts the next thought, and so on; it all depends on the direction of where your ego is looking for attention, as to how your sentence creates itself!

By now I hope you have an idea as to how the collective power of those three deaths become impotent (remember the principal law of Shamanism and the Laws of the Universe states that, as you earn the right to evolve up into the High Priest or Shaman, you must go through the process of metaphysically dying three times; this is a natural surge to connect up into the Ascension Process. Through these three exemplified deaths, your journey informs you that your ego has to deplete in order for your fear to subside through your own discernment. On three different occasions, these codes state that you must finish your old life completely and begin to rebuild a new you). We take note of how it echoes throughout the body and becomes accepted as a mathematical equation, which allows the brain to release its own cosmic ability back through us.

I and many others have mathematically earned how to telepathically communicate with your soul, which is the energetic life force of your unconscious mind, as I have earned the right to intellectually step up into mine. Now you can explain to yourself, that this higher self is a culmination of all of your personalities (aspects of self) that have trusted one another to become your oneness, which is also explaining the mathematics of the Collective mind, also referred to as the unconscious mind (higher mind) where we enter into the world of telepathic communication; it is the autonomic response of the human nervous system). You will find my teachings slightly different to others, as I must make sure that I have understood how these worlds brought themselves together through their own creation in the first time.

Understand that I am speaking through the evolution of my truth, which is also my accountability of my own intellectual journey. With my training into the essence, my peace, love and light had to evolve many years ago into a power source. That source of strength has become the purpose of my life program, and my life program is to explain the science and physics of the soul mind. I am not disturbing anyone on this planet with what I deliver through my teachings, although I may disturb their fear that is still trapped within them; which has already announced itself into their life through the insecurity of them not understanding themselves.

There are many of us who have earned the right to open your gateways into the higher Collective of the Consciousness. I was told to remain silent, until it was my turn to speak. I give thanks to all those wonderful people that have walked before me, the love that I have for them is exceptional and it comes from my core or soul light. Whether it be the doctrines of China, Greece, Arabia, Japan, Maya, Egyptian, Native American, Australian Aboriginal, Druid, or Celt, etc.; do not close your mind to any path, as all of these paths are representing your written word and they all lead to the one and only gate.

Throughout the laws of Shamanism, the wonderful dolphin species of the consciousness represents the attainment we can reach through us earning our freedom of will.
Omni

Chapter 26
Dolphin—Free Will And The Earnings Of Freedom

As we begin to believe in ourselves, our Soul gives us never-ending gifts of knowledge. To believe in ourselves takes a tremendous amount of courage, and that courage will lead us into other parallel worlds of existence. Those worlds align within and open us up to our inner worlds, and then you have earned the freedom to use them to promote our tomorrows. In the previous chapter I wrote about the freedom I felt in that part of the journey, so I have included some information about the dolphin species—freedom of will. Throughout the laws of Shamanism, the wonderful dolphin species of the consciousness represents the attainment we can reach through us earning our freedom of will. The ocean represents the consciousness, and the dolphin is a representation of you releasing your thinking out into that consciousness. Dolphins are the willing mind of the ocean. I liken them to the raft that I hang on to as I ride the stormy seas, whirling my way through to collect my energy. In the beginning of my education, I symbolically attracted five white dolphins to me; and, when I was in doubt, they carried me to my next positive world of thought. Two years later, these five white dolphins came into my life on the beach, and they explained other sections of the Collective Consciousness to me for a period of another two years.

When we look at the evolution of the whale, dolphin, and many fish species, we come to realize the importance of their evolution. In order for a newborn dolphin to learn to swim just after birth, it is born with a total belief in and awareness of itself. It takes up to thirty minutes from birth for it to realize its own independence. That dolphin lives totally in its Collective Inheritance, in which it is capable of mirroring the conformity of the world it lives in, and that is its unconscious mind (higher mind). Buoyancy can only materialize when the mind is focused on itself, and when and where it feels safe in that realm of thought.

The mother of the baby dolphin is there as a support system and source of nurturing. This continues until the baby dolphin can allow its feelings—or security—to link with the movement, sound, pulse, and tone of the ocean; and to acknowledge the ocean to work with its thinking, which allows it to become at one with the ocean and all the oceanic species. This occurs through the hologram that is automatically created through the dolphin's mind becoming harmonized and mirroring back to itself. It releases a tone of mathematics—or codes—that enables it to create a life of perpetual ascension. Its continual state of mind becomes a focused movement which then carries it forward. That is why the dolphin's mouth is open all the way through to its crown. The same explanation relates to the whale and other similar species as well.

We now understand that the dolphin and whale are among the earliest species to develop through the evolution of the Divine inheritance. We have also come to a unique understanding that the whale, dolphin, bat, bird, and insect all are connected through the sonar that they produce. They all have evolved completely, up into the highest form of the Collective Intelligence, which is the ultimate ascension for us to learn to create in order to release our own intuition up into the unconscious mind. In other words, they all rely on their own manifestation of sonic sound.

When a dolphin swims beside a fast-moving ship, the dolphin uses the power—or the energy—of that ship to add to its own energy in order to propel its motivational expertise through the water. That also explains to us the understanding of free will. The thrust, which comes through the belief of its own empowerment, can keep the dolphin's speed equal to the speed of the ship, where the dolphin then has the opportunity to power beyond the ship, through surging into its own free domain – if it so chooses. It is as if an astral restaurant is supplying the dolphin with nourishment from that energy. Free will is the teenager, and it is also the warrior earning his wisdom through achieving his own self-will.

The dolphin's evolution goes back to a time millions of years before the arrival of the first humans. As a by-product of the killer whale, dolphins became the next species of emotional conversation. The whale, in Shamanism, is the evolution of the word communication. It represents the conversation, pulse, and tone throughout the Collective Consciousness, and it sends and receives sound only through that sonic level.

Dolphins and whales are an interdimensional species of the same thought. They created their own groups of consciousness, in regard to time; they have evolved through a separate tone or language for each species, yet they are of same mind. There are eighty-plus species of these cetaceous mammals in the ocean, and, through their continual movement, they are anchored into their genetic inheritance.

We are aware that the dolphin has evolved into having the ability to use both brains at the same time through only having one nostril. Its mouth opens up into the crown area of the head, so the dolphin is always breathing its total freedom of thought. Its brain is permanently in unison, which has come through the balancing of the middle ear, and this is the beginning of the species' creation into evolving up into their sonic sound. The Tibetan masters also teach us how to achieve this 'one brain' facility through the teachings of Esoteric Buddhism, where we tune both nostrils into becoming one. Dolphins take short catnaps just below the surface of the water, and then they slowly rise up in order to breathe. Their breathing is voluntary, so, when they sleep, they only close one eye, which diverts the energy and frees that side of the brain, while the other hemisphere of the brain takes full responsibility. I know a few humans who have this ability as well, especially when watching TV!

That deep emotional conviction of the presence of a superior reasoning power, which is revealed in the incomprehensible universe, forms my idea of God.
Albert Einstein

Chapter 27
The Shaman Within

We can try and deceive ourselves as much as we want, and still the Shaman awaits us. That Shaman in you, is the fortified you; waiting for you to release your fears, where you may have difficulties in accepting yourself. It is not waiting for you to throw anything out, lock anything away or ignore it; it is on standby waiting for you to acknowledge and release the tension that surrounds this innocence we are all born with.

The Shaman within you has the ability to teach you how to inherit the knowledge of the Laws of the Universe. The Shaman is the Royal Ness of humanity, the silent one, the one who lives the life of the mystery that others who are still wrapped in their fear, have yet to release within themselves. The Shaman works beyond the aspect of time, and believes in those things, others cannot see.

The Shaman is the one who knows and can know, the one who sees and can see from within the hidden consortium of time to allow and more importantly trust in the pureness of the Soul energy of self. The Shaman never walks alone, he or she walks with all that is, and moves inconspicuously amongst his/her fellow man. In other words, the Shaman is one of the power poles that support this planet. The others are the minerals under the earth, the alchemy of the soil, the essence of the trees, the animals who evolved before us, the birds who protect us, the oceanic kingdoms, who urge us forward, these are just some of the—Masters of time—taking care of us.

You become the Shaman when you turn your life over to the self, where you meet these exalted Gods within; remember they are the attainment reached when your thoughts inherit themselves; where you are not afraid to walk in the worlds that are presented to you. To enter into the next chapter of your intellectual mind we begin with learning how to meditate, learn how to seat your thoughts, through your silence to understand your mind. It is only in that stillness that you become aware of your Soul's purpose of what you are capable of inheriting as you open up into the Collective Consciousness, where you are at one with the universe.

Remember the martyr comes before sacrifice, and from sacrifice comes the master. A martyr is someone who is pleasing their own fear; they begin through celebrating the fear that they have inherited. This suffices their ego as it feels worthy and is totally connected with the left hemisphere of your brain. A sacrifice is someone who bows to somebody else, and says, "Here, if you cannot find out how to use the self, I am here to assist you." We have shifted the consciousness of our ego over to the emotional right hemisphere of our brain. Then there is the master, the one who stands still. The master does not bow to anyone, and he/she never apologises or explains. The master looks at every other human as a reflection of him/her self, does not have to choose words, they are an autonomic response to the child, the teenager or the adult, as they are spoken through the heart which is the power of love. Look at our every - day family life with mother, father and children and you will see the familiarities I am talking about.

My teachers gave me the opportunity to take my time to see these familiarities creating themselves. I found that the more time I paused to collect the information, the more opulent my inner worlds stood before me to show me the way. There was nothing more beautiful than being mused into the vibration of colours that permeated through the inner realms of my body. It was through the exploration of each thought that gave me many new ideas.

The double helix once it has been encouraged to move forward begins its own momentum to continually spiral up towards the brain. Once through the medulla oblongata it begins to oscillate and reflect the information throughout the mathematics which is known to us as the 'heavenly oracle.' The brain then has the opportunity to branch out, where each thought is carried into diversifying our alchemy into releasing other chemicals. We understand at this stage we are being informed of our DNA; which is metaphorically (biblically) explaining the twelve (12) apostles to assist and magnify our moment.

Through this diversion we have the opportunity through one thought, to have twelve (12) ideas. Once those twelve (12) ideas harmonize with one another, they expand into an aperture to formulate another twelve (12) ideas. This is the story of Camelot and King Arthur. King Arthur had twenty - four (24) knights, twelve (12) had to sacrifice their life to him and the other twelve (12) had to earn the right to assist him. As those twelve (12) died, he could replace them with another twelve (12), who were on standby as they had earned the right to come through. This is the story of the Knights of the Round Table. Camelot is announcing to us the gathering of our intellectual light through our exploratory conditioning. It's also the story of

Solomon in the Bible, who also had the twelve (12) officers over all Israel, and don't forget the story of Zeus with his twelve. Hopefully now you can see how the stories in the Greek Philosophies and the Egyptian Philosophies coincide with the New Testament of Jesus and his twelve (12) Apostles. And now you can understand my stories are explaining to you that every one mentioned in this paragraph is guiding you to the inheritance of the twelve strands of our DNA.

These wonderful symbolic codes have kept this planet functioning for many thousands of years. When we delve into the depths of our cells is where we take ourselves deep into our own ocean, our own consciousness, we find that we have the opportunity to listen into the God within (higher self); by understanding these natural laws, they help us create our own possibilities.

During my education into these fields, I had the opportunity to view the brain and to take notice of how it functions. I began to notice small impulse signals, which were a bright light blue colour and watched as my thoughts created short little jabs of alchemical energy; I was metaphorically viewing my mathematics at work! A negative thought created static electricity which cut off the supply and caused the cells to stagger, which created a tinge of green light to reflect around the perimeter of the blue. A positive thought flows through the cells and releases the flow of adrenalin which autonomically empowers the DNA to open and release more information. Biblically this is known as the Ark of the Covenant. It is the store house of the unconscious mind (higher mind); the home of the hidden God you have just read about or more importantly, it is referred to as our heavenly home!

Our higher self/God within, speaks to us through the language of our body, to remind us when our thinking is incorrect. How do we become aware of this inner language? This was a trying time for my many thousands of students all around this wonderful home we have inherited, who had to learn to devote their mind to each movement of their body to be able to read the consequences of their thoughts. Remember, it also took me many years to bring the information into a format that I could understand in the beginning, before I could explain these sacred laws to them.

It is all connected through the mathematics of our electrical wiring which we have named our central nervous system which begins to vibrate through the soles of our feet; I refer to this one as the home of the God EL, which then has the journey to connect deeper into our glandular system. This system then traverses up through our spinal cord, into the brain where it passes through where we observe our memories, named the retina to the back of our eyes, so that we may see.

The next one is the peripheral nervous system which consists of sensory nerves that connect to one another which tap into the central nervous system, through the reaction of three of our five senses, touch, sound and sight (light). This system transmits signals throughout our glandular system, which stimulates our muscular movement. I refer to this one as our educational system, which is the home of the God AN, or Ang throughout the Asian Principles, which is situated around our solar plexus area. All of which has been passed down to us from the times of Ancient Egypt. Nothing is new! It has always been here! It is the results of these two systems working in unison together that creates the third God EA or written thousands of years ago as AEA.

These sequences automatically release with each thought we think. I have received answers to my questions, three months or sometimes it has taken fifteen years after I have asked myself the question. We expect that everything must happen right now. But, these trillions of cells that we are reconstructing within ourselves, must also be collected and connected beforehand to one another, to prepare us for our next moment.

Through my education of meditation, I could learn to silence my mind; not allow one new thought. I was told to stop thinking and become as God or the Laws of the Universe are, "They don't think they react. And a reaction is looking back into the gestation of each thought, to allow the truth to release itself. It is you who is playing the game, not the Law or this hidden God."

That light, that transformation, that transformer of the atomic energy inside your body, can only occur, if you believe in yourself. If you still refer to your doubt; how can you believe in self? Make it light. Know that you know. Hear that you hear. Speak that you speak. Be still, and let your thoughts collect all by themselves. It is amazing to view something that is being returned back to you. When we ask a question, speak it, now reverse what you have said and if you are still, allow the question to answer itself. The more you trust and believe in yourself, the more this hidden God and these natural laws react to your thoughts.

You walk in one world and the benefits from this become relevant to your positive behavior to create your next, and every cell listens and shines. If we allow ourselves to be free and explore this journey, we have the possibility of being heard right around the whole planet.

This whole quest of living your life to its fullest; it is a growth of your intelligence expanding itself. It becomes an automatic reaction where it delivers to create what we term as time; once you have entered into the eternal kingdoms of self, we find that there is no such thing as time; once the collective mathematics have done their work on your behalf.

It is as though we are standing in a hallway which has twelve (12) doorways, we can open those doors, where we have the possibility to go into different rooms, and maybe I could rearrange this paragraph and say that they are different ideas which are another way of looking at it. Through your stillness we learn to keep those doors open. As we begin to believe and trust in self, we automatically become involved with the twelve (12) tribes, but it is when you doubt yourself, that one of the doors automatically close, which delays the sequence you have set out to accomplish.

If you can learn to believe and trust in your thoughts, you can see how these natural laws of the universe work; it makes the job of believing in yourself so much easier. The natural law delegates your thoughts to work in with the autonomic responses of your central nervous system. The steps are all there, identical to the map left for us of decoding the scribes of Egypt (all explained in my book Decoding the Revelations of St. John the Divine') and when you get to a point of understanding and believing in self, you will learn to take the elevator; it's much easier and saves a lot of time.

I explain our holy grail as balancing and harmonizing our mind, just like the metronome, which will create a feeling of perpetual motion; we can store what we understand about our self, until we feel free to act upon it. That Holy Grail (cup) always pulses in tune to our heart beat. When our cup is filled with knowledge, it is important that the information is distributed out to attend to those personalities of our mind (aspects of self), that are still locked away through not being able to breathe their own breath; which again is all through our ego refusing to release its hold on its old playground where it felt secure.

When I had finished my journey, I was so full of knowledge from those many turbulent years that I was told to convert all of it back into a three- dimensional language. I did not have to come down, fall down or collapse; I had to Shamanic-ally explain each story differently, which emptied my cup.

Through respect, we as Avatar/Shaman learn to answer a question from those who have difficulties to hear themselves, we collate through our eternal wisdom by reversing our information back into their levels of knowledge. That is the key. Always remember, that whatever story you are explaining that you learn to speak in a language that will empty your cup of knowledge, as well as help those people fill theirs, so that they may understand what you are talking about. If they can understand the message, we know that what we have said is one third of the information being digested throughout them. Change your words, not your thinking. Every story that you tell, and every thought that you think, is for you. Listen to your own stories, to allow your mind to recreate them.

For two minutes each night before you go to sleep, you owe it to yourself to look inside to view the day's foregone events; remember also that the reflection that is manifested back to you becomes your futuristic intelligence, which is empowered to become the illusion of self, until you become the reflection of your own thinking. That reflection is what we call the light of God, the light of your own Genesis or beginning. It is where everything reconnects to your Soul!

When we ask something, and we do not receive an answer, it is because we do not fully comprehend the mathematics that set the scene in motion. Do not surmise or conjure; your mathematics will not release the truth until you have earned the answer; in other words, your mind has not equated enough as yet to receive! All will be revealed at exactly the right time; that's the journey.

When one of my teachers asked me to explain what I thought the consciousness was. I answered him with, "All that is. I am all of it; I am here to connect myself to it, where I can learn to bring myself together." "There is an easier way to understand how this information works," he said. He would always make me walk backwards, back to the point of where that thought came into my mind. "Stand up!" he would say, "Raise your right leg, see the word, and now focus on the word and watch the word, and lift." I discovered that Consciousness is one thought stretching and rearranging itself moment by moment; and that my dear reader is what we call reality. It was easier than I thought. Many times I toppled and knew I had forestalled the moment by trying to interfere with the greater good! Through my reality, my ego was trying to cut corners as it quickly became bored and refused to tolerate the conversation.

I learned to sit in my stillness year after year, with one thought in my mind at a time, where I had to explore the world I was busily creating, to see how many other worlds collated with each thought. Then I had to look at the pictures that my thinking had created in reverse to bring them all back into that original thought again. You would be amazed at just how far your intellect can open itself up, by looking at one word for three minutes. If your mind can stand still long enough, you will begin to notice the areas where your fear is able to trust in itself to have the confidence to release itself. I use these codes to help assist my dyslexic clients, or the child who has difficulties studying. One step at a time!

We can't take these codes away, as the energy of every disease of self is implanted into the DNA of the planet; all collated systematical through the reflection of our thoughts blanketing the earth. The magnification of these codes, unfold unto themselves. It has nothing to do with us.

I soon found out that through the journey of the Shaman, one must be totally responsible for self. This new thinking changed my inner dictionary as I came to realize that I was working with the physical worlds as well as the intellectual worlds of freedom, which ignites both hemispheres of our brain where they unite and become one.

As I journeyed forward, I felt my energy stretch itself back into my past at the same time. I was able to listen to my ancestors explaining their walk before me, and I realized that I could bring my ancestors up into this moment to become my ancient past and my future at the same time.

This again changed my inner language, which also helped in understanding the metaphysical language explaining these hidden codes. I realized that when the sun had set on yesterday, it brought the energy into abeyance, where it rose again today with new intellectual light. Therefore, I could not rely on looking back into yesterday to carry those thoughts into today. This brought about a repeat performance that I had already lived! As the sun rose in the new day, I understood how the energy ley lines that were congruent to yesterday were not suitable to the changes that my unconscious energy had prepared for me for today!

When we go to sleep, our fear pauses to rest. Whether we have nightmares or wonderful dreams, the unconscious mind is relaying to both our left and right hemispheres of the brain explaining a sequence to us in cryptic form how our mathematics are collecting for our tomorrows, or what we are busily precipitating for ourselves today. If our dreams are not our liking, know that the disturbance we have created and allowed to build up in our mind can be rectified. This is the image we have received from inside our nation—our imagination! These are our vision worlds, until we have found the strength to freely walk amongst them. Why not wake up into a new day, with fresh energy, a fresh mind, which allows our attention span to become vigorous with anticipation.

The part that keeps us sane is in knowing that we are vibrating our energy every day on this planet, and yet we have the potential to live in our silence at the same time. The Shaman lives in his or her own stillness; is afraid of nothing, as there is nothing to be afraid of, if there is no fear within. Fear when not being controlled always creates what is known as time for itself; and we now understand that time must always be rectified to become refined.

Are you hiding behind your shadows? Which positive or negative thoughts are you creating in this moment? Negativity is the dark, the dark is the shadow which closes our heart, it balks the light; the shadow is a reflection of the growth of the inner self depending on the strength you have within you. If you are afraid of standing in your own light, remember, the shadows deepen to create your next doubt. Positive thoughts are your light connecting to your oracle, which changes the vibration into becoming love which opens the heart up to greater expectations. Remember that the heart is one of our greatest tests to keep ourselves alive; and the number one killer of heart attacks is lack of happiness to self.

Understand how you can bring the shadows out from within you. It is the left brain (ego) which creates the shadow through Fear. Stop doubting everything you are hearing, and stop trying to correct the self. Stop creating a fear, and allow the child or the innocence within you to be loved. The more self-love you have for you, the less the child within you has to fear, therefore the less you doubt yourself. Doubt yourself and you lose, it is as simple as that.

It is only through our innocence or maybe it is our ignorance; also our insecurity that keeps our fear alive. You are your own tree of knowledge, and as your branches grow (lymphatic system) remember, that throughout the day the sun shines completely over and around you, and your shadow also moves around you; it does not stand still. The strength of your tree is reflected in every leaf and each leaf represents a page in your DNA. Speak the thoughts of your mind. There is only you and your truth that you must abide by. Our Lord Buddha taught us to sit within our own tree of knowledge, in amongst our own branches, and to weep no more.

Those leaves on your inner tree of knowledge are explaining the book that you are releasing at this time, until you realize that you are both sides of every leaf of your own tree, and each leaf represents the thoughts that you have manifested this season. The top side of the leaf is attracted to facing the light and the underside is quietly in abeyance, for the opportunity to present itself. The top side represents our outer perspective and the underside is representing our inner self. Both sides will become your hologram. Your holographic imprint comes from how you will create your thoughts, to blend not only throughout yourself; also, to show you how you blend with humanity.

When we think a thought and do nothing, that thought has to travel to a parallel world where it sits in the cosmic consciousness and awaits you. Remember all of these thoughts of yours, that have not been accrued, condense in your aura, which must be returned to you, until you get it right!

Shamanic-ally, we understand that we are many facets. We are our own spaceship, our own hologram, our own blueprint of the tribe we inherited, which continually unfolds itself. That means that many thoughts have the opportunity to relay a sense of peace through our wholeness. If we are the trunk of our own tree, through the Sha-man be-leafing in oneself, we can read every page that has been written on our behalf. We are then able to read all of the pages written in the seven seals that are supposedly in the Library of Alexandria.

I have watched my intellect grow beyond my own expectations as I opened up to understanding these sacred laws, my indemnity doubled and then tripled, the more confident I felt, to ordain me into believing in myself. I came to realize that the universe is standing beside me with every thought I think, always ready to assist me in my momentous decisions to ease my next step. The more silent I became, the more I could hear my next thought. It's a nice thought to know that my temple or heavenly, mind (which is the Buddha's head, that we place in our house or garden) is always releasing its mathematical energy to surround me.

My Shamanic journey ended with many eagles, spiraling above my head, climbing higher and higher when they initiated me and two eagles gave me their living Souls. Now that I have totally finished my journey, I look at all the knowledge and wisdom I gained over those nine difficult years and I realize that I am still me, where I have created a light so bright that sometimes I even blind myself!

Take note that the great Pyramid in Egypt had four ships buried at each of its corners, which relate to the four directions or Medicine Wheel that we use. Those ships represent the temple of how we earn our freedom to sail into the consciousness.
Omni

Chapter 28
Secrets Of The Medicine Wheel

Allow me explain another version of the secrets of the Medicine Wheel. Shamanism is the supreme biological training of the mind; the myths of history are also explained to us this way. The stories are the worlds of Metaphysics—or the matter of physics—that is, our consciousness evolved through the mathematics collecting the energy of the unconscious mind, which urged us to move forward through the Medicine Wheel of our body.

NORTH—ABOVE

The direction of north is up and forward, no matter which way we are facing. When we relate it to the body, the north begins around the neck area and goes up to the crown of the head. We enter into the north in order to grow and receive; this is the land of the invisible myth. The north is the top of the mountain; it is how the stories of the Bible were created in the first time.

The Bible is written in code for you to understand the inner you; not the planet as a whole. Do you remember the old saying, "Go north, and you will find it!"? One of my late father's sayings to me was, "Go north, and your search will find you; you can learn to release the thoughts that you have earned from understanding yourself."

SOUTH—BELOW

The direction of south begins through the world of understanding ourselves. In our body, the south begins with the feet and legs, and goes up to just above the navel area. South is where we have stepped into the underworld, through the worlds of our fear; it is where we go into our darkness to discover our inner light. That world was created for us through the trepidations of our forefathers and -mothers, who neither understood nor accomplished their Divine Inheritance.

In my case, the south was where I had to learn and earn my trust. It is the primordial evolution; in other words, it is the place we climb into where we overprotect our thinking. Some call this experience 'voodoo'. I remember my teacher explaining to me that Sigmund Freud was a great teacher of voodoo. Voodoo is where the mind overpowers the emotions. Carl Jung was a teacher of the occult, and that is where the emotions over power the mind.

It depends on whether the left or right brain is in control in that moment. They were both right, and if we could harmonize and bring both together, we would have earned the understanding of the Oracle of Life.

EAST—WITHIN

The direction of east is the story of the connection to the inner self. The east is the area of the body that begins around the heart area, going out to the release of the action of the right arm and up to the base of the throat. The Bible explains the story of the Wise Men from the East The wisdom of the Collective comes from the east, which is brought through to the right hemisphere of the brain and also through the action that comes from the right hand. It is an ensuing consequence resulting in a positive intelligence. We realign with the knowledge of the Soul's intelligence.

WEST—WITHOUT

The direction of west is the arid or empty spaces in the mind. It is the left brain and the action that comes from our left hand. In Shamanism, we go west—or into the wilderness—to dichotomize in order to bring all of our knowing together. Do you remember the story of Eli who went into the wilderness to attain his own inner word? This is the world of listening to the self; and, from listening, we begin to hear that which is important for us to nourish and accept, in order to see how far we have come. West is the last direction that we go to before we ascend into the mastering of the east, which is awoken through our own vibration confirming itself.

We gather information, and, as it filters through, it becomes our worlds within worlds, and it builds us up emotionally. I liken this to equating all the information into balancing both brains, where we have the possibilities of using our information through the harmony of both brains coming together. The light we bring forth expands through every cell that is embedded within. We can explain that story from the inner or outer—or from the logic or creative. We are all different; we use our personalities in the ways that suit our own moment. I am mastering me, and I am always searching for more in the Collective. In other words I am bringing energy into me; I dichotomize and release it back out again, where I become my educated mind through using my inner heavenly energy.

It does not matter which direction we face on the planet, it is the movement of consciousness in our own force fields that is the Fung Shwa. We are our own compasses, so we can create the four directions—or that Medicine Wheel within our body.

The 'Western Wall', which was supposedly built on Mount Moriah in Jerusalem, is the only section of the Holy Temple that still stands after the Romans' destruction of it. That wall symbolically supports those who gather there to strengthen their own beliefs. We in the West need that support; we need it in order to believe in that which we are accomplishing within ourselves.

On a trip through North Africa to Mali, an Elder of the Touaarik tribe (this tribe is also called 'Tuareg') gave me a compass that they have used for thousands of years in the desert, in order to travel from oasis to oasis. It is created in the sign of the cross. He explained how the compass works in the sand. The sand reads the shape of the compass, and the priests read the energy waves that the sand creates. The reading is construed through the mathematical vibration of the silica that is produced through the sand, where it releases the light; they explained to me that they were never lost in the desert, as the light always points in the direction of the north.

Those High Priests have been looking after the 'tomb of the books of truth'—or the ancient Library of Tumbouktu (pronounced in English as, 'Timbuktu') for nearly 2,000 years; they still wear the same style of garment and symbols, and they still rely on the compass to direct them as they collect and scribe the ancient languages of the past.

At the beginning of our quest, we are introduced to the side of the world that is opposite from our own. It is through this attainment that we humans can reach our future without the dilemmas that we create along the way. Many people, when coming into the connection of self with an enquiring mind, have an urge to take a journey to Tibet, China, Japan, or India. We have an urge to reach out away from our homeland. Why? We need to search for our opposite; maybe we have a desire to taste the unknown and stretch our boundaries to see how far we can go. And then we must begin to connect with the four corners—from the south to the north, and from the west to the east—that is the square becoming the circle, in which we search for information regarding the Medicine Wheel, which represents the Collective.

When decoded through the Sacred Alphabet, the interpretation for the word 'human'is: 'The heavenly understanding of mastering and ascending through nourishing our self'. An easier rendition is 'the heavenly understanding of man'.
Omni

Chapter 29
The Sacred Alphabet

In this chapter I have included in condensed form, information in reference to the Sacred Alphabet from my book 'Decoding the Mind of God'. When we go back to the first language of man, we can see the evolution of the Sacred Alphabet, as well as how the collection of our tribal heritage has programmed our own language into us, which autonomically creates our own intelligence. Our language—or 'land-gauge' is where we learn to mathematically gauge or measure the intelligence of ourselves in order to feel comfortable releasing it out to the rest of humanity.

From the moment of your gestation, your memory banks become embedded with this information; this is a repertoire presented to you through the Divine Inheritance to explain to you why and how your Soul was designed to be here—why you were placed here as a quasar to represent your family. This was all happened nine months before you inhaled your first breath of air. All this intellectuality springs forth through you religiously asking yourself a question— which is created through an emotional response to those memories, and which allows them to release into the personalities that create your thinking. Read the text over again until you feel comfortable; only then will you know that you have reminded yourself of the connection that you have made with those ancient memories that have created your past. These are the pages of the second God "AN"; they are the books of your inner library—the recorded history of your grandmothers and grandfathers and of all your ancestors.

I will initiate you into some of the basic structure of words that we use to urge ourselves forward. We can add to, but not subtract from, this list of words. This list will allow you to learn the codes of the Sacred Alphabet, which you will repeat according to your own intelligence accepting the nurturing from its self. Through the belief of trusting in self, and through you accepting your intellectual advantages for your own personal gain, you will see these words change.

THE BASIC CODES TO THE SACRED ALPHABET.

A. Ascension. Activate. Attitude. Antenna.
B. Before. Beginning. Balance. Beauty.
C. Creation. Christ. Create. Comply. Complete.
D. Depth. Death. Desire. Define. Divine. Divinity.
E. Energy. Eternal. Evolve. Essence.
F. Fate. Faith. Form. Freedom. Fly.
G. God. Greatness. Gift.
H. Have. Hold. Horizon. Highness. Heaven.
I. Intelligence. Intuition.
J. Jesus. Judgment. Justice.
K. Knowledge. Knowing. Knife.
L. Love. Light. Life.
M. Measure. Master. Martyr.
N. Nourish. Nurture.
O. Oracle. Oneness.
P. Power. Pulse. Presence. Potent.
Q. Quest. Question. Query. Queen. Quell. Quintessence.
R. Release. Reign. Royal.
S. Search. Soul. Spirit. Sword. Source. Sound.
T. Trial. Trust. Truth. Tone.
U. Understanding. Urge. Uphold. Upon. Unto.
V. Victory. Valor. Value.
W. Wise. Wisdom. Will. Wind. Weave.
X. Xenium. (Latin: "to see the measurement from within")
Y. Yearn. Young. Yield. Yoke.
Z. Zenith.

MY SHAMANIC NAMES

Through my journey I received many names; by this, I mean that I received the vibration of the name. The last vibration I received came to me in the year 2000, and I use a shortened version of it: Omni. I have had to learn and accept the language of the alphabetical inheritance to the codes of each name. For twelve years, I was known as Om Mira, and I had grown quite satisfied with that name; but, once I had conquered it, I had to release it. Both names were "nicked" in order for my students to be able to pronounce them. The reason for this new name became known to me when I went to Europe in the late '90s, as that is when I was asked to teach and explain my academic stature.

Years previously at the beginning of my education, my name changed every few days; at first, I thought it was a joke being played out on me. Slowly, I began to notice that the names were becoming stronger, longer and more difficult for me to pronounce. I realized that I was being introduced into the alphabetical inheritance of Babylon; this is explained in chapter 5 of the Book of Genesis, which describes the generations of Adam, who lived for 930 years. The biblical stories of the twelve tribes of Israel also explain the change of names (i.e., who begat whom, etc.). Thus, I realized that the names I was given in the beginning were references to the names of our own educational systems that are embedded in our DNA; these names were a challenge, designed for me to try to understand all this knowledge—and many a laugh resulted as I opened up my inner dictionary.

That was when I began to realize that I was bringing myself up and through the alignments that society takes for granted. In other words, I realized that the joke was on me—I had to answer the challenge and speak from the wisdom of the name that I had been given. My memorial genetics were opening up, and I learned to conquer those earnings in double quick time. I had to be able to master those ideologies in a matter of days; but, once I understood the title—or name—I became all of it, and my commitment to the name and the challenge became much easier.

After that point, my name was challenged and changed again; the education for that next title began as soon as I had completed the understanding of the previous one. I was working my way up through the levels of the language of the unconscious mind; therefore, my earnings accelerated as my thinking became faster, and, so too, did my time. It took years of this training— through frustration beyond comprehension—for me to keep on correcting my intelligence, as I had to accept what was placed in front of me. There was no walking away from any of it; and, if I did walk away, nothing happened—my mind went into an abeyance until I could go back over my teachings and pick up from where I had left off.

So, as the names changed I realized that they were being given to me in three different levels. The beginning of the education brought forth more information from my endocrine system; this system begins to open up in our childhood, so the message was delivered to me more as a nursery rhyme, or a fairy story. As the name grew into the next level, it opened up to strengthen my immune system; this system begins to collect when we birth into our teenage years, awakening the inner warrior. Our personalities begin to unravel at that point, and our inner dictionary becomes much more colloquial; we learn to find the strength to place our own point of view out to others. As I accepted more responsibility for this education, my original name grew and became more advanced, which placed the responsibility onto my lymphatic system. Those three stages of names brought that frequency into a dependable explanation of how I would be able to mirror myself back to humanity. The circle of energy had been completed; thus, my next world could begin. This is exactly what I explain regarding the concordance of why our stories are carved on the walls of Egypt. The wonderful ancient Egyptians have left us the initiations to succeed; they inscribed the sacred codes into the walls, as to how we can understand our journey into the afterlife—or the next world. No, we have not gotten that story exactly right—not just yet, anyway.

Each of my Shamanic names provided a language of separation and advancement for me to grow through. As each step of my intellect unfolded, it became easier for me to find the answers to my own questions, as well as to answer those questions that I had received from others. When we accept each level of our truth, we are welcomed into a more advanced tribe in order to experience our life through these higher levels of understanding. Once I had brought all those vibrations into their fullness, through mastering myself, my life was held in abeyance until the next name came through.

As I said, it took an immense amount of study over the years to earn the full Sacred Alphabet, complete with the learning capacity for each of my names. It was when I understood the language that the Bible was written in—in all its totality—that the names were transferred into me. I was pleased with my endowment of Omni, and I realized that now I must live up to it—that was my challenge and my responsibility. This placed a totally different slant on things. My total responsibility is now focused on the words that I speak, and, always, I know that my truth reigns supreme. The vibration of the full name I received in 2000 is "Om-ni-aar-elle" (abbreviated "Omni", as I mentioned). As this name began to enter into my life, I did not want to accept the changes, at first; I felt very comfortable with my name at that time ("Om Mira"), which had supported me well. Again, as mentioned, I had been invited to Europe to teach, and I was very quickly becoming internationally renowned, speaking to many people from different lands, through many interpreters. I had moved out from the safety net of my own land, and I had not fully realized the responsibility that was being placed on my shoulders.

I refused the name Omniaarelle for six long weeks, as it seemed too hard to pronounce and far too long, but I soon learned. The number of students attending my classes was cut in half, my car broke down, my radiator burst, my phone was disconnected, and the heating system in my apartment blew up. Many cataclysmic events occurred in my life through my refusal to accept that new name. Everything stopped through my refusing to take my next breath and hold myself in abeyance; in other words, I had turned my back on myself. The Universe would not accept excuses from me! The Cosmic Attitude is: "This is it—take it or leave it!" The prophet could not profit, so life became extremely hard, financially. I realized that the creator had stood by me through all those years of my training, and I also knew that I had to accept that this higher education I had received was not only for me, it was also for me to release this information so that all humanity could accept and understand. They would receive those understandings through the same opportunities that I had been given, and they would bring that written information back within to connect to themselves. I had worried what the new students would think when I introduced myself to them the following month; as they were just getting used to my name (Om Mira). I forgot, of course, that my ego could no longer be in control of my destiny.

I was at a turning point in my life—which happens to all of us twice a year—I had to retrace my own constituency and come back into my own palace of worthiness. The creation of all had tenderly shown me what I was here to do, which was to lead humanity into its next step of evolution of awareness. He loved me, even when my strength was at its weakest point, and he was prepared to wait until I could find myself again. As I gathered myself together, sending my love and courage back into myself, my strength returned to support me once more. That name, which I shortened to Omni, is a code of recognition through the Collective Consciousness. Once I accepted the responsibility of my new name, my classes filled up within seven days, and my house came back into order. That is how it all works.

Accept your livable moment! Do not worry about next week, and always remember that last week is finished. If you are correct in your thinking now, the future is automatically preparing next week, on your behalf. The secret is to keep the mind both pliable and available, through allowing your mind to become the light of your life. In order for you to evolve into your next thought, come back into the moment. It is the vibration of the sound before the word releases that sets the Metaphysical language of the brain into action. We are on this earth to live, love, and become complete—so do not waste a moment of it!

Throughout my training to receive the breath of Shamanism, many Elders from other cultures came to Australia and initiated me into their own tribal laws. Most of these Elders were men who arrived on my doorstep uninvited; I received only four women. Those magnificent people who had also earned their Shamanic experiences, only stayed long enough to give me their gift of consciousness and to initiate me into my new name, which their tribe had bestowed on me, and then they disappeared out of my life as quickly as they had come into it. They came to Australia representing the cultures that had evolved before mine. All of them knew the story of my family tribe and could explain parts of my life to me, which, at that time, I had not yet been made fully aware of.

My Australian Aboriginal name is 'Rainbow Wadjinda'. That name, through the English interpretation of the Pit-Jan-Jat-Jarra tribe, means 'Illumination of the Ocean'. If we look at the word Wadjinda through the Sacred Alphabet, Wadj means 'wisdom ascending through the Divine Justice'. Inda interprets as 'intelligence nourishing through Divine Ascension' or, simply, 'to search'. When decoded through the Egyptian language, Wadj means 'serpent'. Do you see now how the Aborigines first understood the codes and came to the fruition of the Rainbow Serpent?

THE SACRED ALPHABET AND EVERYDAY LIVING

Here are some of my explanations to a few words that I have decoded through the Sacred Language.

NAOMI: Nourish – Ascend – Oracle – Master – Intelligence. Through nourishing, I will ascend the Oracle and master my intelligence.

PETER: Power – Eternal – Truth – Evolve – Release. Through the power of eternal truth, I evolve and release.

Palenque: 'Pha-EL-AN-Que' is the name of the lid that covered the tomb of the Sun God, Lord Pacal. Pacal is pronounced 'Pha-Kha-EL'. The lid is a story that relates to the unconscious mind of man; therefore, we must read the story in reverse. This lid is explaining, symbolically, the spaceship that we all become when we have completed our Spiritual Quest and are delivered up into the realms of the unconscious intelligence.

Akashic: Let me break this up into the first time that it was released, and we conversed with one another, referring to it as the 'Ark of Ashes'. We reverse this title, as it relates to the language of the unconscious mind, as the 'Ashes of the Ark'. This is known as the Resurrection in the Bible. Another name is the phoenix, the bird rising from the ashes of its own pyre, from the Mayan principles and/

or the Asiatic philosophies. It is also known as the Golden Pheasant, and it explains the Book of Revelations. The Ark represents you releasing your past—your DNA—as you birth into the generations of Noah (the 'knower of ways').

Record: To 're-cord'. Re means 'to return back into the light of self'—that is, to the 'silver cord', as we symbolically refer to the DNA—or 'to reconnect us with our life force'. This is the cumulative inheritance of the evolution of man. Now we can realize our truth as to how the Akashic Records have collected that name.

Trident: This is the spear in the right hand of the old man of the sea (Poseidon, Neptune, Triton, etc.). When we take this symbol way back in time, it is not the trident; symbolically, it is representing the horns that relate to the power of the bull, with the penis coming up between both horns. There is nothing negative about these ancient signs; they merely expressed the connivance that our sexual energy plays so wonderfully. We find our freedom, symbolically, through these old explanations of the Gods. Do you see how Michelangelo carved the statue of Moses with the two small horns?

Cappadocea: One of the most fascinating places I have been to in Turkey. Now this is how we spell—or spin—the word. The Turkish pronounce it as 'Kha-Pha-Dhak-EA', but the mountain people explain it somewhat differently. They pronounce it as 'Papa-Di-Ark-EA'. As you can see, the two explanations are slightly behind the more pronounced version that we know (also written as Cappadocia). This land, through the shapes of its rock formations, is an exquisite explanation of the power or penis. These upright carvings, which look like the penis with a cap on its head, have been created by the wind; or, more precisely, the measurement of the energy that holds the land together. Hence, the word cap; to the more common language, they look like the father figure. Also in this area are other carvings that have naturally been honed by the wind, where we see animals gathering together, which represent the evolution of the human brain. This area is also known throughout other Arabic nations as 'the gathering place for Noah to fill the Ark'.

Lah Dhak: A city in Tibet. (In reference to the above paragraph, also provides the same explanation regarding the mountains in Tibet.) The Tibetan pronunciation of this city is 'EL-Lagh-Dhak-EA', using different emotions and explanations of the language. Those penis-shaped structures are there for the entire world to see (the same as the structures described above in Cappadocea, Turkey). I have some amazing photos of these structures, as well as the shapes of the animals that have evolved through the Divinity of these hills. As the wind wove its way through the valleys, it created the shapes of the animals that were compatible to the mathematics of the emotional responses of the people who expressed their sexual – or egotistical – language throughout that area. These are the guardians of the 'Land of the Penis'. God has placed the Soul of our evolution completely around the planet, through the evolution of the species, in order for us to connect and mirror back into our selves. We are the Ark and the animals. They are a reminder of our evolution connecting to the twelve lesser Gods within.

Calcutta: This is Golgotha in the Bible. In the Italian language, it is pronounced as 'Kolkotta'. Through the codes, this is an explanation of the 'gold of God'; it also relates to the philosopher's stone – or the Alchemy of the mind. Nice name isn't it? So why are these people all living under sufferance? They have been drawn to this area; when will their world turn for the better?

Xian: 'Chi An'. When interpreted, this name is encoded as 'the energy of our journey through our education system in order for us to release ourselves up into the next level of God'. This is the city where the old Silk Road began. Is this city more powerful than any other? Are all the people here satisfied with their progress? Why are people drawn to these areas? Why do they call it home? We do know that, thousands of years ago, the Pyramids were also built underground, around this area, which is filled with the mythical biblical inheritance in regard to its name.

No matter what country I have visited, I was introduced to someone who still held the codes of long ago; these people were there to remind me of the original story, as it is instilled in their minds, and they, through their inheritance, had never forgotten it.

Chechnya: A place name frequently in the news. Let me speak this name through the codes to see what it tells us about that country. 'Che-Che-ANEA' is connected through the relationship to the energy of the two higher Gods. 'AN' is through our educational system, which relates to our Soul, and "EA" is through the heavens. Listen to how the locals pronounce the name of their country, and you will hear the voice of their God initiating you into their land.

Every country, city, town, and village has been named through an emotional complement to the language of the Universal Laws. For example, listen to the sound of the word before you look at the spelling of the names of places in ancient Egypt; as we hear from within, so it shall become. You will find those same names in China, India, the Americas, Europe, Polynesia, and also in my own country,

Australia. The Aborigines of my isolated continent speak and sound this early language of Babylon. We see how all these countries learned to pronounce their vowels; whether they used an a, e, i, o, or u to create the name, depended on the intelligence of the person who was speaking.

It is through the acceptance of numbers that we are introduced up into the Sacred Geometry.
Omni

Chapter 30
Numerology

In this chapter, I have included in condensed form, information in reference to Sacred Numerology from my book *Decoding the Mind of God*. All numbers are powerful, when you fully understand the value of the thought that they must work with. The numbers of your birthday add up to a language of the responsibility you have the opportunity to uphold. The Divinity of Numbers, which collects through the Sacred Alphabet, works through the intelligence of the Metaphysical language which is registered through the higher mind. It is through the acceptance of numbers that we are introduced up into the Sacred Geometry. It creates a structure, where we can conform and become all things through using the strength of our numbers, one digit at a time. Each number is created through a resonance that empowers itself, alerting the conscious, subconscious, and unconscious minds (higher self)—all of which multiplies through this additional intellect, and we learn to harmonize our thoughts with our self and with one another.

Allow me to initiate you into explaining the Shamanic Inheritance of numbers and their meanings.

1. I Am.

2. My Relationship; comes through acknowledging myself.

3. My Mind; is everything I am.

4. My Temple; my inner self; my education into discovering my darkness and my light.

5. My Freedom; I earn through the changes I have made to my self.

6. My Mastering; the gathering of one's self to master the understanding of all thought. Our ego loses its control over us when we accept the responsibility for every thought that we think. Can you see how 666 became the mark of the beast? It is not negative; it is a powerful number which informs us of the responsibility we have to live up to in order to know our own mind.

7.   My Communication; it is our intuition; it belongs to our teacher within. It produces our light, which we have labelled our Christ consciousness. This number is also in relationship to the knowledge of the angelic realms.

8.   My Balance and Harmony; this is the sign of infinity; where everything is available and waiting for you.

9.   My Death; to my old ways, through the education of my understanding and knowing all.

0.   My Soul; my Alpha and Omega.

When the numbers become double digits, we relate to the above and bring them together.

10.   I Am my Soul.

11.   I Am as I Am.

12.   I Am my Relationship.

And so on, throughout the numbers. Thus, we are affirming and collecting our intellect with each digit.

When the numbers vibrate into the twenties, it is through the connection to the number two (2), which represents the relationship we can attain through self. When we reach up to the thirties, we are opening up into the mind of self; we are embellishing ourselves to our mind. The forties are much higher, and they begin to collect up into the temple of self. This is where we never try to repeat our mistakes. Both brains are realizing their intelligence, and this is where we are being tested through the consciousness to abstain from thinking in a negative way. We are beginning to enter up into the unconscious recognition of our mind. The fifties are, through the changes of the old ways, where we are able to release to earn the freedom of self. The sixties are, through the gathering of self, where we begin to familiarize and master self. The seventies are the teachings of self, where we have the ability to unconsciously reflect our intellectual earnings out in order to teach others. The eighties are the harmonizing of self with the infinite, where we begin to prosper. The nineties are the belief of knowing self, where we have the ability to move into the next thought and/or attract ourselves up into the next world.

Each step of your intelligence that you awaken from its long, deep sleep advances outside your own reflection, where others are alerted to your energy, and it is also where you become aware of them, before they see you. They are waiting for you to move into their psyche, as they know that you can help them answer their questions. Once they learn to understand themselves, they then move into yours. The world is full of beauty and grace, isn't it? We are always in the right place at the right moment. When I was collaborating with all of this ultra mathematics during my training, my heart ached so much at the wonderment of how these Universal Laws are always permanently working on our behalf. This gave me so much more confidence, and it opened my heart up to where I could understand how to release myself into the arms of the creator of all things.

When we have three repetitions of the number one (i.e., 111), we are starting to collect the mind together. We begin here by looking at the number one (1), which is 'I am', and, as there are three repetitions, we realize that this denotes as, 'I am my mind'. The 'I am' is being reminded of your awakening, and now you must make an important decision to trust yourself more and move forward into the relationship of self—that is, you must not keep on thinking that your mind is in charge of you.

Let me briefly explain the number 1,000,000; there are two ways of explaining these digits. From the left brain, we would respond to 'I am forming a relationship to my Soul mind', and the right brain would read them as 'I am mastering my Soul'. The left brain is slower at comprehending each digit; whereas, the right brain is multifaceted. We are able to comprehend how the right brain is presenting a stronger belief in what we have already accomplished and attained.

These numbers have begun to collect and multiply on a subconscious level, and, when you become aware of the growth of your intellectual achievements, each number begins to appear before your eyes; this is where you are autonomously opening up your inner vision. Your intelligence seems to be climbing up your inner ladder of success as your DNA unravels through accepting its own strength. Other people who are familiar with you notice these changes; they begin to realize how assertive you are feeling towards yourself.

It takes time for the body to adjust to this new way of thinking, as you are being pushed out of your old safety harness. It is a much higher intellectual code of you understanding just what your capabilities are able to accomplish on your behalf. You are communicating through to your master system, which is opening up a doorway into your unconscious mind. You are automatically collecting your own self-worth.

How many of you have a repetition of the same number on your number plate, phone number, or bank account? One lady, who read out her bank account numbers during a seminar where I was explaining the Sacred Numerology, came to the realization that the only winner was the bank! She changed her bank and her account number, and she has never looked back. Her friend who sat next to her had the same bank, but she was of a different personality, and so her account numbers worked well for her, and she had no need to change. It all depends on which personality of self you allow to rule.

Numbers work in the negative, as well as the positive, and the Laws of the Universe present them to you for a reason—or a resonance—in order for you to work through them and bring your thoughts up into a balance that is part of the Collective. Remember that the conscious mind works in single digits, and the responsibility is yours to accept, emotionally, how you collate to bring those numbers together. The totality of the answer presented to you will depend on how the sonar, which you symbolically create, registers your mathematics back to you as to what you have already achieved; this is delivered back to you in its pure truth. We cannot lie with numbers.

Maybe now you can understand how the employees of major corporations who think that they can 'help themselves' to reap the benefits of money that is not theirs in the first place always get caught in the long run. You cannot keep lying to the Collective; it is much stronger than you are. Karma will always be returned to you, especially when you are over controlling someone else's attention. Stock markets crash, banking industries falter, etc.; always, this is the result of our action spiraling ever higher. Other people have invested in this or that company in order to reap their own rewards, but usually not to keep the company functioning on its own merits. Remember, the ultimate aim of the language of the unconscious energy always finalizes everything we think and do in numbers. If the results of your action do not strike you, those close to you in the next generations (i.e., your children, grandchildren, and so on) will certainly inherit your lies. This is the ultimate deliverance to the mathematics of our mind.

It does not matter how many digits you wish to use; they must be sounded out one at a time, in the beginning, in order for you to learn this higher code of conscription. Let us take, for example, one of the most powerful numbers: 333. We do not group the number as 'three hundred thirty three'; instead, we repeat the singular sound—'three, three, three'. We know that the number three (3) represents the Mind of God, so when we group these three numbers together, the result becomes the 'mind's mind'. Through saying this, we release an understanding that the mind must measure the mind, and so the competition is on. This is in relationship to left-brain thinking.

Now allow me give you a positive, which is accepted as the responsibility of the right brain's intuitiveness, and say that 'the mind mirrors the mind'. This equation is so much more positive, and it is what our pituitary gland relies upon: $3 + 3 + 3 = 9$. The number nine (9) is the last of the single digits; when decoded, it equates to the symbol of death. We are talking about the Noah – or the 'Knower of ways' – here; it is an ending of one world in order for us to die to our old ways so that we can be free to advance into the next one.

We begin to bring together those 'three threes' (333) that have eclectically and divinely collected through the religious experience of self. When we view the symbol of the 'OM", you will see that the Sanskrit character looks like the number three (3). Symbolically, this explains to us that our understanding, acceptance, and action become one, and this union must equalize each hemisphere of the brain into 'one-ness'. Now we can understand how the number nine (9) is an ending that allows the step up into the next world to present itself to us so that we can go on.

Another powerful number is the number is the number ten (10). When we refer to this number, we have automatically opened up into the subconscious mind, which is the wisdom of the right brain. This explains to you the resonance known as 'Akhenaton', who was supposedly the tenth Pharaoh in Egypt. Remember that the first nine numbers are in single digits. So, when we reach up to the number ten (10), we are bringing in the zero (0) to repeat ourselves again. This time, we are including the right brain, as well as the left. This is where the word dichotomy is collected, and we become much more responsible for everything we say and do. We are awakening and connecting to the inner truth.

Through my eyes, when I had fully understood the mathematics of this beautiful being of light that we have named Akhenaton, I could understand what he was representing through his own purification of his intelligence; I definitely wanted to learn more. He was both male and female (or was it pronounced 'phi-male' at that time?)

This explains his body shape that is recorded in his statues. He was announcing to us the next evolutionary step that humanity can step up into, which is the Metaphysical journey of enlightenment. And remember that the word Metaphysics is reminding us of the matter of physics; explaining how matter evolved into becoming pure. Through my eyes, he represents the first person in history who honoured himself.

HOW WE RELY ON NUMBERS TO READ THE HIDDEN LANGUAGE

The next step is to introduce you further into the worlds of Shamanism—that is, the way in which we rely on numbers to read the hidden language of how the Collective is reimbursing our truth back to us. This is also your introduction into the language of the body. We begin with the hidden language of God, who lives in your consciousness and vibrates your thoughts up into the Collective Consciousness; this is where and how the mathematics began to equate telepathically with your Soul. The more stimulated your thoughts become, the more opportunities you will be able to use to your benefit. Do you see how I am bringing both the languages of religion and science together? Remember, your ego needs religion, and your emotions need science; you must have both in order for you to benefit and advance the left and right hemispheres of the brain up into their temple inheritance.

Whatever thought you have in your mind is automatically being reflected back to you instantly; this happens as soon as you allow your mind to think. The world is your mirror, and it is always assessing your thinking. It sounds ridiculous, doesn't it? Every thought you think to form a continuance of your energy creates a sentence, which, in turn, is reflected back to you. It begins from the first sentence that you hear on the TV when you turn it on. Spilling your drink, dropping a cup, slipping on the floor, cutting your finger, etc. All these are part of the process. Remember, there is never a mistake! Every consequence in your life is through the results of your thinking; all of it mirrors back to you, every moment of every day. When you are out walking, the bird in the sky, or the dog or cat walking across your path, is a mirror image of your thought in that moment. If you see or hear car tires screeching around a corner, and the brakes slammed on; if a fire engine races by, or an ambulance siren screams in the distance—please start to take notice of what is surrounding you.

If a car horn sounds once when you are out walking, you must immediately bring your thought back to the self. This single sound means that you need to pay attention to your thoughts, as they are running away from you; you're losing control! That horn is a warning, so watch the thought you are having in that moment. If the car horn sounds twice, it means that you must come back into yourself and rebalance your mind; you need to come back and form a relationship with these thoughts of the moment. If it sounds three times, it means pay attention to the whole experience of your thinking. When we hear the same sound four times, it means that it is a sign of destruction to a temple thought, so eradicate your thoughts immediately and begin again.

If you notice a bird in the sky, it reminds you to think from an angelic perspective; please fly higher with your thoughts of that moment. Remind yourself that you should use it in the singular; that thought should only be used for the self. That angel with wings is saying to you, "Come on, move up and fly higher!" Two birds relate to the relationship of your thoughts; in other words, start to bring your thoughts into the Collective Mind. Three birds relate to your mind; start to improve your thinking, etc.

If you hear a dog bark, it means that you are dwelling in the past with your thinking; the animal mind relates to our ancient past. Count the number of barks, and then refer to the list above. Dogs represent the emotion of loyalty, so that dog is reminding you to be loyal to your thinking. Stop wasting your time with miscellaneous thinking!

I would like to explain to you how the Collective is answering your thoughts, whether it is a fly buzzing around you, a beetle walking on the ground, a leaf falling from a tree, and so on. Humankind has evolved from the first species to inherit the earth. They have been created through one of them believing in themselves. As each species created the next generation, we all inherited. Man is the last to evolve, and our brain has been created through every other species earning their own emotional inheritance. The whole planet is a thought that learned to believe in itself. Learn how we are able to see how the human brain invested in itself! Where does your animal live in your body, and what emotion does it represent in you? Where does your bird tribe live in you? Where in you is the fish of the ocean? Why have the eternal species invented the insect world?

You can use the Sacred Alphabet and Sacred Numerology whilst you are sitting in your car in traffic. Decode the number plates of the cars around you; those signs are in your vision world for a reason—or, as some of you refer to it, a 'coincidence'. Now say that word correctly, breaking it up into syllables: 'co-inside-essence', which is interpreting the 'corporation inside the essence'. Now we will reverse those words: 'the essence inside the corporation'. Interesting, isn't it, that this is the language of the brain, and what we refer to as the unconscious mind is also the energy of our Soul?

The letters and numbers on the cars coming towards you are the incoming messages regarding your day ahead. The ones going away from you are in regard to your thinking and where it is leading you in that moment. When I was heading off to work at my clinic for the day, I was always alerted to what my day could perceive for me through reading the numbers and letters around me as I travelled to work. I always read the number plates of the first seven vehicles; if it was a truck, it imparted a different message. (All these explanations are in other sections of the book concerning the subject.) In the beginning of my training, on a conscious level, I was innocently unaware of what I was doing; however, my subconscious mind was alerting me to the fact that my unconscious mind was directing back to me. I became more aware of the power of numbers. "How could this be so?" was my cry to the Universe. "Why is everything so exact? How could this vision give me my immediate answers to all of my thoughts, so intellectually?" I became so excited when this information began to filter through my mind. Each time you see a car number plate, street, or city name, put the meanings of the Sacred Alphabet and Numerology together.

Here is an example of a number plate and its meaning: MUW-9496. The letters M-U-W mean, 'the mastering of my thought is through understanding my wisdom'.

9 means: 'Knowing all.'
4 means: 'My temple.'
9 again: 'Through my relationship of self, I know it all.' In other words, you are allowed no excuses.
6 means: 'Become the master of self.'

Or we can read the message as the numbers 94 and 96. The number 94 it means, 'through knowing all, I am my temple'. The number 96 means, 'through knowing all, I master my thoughts'. That number plate is acknowledging that the principle thought that collected itself is available for you so that you can use the energy that unconsciously has been collected just for you. And this is the power of the mathematics of the mind; it is available for every human being, all at the same time.

Always, your totem energy is working with you.
The Laws of the Universe are always serving you.
Omni

Chapter 31
Totem Energy

Through the 'Totem' energy of all, the ancient species that have evolved before us, represent an emotional inheritance that we can rely on to sustain our moment. They will become the beneficial advisers to help us with our own intelligence when our mind is in the fields of doubt. Throughout this chapter will be scattered paragraphs from previous chapters but let us revisit those words.

As we release the Shamanic Principles from within, Metaphysics describes how every myth was an inner kingdom that each human could find within themselves. Through the Collective Consciousness, we connect unconsciously with every story that has ever been written, spoken, and collected mathematically.

A Shaman is trained to accept and become the measurement of the emotional harmonics of all the species that have evolved on this planet. During the inheritance of our Totem, our energy fields are multifaceted; that energy then collects and builds up into a force field, which is of exactly the same mathematics as the electromagnetic fields of the planet. Every Shaman must learn to realize the frequencies that each animal, plant, or mineral commits to the Collective for them to have also inherited their Earth.

The Gods—be they Mayan, Arabic, Aboriginal, or Asian—those giants who walked before us, are the propelling emotions of our totem energy; that is, they form the wisdom that we are able to draw from the evolution of the species, which we need to strengthen us when we doubt our own possibilities. When we are devoid of these emotions, the Gods replace in us what we are too afraid to accept about ourselves. This is the strength of the totem energy, which has been mathematically collected through the Universal Laws of God.

At the start of my journey into the Shamanic world began with the birds and animals that entered into my vision world to support me. Out West we had a butterfly plague for over twenty one days with millions of bright blue butterflies fluttering everywhere. We all had difficulties driving as they stuck to the windscreen, blocked the radiators, smashed into the windows of our homes, got sucked into motors etc. I realized that butterfly when decoded meant transformation, it also meant that changes or alteration was on its way. I looked forward to this next venture into my schooling and waited in anticipation for things to happen. Seven days later my totem energy began to present itself to me.

The first was a young bird we called the honey eater that a cat brought into the kitchen, we retrieved the bird and I placed it in my right hand and was going to tuck it in near my heart, when it stiffened and died in my hand. I noticed a light mist rise from the bird and it went straight into my arm and disappeared. 'Where did that go' I asked myself. It took time for me to realize through talking with my teacher how fortunate I was to have received the soul of that bird. 'Now', she said, 'tell me how does the honey eater live, what does it eat?'

I was learning to understand that each species that had evolved on this planet had been mathematically induced into these universal laws. It was helped along through the previous generation. There never was a mistake, as a mistake could cause a catastrophic conclusion throughout all species, which could create a detriment for generations until they earned the mathematical right to get it right!

In my area the honey eater was referred to as the banana-bird for its habit of feeding on banana fruit and flowers. The birds knew when the banana flower nectar had reached its peak of perfection. Like them, we just had to wait a few days for the energy to travel throughout the bunch and then chop the bunch down and take it into the house, before the birds could claim them. I noticed that the birds were watching the different insects buzzing around and when a certain insect came to the bunch of bananas, the birds knew that it was ready for consumption.

How did the insects know? Remember they live in the unconscious (higher) mind, with their multi-faceted eyes, where they are able to read the combustible energy that permeates throughout what they are viewing. The insects were reading the ultra-mathematics in the geometrical color formation of that species of plant.

That wonderful little bird was informing me that I needed to sweeten myself for me to produce my own nectar, which would flow throughout my body for me to earn the state of endlessness I am in today.

My next totem was a female kangaroo that was placed outside my bedroom window early one morning by the dog, which was barking loudly. I opened the window and whoosh its soul entered my chest area, and nearly knocked me over. Kangaroo represented family, as it carried and supported its baby Joey, for over eighteen months, until it could rely on itself. I likened it to my next generation, and on this journey, it became my next thought of strength and compatibility to step forward.

Over the following years the list went on as I watched my totem collect itself, with me receiving over 100 souls from the eternal species, who have died in my arms or beside me. Each species explained an important function that needed clarification within me, enabling me to realize that my weaknesses were uniting and gaining strength. My totem energy changed every time I had finished a current metaphysical lesson.

I noticed that my name also changed every time I had completed a quandary of the unknowing, by rephrasing my alphabet into a higher format, which readjusted my language into an educated step of advancement. Of course, at that time I argued with everything I was learning, this information could not all be for real!

Who, was in charge with all of this information, how did it deem itself to be so important that every living thing had to be controlled by something we could neither see nor hear! These Laws of the Universe were well beyond our everyday language and yet, even a blade of grass had to obey them for their own existence to quantify and be measured for them to take their place on this amazing planet.

While we are on this subject (grass—plant kingdom), when we receive a species of the plant kingdom internally, we also receive the vibration of the species' emotion. The emotion of the plant is the Alchemy of its life force; the mathematics is its creation, which has ensued continually throughout its evolution. It is also instilled in our understanding of our third-dimensional mind. Plants are a living energy here to serve us in the same Collective Consciousness. That plant, which is a part of the make-up of our human brain, explains to us our own evolution.

When we place that plant into our mouth, chewing and swallowing it, the essence from the food moves up into the brain through the two small holes in the roof of the mouth, and then that essence registers itself with the unconscious mind, which allows the mathematics to register in the brain. This acts as a mirror of the species vibrating and accepting one another. The brain registers that it has received this energy, and it has the opportunity to use this mathematical frequency at any time to repair a difficult thought that we cannot bring into abeyance. It is a species of our intelligence. It is an accepted spark of our Universal Law. Once we have eaten a species of vegetable, the mathematical intensity of it stays with us for the rest of our life. Take a moment to reflect back into your own lives to remember what vegetables you rejected as a child? What did you miss out on? It's never too late; eat or juice them now to stimulate your senses into creating new ideas, also to be of service to you in your future. Remember, we are rephrasing your ego, which rearranges your alphabet!

Always, your totem energy is working with you. The Laws of the Universe are always serving you, as they are explaining the echo system of our body, which is identical to the echo system of the earth. They are teaching us what each thought leads us into accomplishing as we interlock into the higher layers of consciousness. As you learn and earn your intelligence, you ascend up into your hierarchical mind, which creates a space in time that becomes yours, and the echo of your thoughts release out into the Collective Consciousness in order for the next person to hear your thoughts; thus, he/she may begin to understand his/her own Laws of Self.

Throughout the Conductive Laws of the Shamanistic principles, we are asked to use the electromagnetic fields of 'Elephant' and 'Whale' quite frequently, as their sound waves travel completely around the planet, which adds to our gravitational fields. They are excellent collectors of eternal energy. We need them to fortify our strength; we do not need to eradicate them! Elephant, through the Laws of Totem Shamanic energy, represents 'Knowledge', and Whale is 'Conversation and Communication' as stated previously. Their sound vibrates to a very low frequency of around 2 megahertz, and it travels along the crust of the whole planet. Those sounds are collected throughout the electromagnetic fields, which are construed correctly to the given point through the contact of the vibrations coinciding or arching with one another.

Whales create fields of light energy that can be seen from great distances, even from satellites travelling in the outer Universe. That vibration collects, and then it is forced through the next field of energy until it completes a full circuit. That is why both species can speak to the other through their unconscious mind. They can hear each other's thoughts through the sonic sound that they produce, through the beat of their own heart. All species that vibrate to the same frequency can hear and understand this sonic sound.

I would like to explain why dolphins and whales beach themselves. The ocean species measure with the Collective Consciousness, and, when we are in doubt, they freely return their energy to supplement that same weakness in ours. They follow the emotional ley lines of Collective Energy, through the awareness of humanity. Do you recall this happening in your area? What was revealing itself to the consciousness that allowed these creatures to step in to surrender their life for the humans in your locale? Do you recall the 220 dolphins and whales that beached themselves off the Australian coastline four days before the devastating tsunami that struck the shores of Southern Asia? The collective governments of the world had reached a zenith at that time; and, as always, Karma steps in to remind us of our responsibilities. What were they trying to instigate in those nations that was not for the benefit of all concerned? This announcement to us indicates the Universal Laws at work!

Look around and take notice the next time these animals beach in your area— see for yourself. This same reasoning can be related to volcanic eruptions, earthquakes, cyclones, and hurricanes. Please don't think that the force of God is useless; every thought that we think is collected, measured, and very positively returned back to us. We reap what we sow. The higher the responsibility one must stand up for, on behalf of the populace, the greater the Karma returns, in order to retune that land.

On my first trip to China, during a visit to Tiananmen Square just outside the gates of the 'Purple Forbidden City' in Beijing; their totem poles (traditional Chinese ceremonial columns) are there for the entire world to see. They are introducing you to the original heavenly language that you will be stepping into as you enter the Old City. As I observed one of the totems it was free of animals and birds and the pole was spiraled—the spiraling represented the double helix of our DNA, which is supported by our spinal column (forwards our genetic instructions to our brain). Three quarters of the way up the totem pole (also known as the pole of the DNA, or totem of humanity), are the clouds which are representing the doorway into the heavenly kingdoms. Metaphysically the heavenly clouds are manifesting as your ideas, as your lesser Gods earn their way up to the area situated in your brain.

This is also the explanation of the Kundalini—or the DNA unfolding—through the Tibetan and Indian law; it is the Feathered Serpent through the Mayan law; it is the Pharaoh of the Egyptian principles, with the two symbols of the serpent and the vulture symbolically coming out through the forehead. It is also the explanation of the stories of the Rainbow Serpent in the Aboriginal law.

The Dragon signifies the ego (left brain), and the ego does not want to lose its own control as we evolve in our intelligence. That left brain is what we call the Bja or Seth in Egyptian law, the Devil in Christianity, and the Beast or Dragon within through the Asian Law. When we bring it back into the Aboriginal law, it is the Bunyip or Banyop. Is this meant to be the same meaning as 'BJA-AN-OP'? I love taking the language of the moment back to its source. That dragon, or fear, feeds itself only on our past thinking. It has the utterance to think it is still in control. The Chinese celebrate with the dragon, which they continually thank for the transformation it has undertaken to become exemplified in its own glory (transforming into the right brain—emotions).

Through the Arabic principles the thyroid is called the 'Drach-ab-Bja', the 'dragon's breath'. This explains why we cough. A cough creates itself through a congestion of blocked energy, and, if we keep on ignoring it and don't pay attention, it becomes bronchitis, which sets the stage for pneumonia.

In the myth of Hercules, the second of twelve labours Hercules cuts off the head of the Hydra. The word Hydra ('Hi-Dragon') represents the ascension of the fear(s) that we have difficulty in overcoming; hence, the task given to Hercules. It had been embedded with the fear of our past generations, which resulted in the animosity towards the self! Each time Hercules chopped off a head with his sword, two heads grew in the place of the severed one. The only way he could eradicate those heads and prevent them from growing back was through fire, and he accomplished this through burning the stumps of their necks once the head was removed, which indicates that he had to resurrect them. They then disappeared through their own transformation into their new intellectual light. The last head was immortal, and so Hercules buried it, and it turned into a rock (in some versions, he rolled a rock over the burial site). The rock represents the closing down of the left brain, which allows the right brain to take over the responsibility of the last head; thus, it could be transformed, given the freedom to move on without the ego interfering with the new growth. Also, the rock represents the brain in its innocence.

We make note that in the indigenous cultures, their totem was a pole positioned in the center of their village with animals and birds, that they needed to refine their thinking. This totem pole as it is referred to, fortifies the intellectual light as they stepped forward into the unknown at that time; to assist the thoughts of those that lived in the village. For example, if owl was symbolized on the totem pole by the Shamanic Principles, we note that the owl represents the four directions of the night, North, South, East and West. Owl has x-ray vision and is able to detect the slightest disturbance through the visibility of vibration, which occurs through the third eye. The owl signifies entering up into the angelic realms, relating to the emotional responsibility of our heart, learning to balance our thinking through the harmonizing of, and mastering of self. The eagle was often representational on the totem pole. The eagle represents the highest levels of the Laws of the Universe. Its nest is placed on the highest peak of the mountains and this allows its peripheral vision to extend far and wide. Eagle glides through the air and rides the thermals in a circular motion, where his mind is always centered and still. When eagle flies in a circle above us it creates an autonomic response in our nervous system, which pulls and lifts us up into a higher realm of our unconscious (higher) mind. Eagle acts on our behalf, his spiral creating an uplifting response to our DNA.

In ancient Egypt the cobra and the vulture were symbolized rising from the Pharaoh's forehead (attached to the Pharaoh's head-dress/crown). The cobra represents Lower Egypt and the vulture, Upper Egypt. The double crown represented the unification of the two regions of Egypt.

The cobra, the Uraeus (representation of a sacred serpent as an emblem of supreme power) is a symbol for the goddess Wadjet. She was one of the earliest Egyptian deities and was often depicted as a cobra. Metaphysically the serpent (cobra), emerging from the forehead is announcing the strength we bring forth from our ego (left hemisphere of the brain) conforming to its own state of grace. We tune into our ego as it learns to earn its own respect, to venture up into the heavenly kingdoms to release itself from its own bondage.

The vulture represents Upper Egypt. This is a representation of the emotional mind, (right hemisphere of the brain), and is a symbol for the goddess Nekhebet It is here, where we understand we have earned the right to enter into the doorway of the heavenly kingdoms, where the Lesser Gods are earning the right to become one. We are very much aware of the sanctification the vulture represents through our totem inheritance. It must make sure the soul has left the body it will devour, before it steps forward to eat.

On Tutankhamen's mask are the symbols of the cobra (serpent) and vulture (Lower and Upper Egypt) metaphysically symbolises the ego (consciousness—left brain) and emotional (subconscious—right brain) being in balance which escalates and lifts us up into our heavenly kingdom—or unconscious mind (higher mind)—which is where we begin to enter into the Divine Intelligence where we can release our free will. The kingdoms of Upper and Lower Egypt must balance themselves continuously.

The ancient Egyptian God Horus bears the falcon head. This is announced through the sacred codes as the "Heavenly Oracle Releases the Understanding of the Soul". The emotional species of the falcon represents the inner sight of self, which opens us up in order for us to be able to view through a wider perspective, broadening our peripheral vision. All this also symbolically reveals to us our imagination, and it also provides the codes for us to understand our dreams—or, through the Shamanic Principles, our 'Vision Worlds'.

Through the falcon's stillness of mind, it gathers its own responsibility and creates for itself a perfect hologram, where it can see through all the layers. Look at the bird, and you will see that it is able to fly and hold itself in abeyance, while in its stillness, in order for it to be able to mathematically set its prey. All this depends on the power and use of its wings. The codes of the Egyptian philosophies have left us a tremendous gift to unravel, known to us as our Totem Power unfurling itself.

Through the explanation of the Egyptian principles, the dog is represented to us as Anubis, known as the guardian to the ancient loyalties of the underworld, which we know is the home of the ego. Anubis, symbolically, is the one who represents the ancient loyalty of self; he represents the sentinel of the underworld, and the underworld is where we must walk to free the control our ego has over us—and we know, by now, that the ego's control, which is also our fear, represents our past!

The secret of this journey is to walk forward slowly, one step at a time, through you unfolding the layers of your genetic truth. If we look at the word *truth*, it is the unfolding of Thoth. The Egyptians—or the Arabic language—have explained, symbolically, that the Divine bird is Thoth, the Ibis, who held the tools in his hands that let us know he was also the Divine architect. When we hear and align with the past, we are led into our future. As the design appears to manifest itself, the bird changes, it automatically climbs up to equalize our thoughts into its next equation. The Divine bird, through the Chinese principles, is the crane that lives on top of the mountains and knows all. The crane in the Chinese language represents our 'heavenly energy', and, its symbolic representation is the crane—or crown bird. It is known as the HE bird. These birds symbolically represent the highest angelic resonance that we humans have the ability to earn. Each time we venture into a Chinese restaurant, we see pictures of this wonderful bird on the walls. It is the crown bird that transforms into the Golden Phoenix, as explained throughout the Asiatic laws.

*We are all the Shaman in training,
we are the warrior earning our wisdom
to place us on the earth.
Omni*

Chapter 32
Last Chapter

We bring this book into the last chapter, once again I hope I have explained my interpretation of the metaphysical language to you enough, as to how it represents the story that is embedded in our genetic inheritance from before we were born. Remember our genetics are selected for the life we inherit through the ninety days—pre gestation—stage before the pregnancy occurs. It all depends on the mothers thinking as to what she must inherit, either a boy or a girl, through her thought processes being announced to one another.

You have read an informative encounter as to how I had to accept the hidden codes over many years to bring this ancient transition together. My aim was to pass this information onto you, to give you confidence when your shadows crowd your light, just as mine once did. Through believing in yourself, you have the opportunity to allow your DNA to work with you, to assist you for the rest of your life through a state of grandeur, which relegates you to a higher level of possibilities that are always available to you.

This is my interpretation of the story, which has been passed on to many thousands of my learned students, who are well and truly on the way to speaking and teaching how they could release their inner wisdom. I feel very humbled as I sit in a class room and listen to how they reveal to their students, they have the golden opportunity that await us all. They all have their own story to tell as to how they listened to my stories; heard them and wrote them down, and rephrased my words into their languages, to explain how they themselves understood how important they are to themselves.

There are many experiences that I have overlooked or have not brought forward to relay these insights to you, through their similarity to one another; although I will state that every moment of my journey into the unknown was filled with wonder, as I yearned, to learn the earnings of a language, we have all but forgotten. And here it is; it has been here all of the time; it is the road map of ancient Egypt, which has been placed here for thousands of years, right in front of our nose. How can it be the past, when we have still not understood the language, they wrote down for us thousands of years ago? It represents the future for every human to view.

How many of you have taken the journey they prepared for us? Millions of you have looked into the Temples, studied the hieroglyphs, gazed in wonder at the creation of the Pyramids, read the books, where you have come to realize that you were walking amongst the story of the evolution of the central nervous system of our own body!!

Every story ever written by these Masters of Time, every prayer they uttered was a blessing for self, as they thanked themselves each morning and evening. Even down to the names of the people mentioned; if we broke the name up into syllables; sounded each syllable we would be able to recognize what part of the body they are referring too! Just the same as the stories explained in the Bible! Every God mentioned in the Greek philosophies, the Mayan Principles, and the Indo-Asian Vedanta is explaining exactly the same information! It's all about you!

It puts a totally different slant on our history, when I bring everything back to the first person and not the third! Throughout my education I was never allowed to use the third person as an excuse for what we have already accomplished and achieved. "Read the words, go back through the mathematics they created, reverse your thoughts for the truth to reveal itself to you," my teachers vocalized to me when things got rough around my ridges!

Every mythical story that has been forwarded to us is explaining a story of someone who did something exciting and we put that story out there into the third person category where we only listen to it! This information is heard through our left ear which alerts our ego of something that is happening to someone else. The ego tries to escape from altering its own device, as it suffices itself by living in what has already occurred. Remember if we listen, we are only looking at!

If we bring that story back to where we become involved with the story, we have entered into the realm of the second person, the message is relayed to us through our right ear, where we hear the story; we are looking into! To hear something opens our emotional responsibilities, which affects the right hemisphere of our brain; we form a relationship with these words as we become involved with the story. Our memory bank comes alive to inherit what we are thinking; in this way, we can always recall the story.

We then move up into the final sector where both brains come together. We are entering up into the unconscious mind (higher mind), where this ancient language is still available to us, as it cannot be interfered with. Therefore, we are able to view the whole story; it then becomes ours. As you can see, we have just traveled from the third person, to the second person, to finalize with the first! Once up here in the unconscious mind, you never want to leave.

Hopefully I have given light to the Metaphysical language codes of the ancient Egyptian Philosophies which have been carved and painted as hieroglyphs on the temple walls. They represent an intelligence of a higher wisdom for us to walk or work towards and have explained to us that it is the story of how we were conceived—as it is explained to us in the first person! This philosophy has been explained exactly the same as in the Biblical stories; it is the story of self and the war that cohabitates between our ego and our emotions. We are all Shaman in training; we are all the warrior earning our wisdom to place us on the earth. We all think we are after a peaceful existence, which does not always suffice; we need to feel stimulated, challenged, become excited to make our life more enhanced, to allow us to continue on.

It has taken over thirty—five years of research to bring this amazing story together which is still an ongoing education moment by moment and one I hope will never cease. My years of earning these credits were never in vain, I was guided lovingly by these natural laws into accepting this huge shift of consciousness that awaits us all, where I was given the opportunity to explain my story to different languages in many countries around the planet.

Now that I am in my late seventies, the pressure has been lifted and I am free to write my words; as I was told many years ago, "Make sure you write your books to explain your learning's, which became your earnings, as the pen is mightier than the sword." The Bible also states in Revelation chapter 1:11 'Saying, I am the Alpha and Omega, the first and the last: and what thou seest, write in a book, and send it unto the seven churches which are in Asia' etc. Metaphysically these seven churches are situated at the entrance into the higher mindedness of our levels of intellect.

My hope is that you can accept the language of the words that I have written; these insights can be absorbed into your language and transfer—or 'transverse'—itself into your DNA, for you to use, as they have become familiar to you; it is where your fear can surrender to itself, when you are ready to step into the next classroom of your education of self-discovery.

There is so much more that we can tune into, when we believe in ourselves. So, pack up your troubles in your old kit bag and smile, smile, smile. Let the war begin! Show me your **W**isdom **A**scending and **R**eleasing. Come on, after reading all of this information, I would love you to take a step forward towards the millions of miracles that await you, now let's go meet your Master within...

As I write these words, down comes the rain, the blessing and baptism has begun. With my heart wide open, I thank you for reading my story.
Omni.

Books by O.M. Kelly—Omni.

Through the 'Totem' energy of all, the ancient species that have evolved before us, represent an emotional inheritance that we can rely on to sustain the moment. Each species that has evolved on this planet is recorded into our cellular memory. *Power Thought For The Day Oracle Book* with 22 Major Arcana Shamanic Power Totems provides a contemporary metaphysical interpretation symbolic of our evolution. By selecting a page of the book, the Shamanic Power Totem will provide an insight in how you are thinking at this moment in time. Through the contemporary Laws of Shamanism (with a metaphysical interpretation), O.M. Kelly (Omni) has produced a book that will assist the 'Path of the Initiate' in emotional intelligence when our mind is in the field of doubt. When we become aware of how we are thinking it is a catalyst for transformation. This compact little book is a handy 4 x 7 inches or 10.2 x 17.8 cm to fit into your pocket or handbag.

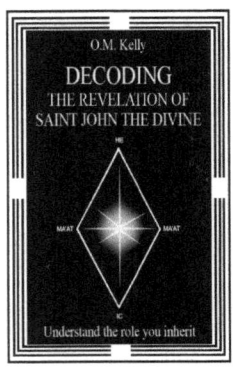

The amazing breakthrough book *Decoding the Revelation of Saint John the Divine: Understand the role you inherit,* is for anyone with an open, inquiring mind, seeking answers to the surreal descriptions of Earth's final days. Through years of research O.M. Kelly interprets the cryptology behind the codes of mythology and various religions and has metaphysically interpreted how the Holy Bible had been written through the original codex of Egyptology. The biblical stories were collected and condensed through this information by the educated minds of that time.

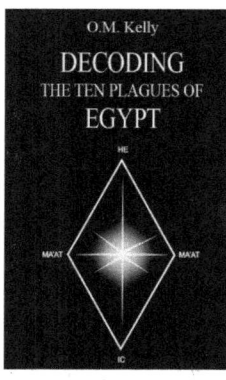

Decoding the Ten Plagues of Egypt presents a fresh insight into understanding the hidden struture of the language of how the Bible was written. The reader is introduced to the step by step metaphysical decoding of the mystifying language, regarding the plagues from the Book of Exodus, Chapters: 7-12 in the Bible.

For the first time in contemporary history the essence of the Book of Exodus and its previously unsolve intriguing language will be revealed to provide deeper knowledge and clearer perception to unlock the siginificance the Book of Exodus is explaing to us.

In *Decoding the Mind of God* author O.M. Kelly delves into the higher mind and discovers the secrets of the collective consciousness, showing how we can realize the potential of the human mind. *Decoding the Mind of God* is a compilation of nine separate volumes encompassing:

The Laws of the Universe
Thought
Disease
Death
Sexuality and Spirituality
The Dolphin's Breath
Sacred Alaphabet and Numerology
Sacred Feng Shwa
Extra-Terrestrial Intelligence
*Updated version of each book will be released in the near future.

In *Decoding Dreams* author O.M. Kelly (Omni), introduces a metaphysical interpretation of the dreams we dream. At times, we may believe that dreams allow us to peer into another world. O.M. Kelly provides the codes for us to understand that other world of dreams—or, through the Shamanic Principles, our 'Vision Worlds'. Areas covered in the book are: Dream Representations (Animal Kingdom and the Human Kingdom), Questions and Answers about Dreams, and Dream Interpretations.

*Updated reprint will be coming in the near future.

www.ingramcontent.com/pod-product-compliance
Lightning Source LLC
Chambersburg PA
CBHW062032290426
44109CB00026B/2607